INVICTUS

THE FORGOTTEN REBELLION AGAINST ROME

(14th Book of the Kahana Chronicles)

By

Allen E. Goldenthal

Copyright © 2025 1ˢᵗ Edition

All Rights Reserve – Allen E. Goldenthal

No part of this book can be reproduced or transmitted in any form or by any means, graphic, electronic, or mechanical, including photocopying, recording, taping or by any information storage retrieval system, without the permission of the publisher in writing.

VAL d'OR PUBLISHING

ISBN: 978-0-6488083-9-8

LETTER FROM THE AUTHOR

What exactly is the meaning of 'Invictus'? If one goes to the dictionary for an explanation, then they will find that Invictus is the Latin term for 'unconquered' or 'undefeated', representing the indomitable spirit that enables people to surmount the most daunting of circumstances. In no other instance is this word more appropriate than in describing the resilience and persistence of the Jewish people to live in their indigenous homeland of Israel. No other nation has suffered occupations by so many civilizations but despite these repeated travesties, the Jews have refused to disappear from existence and remain steadfast in their adherence and loyalty to the land that was given to them by God. Where other empires have come and gone, becoming nothing more than footnotes in history texts, the Jewish people still remain, speaking and writing in their ancient language of Hebrew, following their religious practices as laid down by Moses over thirty-three hundred years ago, and living in the land where they have been a continuous presence for almost four millennia. That is the true meaning and essence of Invictus.

In today's politically charged atmosphere, there is this misconception that today's modern Jew is somehow unrelated to the Jews that are historically associated to the ancient land of Israel. Despite the fact that today's modern Jew still speaks the aforementioned ancient language of Hebrew, still believes and practices the same ancient religion, and genetically still shares the same haplotypes as the ancient races of the Levant, there are those that perpetuate the myth of a Palestine in which the Jews did not live or if they did, then those particular Jews no longer exist, and those calling themselves Jews in today's world are a fabrication of the imagination. As ludicrous and ridiculous as these assertions may sound, they are still believed to be true by millions with no logical nor evidential material based in historical or scientific facts to support such absurd notions. Nothing could be further from the truth, yet they still choose to cling to these falsehoods.

What one must first appreciate is that the term Palestine has nothing to do with the Arab world at all. The concept of Palestine was strictly related to Jewish entomology, in that the Romans drew upon a name that they knew would humiliate, intimidate and subjugate the Jews of Israel after their defeat following the Bar Kochba's war against Rome between 132 and 135 AD. Following this Second Jewish War against Rome, Hadrian's armies had been devastated so badly, that in the Emperor's address to the Roman Senate in 136 AD, he avoided the usual quote of, "The Emperor and his army are well," a comment that had never been deliberately avoided before. It was embarrassing for the emperor to admit to such, and as a punishment, the rebellious Judeans and their refusal to abandon their belief in a liberated Kingdom of Israel, had to be eliminated once and for all. What couldn't be achieved by dividing up their nation into numerous provinces, each ruled by a Roman governor following the first war, would now hopefully be achieved by erasing the existence of a kingdom known as Israel by replacing its name on every map. As David was the Jew's acknowledged first King of a united country after he defeated the Aegean Greek Sea people, called the Philistines or Paleshtim in Hebrew, then the new name of the territory would be Palestina, intending it to be both an insult and a constant reminder how an ancient enemy finally prevailed. The territory would be amalgamated with the Province of Syria as Syria-Palestina, with the intent that the name of Israel would become forgotten from history.

The most significant misconception made by those falsely preaching that Palestine was never a home to the Jews is that the Romans in some impossible manner managed to deport millions of Jews out of their native homeland rendering the land to be 'Juden-Frei' as the Nazi's liked to describe those cities where they forcefully removed every Jewish family as they loaded them on the trains heading to the death camps. There were no thousand mile marches of millions of people, nor were there that many ships in all of the Imperial navy to transport that many people and displace them from their homes scattered across the Judean and Galilean countryside.

During both the first and second Roman-Jewish wars, tens of thousands of slaves were exported across the Empire, but these predominantly consisted of the Jewish elite classes, as they would be the ones needing to be closely watched under constant guard to ensure that they could never promote another uprising. It was reported by Roman historians that half a million Jewish soldiers died in each of the first two rebellions against Rome, a likely exaggeration to make the victory more sensational, but even if it were true, taking into consideration all these deaths and exiles, there would still be anywhere from half a million to a million Jews that were still living in what was now called Palestina. As such, they were still the dominant population.

As just stated, not even the Roman Empire's two victories over Israel left the countryside free of the Jewish presence but there are still those that insist that the deportation by the Romans after the defeat of Bar Kochba in 135 AD was complete. A myth that purposely overlooks the fact that Jewish schools were flourishing in cities such as Tiberias and Sepphoris, resulting in the publication of the Palestinian Talmud in the late fourth century and early fifth century. There's that odd use of the word Palestine once again being used to describe something that was completely Jewish, the Talmud. It's use as an adjective or descriptor of a Jewish object or noun should clearly imply to an unbiased reader that the word had nothing to do with a non-Jewish homeland, nor any Arab population. But the greatest undeniable proof that the Roman administrative region called Palestina was nothing more than a reference to the Jewish state was its use during the third Jewish revolt against Rome. A war that lasted from late 350 AD until 353 AD, involving tens of thousands of Jewish rebels against five Roman legions under General Ursicinus. One doesn't need a census report to know that the Jewish resistance force must have consisted of a massive number of soldiers if they could stave off defeat by the superior Roman legions for over three years. The fact that this highly significant war went unnoticed and underreported for over a thousand years is a reflection of the fear and weakness of the Jewish establishment, such as the Talmudic Sanhedrin, to antagonize their Roman overlords. So, they remained silent, concealed their own history, and policed against their own people to suppress any that voiced a desire for a restoration of Jewish control of their own homeland. Those promulgating the misconception of a Palestine in which there were no Jews, misinterpreted Jewish silence to mean they were not present in the land and therefore they must all have been in exile.

Again, there will be those that will try to argue that even if the Jews were present, their numbers had been so severely decimated that they could no longer be considered as the indigenous race of the land. This blatant misunderstanding of the word indigenous, intentionally designed to spread misinformation, overlooks the legal acknowledgement that indigenous rights are not determined by the exact number of the people that still exist in the land, This argument concerning numbers falls apart when one examines the numbers of indigenous people in North America that were slaughtered by the colonizing Europeans. Fewer than 238,000 indigenous native Americans remained by the turn of the twentieth century, out of an estimated 5 million that were spread across the continent prior to European contact. These numbers are not that dissimilar from the number of Jews that were expelled by the Romans from the land of Israel over three wars, and the number remaining, yet at no time would anyone even suggest that the Native North American is no longer to be considered the indigenous people of that land and that somehow they have forfeited all of their rights and privileges due to declining numbers at the hands of those that became the occupiers of their land.

The story of Invictus is about that undeniable tie that the Jewish people have to their homeland, whether it be called, Israel, or Palestine, or even referred to as Judea, Galilee and Samaria. It reveals that even after two centuries had passed since the Bar Kochba rebellion, the Jewish population of the land was still willing to fight against the military superior occupying forces of Rome. They could not be defeated spiritually and as a people they could never be broken. Even if they did not have the full support of their religious council they were still determined to throw off the yolk of foreign oppression, no matter what the eventual price in lives might be. As they marched to war, one can imagine they sang a song of freedom, it versus a reminder to all of what was theirs: "From the River to the Sea, Judea and Galilee will be free!" It decries the indomitable spirit of Jewish people, who time and time again have been willing to make the ultimate sacrifice while simultaneously making the declaration that Israel is their home, whether it be the past, the present or the future. Jews will fight and die for their homeland but they will never be forced to leave again. This is INVICTUS, and this is their story.

Dr. Allen E. Goldenthal

INTRODUCTION

The Jewish revolt against Constantius Gallus, commonly referred to as the Gallus Revolt, erupted during the Roman civil war of 350 to 353. As General Magnentius rebelled in the West against Emperor Constantius II, it created enough destabilization across the Roman Empire that by the end of the year 350 AD, the Jews of Roman Palaestina saw an opportunity to revolt against the rule of Constantius Gallus, brother-in-law of Emperor Constantius II and Caesar of the eastern part of the Roman Empire.

Taking advantage of the mid-fourth century's dynastic struggle, theological ferment, and shifting loyalties, the perfect environment in which to raise the flags of rebellion was created. By 350 AD, Constantius II elevated his cousin Gaius Vettius Aquilinus, known as Gallus, to the rank of Caesar, entrusting him with the governance and defense of the eastern provinces. Though his tenure lasted scarcely three years before he fell victim to imperial suspicion and execution, Gallus's brief rule left an oversized imprint on the politics, military affairs, and religious controversies of his day.

Gallus governed at a time when the Roman Empire was wrestling with its doctrinal definitions. Constantius II was a dedicated Arian Christian, suppressing both pagan cults and Nicene orthodoxy alike. Gallus, though never demonstrating any strong theological leanings, largely accorded with his cousin's belief in Arian dominance.

Emperor Constantius II, like his father Constantine the Great, believed in the supremacy of the Christian religion, favoring it over all others, including Judaism. Unlike his father, however, Constantius permitted Christians to persecute both the pagans and the Jews. This persecution often resulted in violent attacks and destruction of synagogues and temples. It was therefore not surprising that that this permitted persecution ultimately resulted in the Jews reacting, by opposing Christian proselytism and showing intolerance toward those that considered themselves to be Jewish Christians or Mineans. Sermons were preached in synagogues against Edom, which was the Jewish historical codename used for Rome, accusing the empire of not being satisfied in simply removing their political independence, but were now repressing their Jewish religious beliefs in order to force religious annihilation.

Initially, Emperor Constantius II was engaged in a campaign in the East against the Sassanian Empire but he was forced to return west in order to confront the usurpation of General Magnentius, who had just murdered Constantius' brother and co-ruler, Constans. In order to continue the war against the Sassanid emperor Shapur II, before heading west, Constantius appointed his cousin Gallus as Caesar of the Eastern Empire. Gallus arrived at Antioch, Syria, which would serve as his capital, on

May 7, 351 AD   During the period between the passage of Constantius in the West and the arrival of Gallus in the East, the Jews of Syria-Palestina rose up in revolt and declared themselves to once again be a free and independent people, liberated from the heavy hand of Rome.

This Jewish Revolt against Constantius Gallus began at the end of the year 350 and continued well into 353 AD. As one of the many eastern provinces of the Roman Empire, it represented one of the lesser-known uprisings but contrary to its small stature as a country, by way of its subsequent impact on the Roman government, it was undeniably one of the more historically significant moments of that era. Jewish resistance during the period of Later Antiquity was not as highlighted as the two wars during the early history of Imperial Rome, but it was by no means any less significant. The Constantinian Epoch was a time of political upheaval and major religious transformation within the Roman world, and this revolt was emblematic of the strained relationships between minority populations within the empire and an increasingly Christianized imperial authority that was both prejudiced and intolerant. Where once Christians were persecuted, they were now the persecutors and they had a noticeable disdain for Judaism. But whereas most of those other nations permitted themselves to be subjugated, and eventually absorbed, that was never going to happen to the Jews.

Following Constantine the Great's death in 337 AD, his three sons, Constantine II, Constantius II, and Constans, divided the empire between themselves, but it was obvious from the onset of the arrangement that it had no possibility of being successful, due to the inequity of the division. The battles between the three brothers ultimately led to Constantius II becoming sole emperor, but only after a heavy purging, leaving most of the relatives either in exile or dead.

Under Constantius II's reign, Jews were banned from public office, forbidden from proselytizing, and not allowed to build new synagogues. Christian bishops, incited pogroms against the Jews, leading to numerous acts of violence against the Jewish communities. The taxation on Jews was heavy, often so excessive that entire communities were bankrupted by corrupt administrators. The Jewish communities in Palestine bore a disproportionate burden of taxation, which led to property confiscations and extortion by officials. Under these conditions, revolt was inevitable.

One would think that under constant persecution, everyone in Palestine would be in favor of the rebellion, but such a broad statement usually only applies to those on the bottom rungs of the social ladder. It is a universal reality that those having authority, power and wealth, even in the worst of times will cling strongly to preserving what they have, even if it means opposing the will of the majority. During the first Roman-Jewish War, these men in support of Rome tended to be the aristocracy, the high priesthood, and members of the Sanhedrin willing to dance with the devil and betray their own people in order to retain their wealth and privilege. With the destruction of the Temple by Titus, these particular social classes disappeared, but the vacuum was quickly filled by the Pharisees and a new social class of religious scholars, the Rabbim, a council of chief rabbis that reinitiated the Sanhedrin and filled it from their own ranks. By the time of the second Roman Jewish War, it was now their turn to betray the Jews fighting for freedom, once again due to the fear of losing their power and social status. To see exactly how deep and cutting that betrayal was, I invite you to read **Beneath A Falling Star**. By the time the third war began in the fourth century, it was already obvious, or should have been, that a betrayal would be in the works like every other time, as the old adage claims that history constantly repeats itself and this could never be truer.

Archaeological evidence in Galilee supports the few historical accounts of this mid-fourth century rebellion as seen by burn layers and debris from the destruction of walls and buildings at sites in Sepphoris and Tiberias. Synagogues from this time period show signs of conversion into churches or closure, the common means of retaliation by Christian authorities.

We have a name passed down by the few chroniclers that did record the events of this war. That name is Patricius, who's actual name was Natronai. From a historical perspective, one of Patricius's most intriguing characteristics was his fusion of priestly symbolism with secular rule. While no evidence survives that he performed the High Priest's cultic functions on the Temple Mount, he did claim authority over synagogue courts and insisted on the reinstitution of certain liturgical practices banned under Constantius II. In this sense, he blurred the boundary between sacred and profane power, an approach that both inspired his followers and alarmed the more cautious rabbinic leaders, who left his movement unmentioned in the rabbinic corpus.

Contemporary Christian chroniclers painted Patricius as a fanatic bent on sacrilege, while later Samaritan and Jewish polemicists alternately demonized and lionized him. This polarization reflects the broader anxiety provoked by someone who could fuse the language of temple-centered piety with the trappings of kingship. The mere fact that someone existed that could legitimately call himself 'King of the Jews' was the single most existential threat to Christianity in their three hundred years of existence. As for the Jews, to some he was a heretic who endangered Jewish survival; to others he epitomized the last hope for a free Jewish nation.

Perhaps the most remarkable aspect of Patricius is how little memory of him persists. One would think that a man that led an uprising for three years against Rome would have been immortalized by historians. But unlike the first war, or Bar Kokhba's revolt, or even the Samaritan rebels of the fourth and fifth centuries, Patricius left no sustainable tradition. His failure and the severity of Gallus's reprisals seem to have discouraged Jewish chroniclers to even dare to record his story. But one can conclude from that seemingly enforced silence and attempted erasure of his existence, that his true impact on Rome must have been both extensive and terribly significant. Roman historians always preferred to ignore any event that the Emperor could not claim as a brilliant success. Their silence only serves to underscore both the severity of Patricius's challenge to Rome and the subsequent price exacted against the Jewish people because of it.

Patricius emerges as far more than just another rebel commander in a long history of revolutionaries that took up arms against Rome. By nature of his birth, he was a proto-messianic king, who by challenging Rome, was all at once a political insurrectionist, a cultic revivalist, and a popular hero. His ready acceptance by the people emphasizes the enduring prophecy of a Davidic messiah in Jewish religious-political thought and the unquenchable desire by the Jewish people to be free in their own land.

CHAPTER I: THE DREAMER OF MAHOZA

The morning sun crept through the lattice of palm branches overhanging the garden pavilion in Mahoza, dappling the mosaic tiles with shifting light. Birds stirred in the tamarisk trees, and the perfumed breeze of the Tigris curled into the palace corridors, softening the sharp scent of parchment and ink. Inside the airy hall, between a marble column and an open scroll of Ezekiel, stood Natronai ben Nehemiah, thirty-three years old, son of the Exilarch, youngest of the House of David, barefoot and muttering prophecies as if he was rehearsing for a play.

He wore a simple linen tunic dyed in blue, the kind favored by Babylonian scribes, though it hung open at the chest, his dark hair tousled, his beard untamed, his eyes, deep, fervent, glowing with an intense fire. The dawn had found him as it had for the last few weeks: pacing the corridors, quoting scripture, eyes burning with dreams no one else dared to carry. He had the unkempt elegance of a man too consumed by vision to bother with appearances. He deliberately rejected the princely silks his station afforded. There was something wild about him, as though the walls of exile were far too small to contain the immensity of his longing.

"I have heard it," he declared to what appeared to be an empty room. "Not in sleep, not in madness, but in the deep hush between breath and word. I know it was the voice of the Holy One. He said to me, Arise, my servant, son of David. Go and take what was promised."

Behind a curtain of reeds, at one end of the room, his mother Rachael listened patiently, but the sadness in her eyes suggested she was deeply concerned for her youngest son. He had always been a dreamer, a zealot, a mystic, perhaps one could even say a man aflame with divine purpose. But this trait had always been both inspiring and maddening to those around him. Idealistic to the point of recklessness, he refused the pragmatic politics of his father and brothers, seeing himself not as a courtier or steward, but as something more, something greater than the pampered life their lineage had afforded them. Though he spoke with authority and poetic grandeur, using language that dripped like honey off his tongue, he was not calculating like his elder brother Nathan, nor pragmatic like Huna. He didn't think he had to be, convinced that he had been gifted with a true sense of destiny, unlike his brothers, and therefore he need not be concerned regarding the dangerous charisma that flowed from it.

She had not yet spoken, permitting him to ramble on without interruption. Perhaps she didn't know how or what to say. This was not the boy she had cradled and smothered with honey-cakes, the one she had shielded from his elder brothers' mockery, who wept when a sparrow died or begged her to delay his Torah lessons for one more night of childish games. The boy she coddled and adored as one often does to their youngest. But that love could not protect him now. His brothers saw him as dangerously idealistic, possibly even deluded; a threat to the stability they enjoyed as the ruling house in Mahoza. He, in turn, saw them as being too cautious, too satisfied with Babylonian comforts to notice the real suffering of their people. There was love in their household, but it was strained, increasingly eclipsed by Natronai's messianic fervor. No, Natronai had become a man, no longer a boy, though not the kind of man she had hoped for.

His brothers had grown into practical men. Nathan Ukba, the eldest, was groomed for rule: calculating, patient, devout. Huna, the second, had the charisma of a general and the lean cunning of a market hawker. But Natronai? He was simply the third son, the irrelevant one, his mother's pet. In his own mind he was the storyteller, the questioner, the one who could vanish into the fields for days and return speaking of stars and signs and the scent of angels.

"You're not listening," Natronai said aloud, taking her silence as a refusal to hear what he had to say.

Then, as if to say she had been listening all along, the curtains parted, and Rachael smiled, her veil draped loosely over her graying hair.

"My son," she said softly. "Have you slept?"

It was not the question that he was wanting to hear from her. "I don't need sleep," he replied, not unkindly. "I've been woken."

Rachael sat on the cushioned bench near the scroll. "And what did the voice say this time?"

"The same as always." He looked at her with a strange tenderness. "That I was born for more than exile and compromise. That I am not the third son of Mahoza, but the firstborn of Zion. This household has become too comfortable in its position."

She reached out and touched his wrist. "You are beloved. But don't mistake love for license. These are dangerous dreams you speak aloud."

"Dreams?" he said, laughing. "Is Moses a dream? Did David dream when he ran from Saul? Or Judah Maccabee when he took up the sword?"

"You are not Judah," she whispered.

"No," he agreed. "I am more than Judah. I carry not the sword alone, but the crown. This title we bear of Exilarch is a hollow inheritance, a compromise with our oppressors. Instead, we must seek the throne of David in the land of Zion. The time of redemption is at hand. Our lineage is not intended as a relic but as a mandate. We are not to be content with peace and survival in exile, but of revolt, restoration, and the rebuilding of the Temple."

A heavy silence fell between them.

Rachael's eyes searched deep into his. "And what of your brothers? What of your father's house? Have we not held the line here, in exile, for five hundred years?"

"And what has it gained us?" Natronai snapped, pacing once again. "A seat at the governor's table? An invitation to Ctesiphon to parade along with the Emperor Shapur when it is at his convenience. Permission to worship in silence while Rome rules our land and names it Palestina? We wear titles, not crowns. We walk with the Sassanian kings of Babylon while our people kneel under the crushing boot of the Caesars. This is not a kingdom. This a nothing more than a gilded cage."

Her voice was firmer now. "Nathan will succeed your father, not you. You are not the one to make policy. He is ready. He will be the next exilarch."

"I know," he said. "Let him have Mahoza. Let Huna even have Babylon for all I care. I want Jerusalem."

She drew a sharp breath.

"I will go," he continued, almost to himself now. "I will cross the desert, gather the remnant of our people, throw down the idols or Rome and Constantinople, and rebuild the Temple. Not in theory, not in ritual, but in stone and fire. The Messiah has not tarried, Mother. He is awake. He walks. And his name is Natronai. You asked what God has told me, and that is what he said."

She shook her head slowly, tears trembling in her eyes. "You think madness sounds like purpose. But that which you speak of will kill you. This dream of yours will be your death."

He knelt before her, not with shame, but with fire in his eyes. "Then I will die with purpose."

Behind them, a servant announced the arrival of his brothers.

Nathan Ukba entered first, dressed in fine wool robes and accompanied by scribes and a Syrian steward. He was not a cruel man, but his expression betrayed his irritation when he saw his mother's tears. He knew exactly what she had been discussing with his young brother.

"Again?" Nathan said, sighing. "Brother, you cannot keep making such proclamations before the city's rabbis. It does not reflect well on us."

"They must prepare," Natronai answered simply.

"For what?"

"For liberation."

"Think of what father would say," Nathan Ukba urged. "He would remind you that we have labored to keep this community from crumbling under Babylonian scorn and hatred. He would accuse you of quoting the Prophets while ignoring the consequences. Do you not understand what emperors do to men who claim to be kings? Father has. He has seen them nailed to trees, burned in arenas, left as warnings at city gates. He would laugh at your thinking that the House of David will be restored with poetry and prayer?"

"Is that not what the Messiah is all about?" Natronai questioned. "If not prayer, then why do we even bother to pray for our redemption?"

"You may think that you are the Messiah but to lead a people, you need more than a vision. You need patience. Diplomacy. The will to survive long enough to make change possible. Our father has kept this house intact through four emperors, through riots and famine and Sassanian suspicion. You think we live too quietly and prosperous but it is that quiet that has preserved our people for all this time. What you call life in exile, we call stewardship. Father would never risk our community, our family, or our people on a whisper in a dream."

As if listening to Nathan was not enough, then came Huna, broad-shouldered and blunt, arms crossed. He didn't even ask what everyone was talking about, he already knew. "You think you can waltz Into Judea, raise a banner, and Rome will collapse like Jericho's walls? Enough of this foolishness brother. It grows wearisome."

"I think God will do as He did before. I at least, choose to believe."

Nathan glanced at their mother, who said nothing, only wept silently.

"Listen to reason," Nathan urged. "You're not ready. No one is. Let's say you were the Messiah, what have you done to prepare yourself for such a role. You'll die out there, or worse, you'll get others killed for your dream."

"It's not a dream," Natronai said, rising to his full height. "It's a summons. I have heard Him. And you, none of you, can unhear what has already been spoken."

A hush fell over them all.

Then Natronai walked to the open terrace and looked toward the west, where the sky was stained with the smoke of morning fires, and beyond that, far beyond, the unseen hills of Judea.

"I am going," he said with such determination that his brothers thought he might be serious this time.

No one moved.

He smiled faintly, almost pityingly at his brothers. "You may contend yourselves with the governing of Babylon. It is my intention to reclaim Israel."

And with that, the third son of Nehemiah turned and walked from the room, his sandals slapping the stone, his shadow trailing regally behind him, as if the floor of the palace had become a road, and the road was a prophecy.

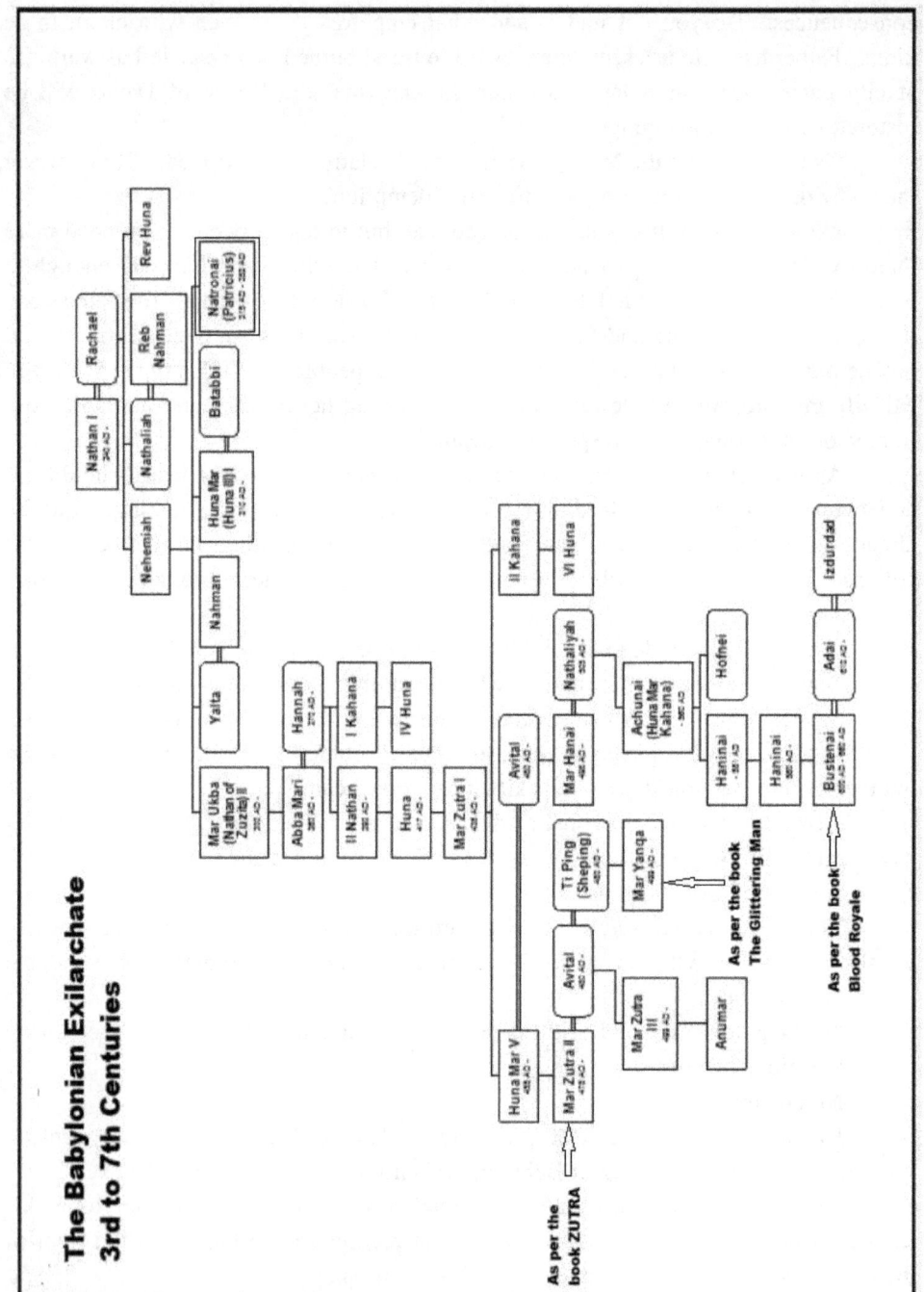

CHAPTER II: THE DREAMER OF NICOMEDIA

She was young, perhaps sixteen, and her name eluded him. Gallus stared at the painted ceiling of his chamber as dawn crept through the half-drawn curtains, casting long bars of light across the tangled sheets. The girl lay beside him, silent, breathing shallowly, her body half-draped in linen. One of his hands rested on her bare back; the other held a goblet still wet with last night's Falernian.

"None of it matters," he muttered, slurring just slightly. "Empires, gods, lineages. All ash, all rot. We'll all be bones soon, and even the worms will forget our names."

She turned her head, wide-eyed, uncertain whether to speak. He didn't look at her.

"Do you think they'd weep if I threw myself from the balcony? Would you weep?" he asked, his voice heavy with wine and something darker.

The girl sat up, clutching the sheet to her chest. "My lord..."

He laughed bitterly. "Lord of what? These walls? The gossip of eunuchs? My father's ghost" He rolled over, faced her at last, his noble features shadowed and unshaven. "You'd be better off dead, you know. Pretty little thing like you. They'll marry you to some potbellied scribe or toss you to the kitchens once I'm done."

She shrank back. "Please..."

"Go," he said, suddenly quiet. "Get out. You're boring me."

She fled, the door closing softly behind her.

The palace in Nicomedia was not a prison in name, but Constantius Gallus had long understood the difference between gilded captivity and freedom. As a child, he had run its corridors like a colt newly foaled, marveling at the marble statues and the basilicas that groaned with imperial history. But as he grew, the guards grew more numerous, the courtiers more watchful, and the doors, which once upon a time were left ajar, were now most often sealed behind him.

He was thirteen when he understood that his father was not coming back. Julius Constantius, half-brother to Constantine the Great, had been caught in the slaughter that followed the great emperor's death in 337. A storm of blood swept through the Constantinian dynasty, purging those whose lineage posed a threat to the fragile balance of imperial succession. Gallus, too young to be considered a threat, and his younger half-brother Julian, had been spared. But the absence of steel did not make the chains any lighter.

Gallus rarely spoke of the day he learned his father was dead. He had cried for hours in the chambers of his Greek tutor, a bent and patient man named Theon who had simply waited for the boy's sobs to subside before handing him a copy of Homer. "Read," he had said softly. "That is where the dead live on."

So, Gallus read. And learned. And dreamed.

In the mornings, he studied Greek rhetoric, practicing the flourishes of Demosthenes, the biting irony of Lucian. In the afternoons, he was drilled in Latin law, the corpus of the res publica that still clung to a shadow of Republican virtue even under an emperor's hand. Horsemanship came next, and then the rudiments of military command under a grizzled centurion with one eye and a voice like stone dragged over bronze. Gallus learned to hold a sword, to mount and dismount, to command a small unit on the parade grounds of Nicomedia, though he was never permitted to lead men into war. That would have made him a threat.

He was educated but not cultivated for succession. Never once was he given control over a province or entrusted with a garrison. His name, noble as it was, had been shelved as an heir preserved in amber, a tool that might one day be useful, but not now, and perhaps not ever.

And so, he waited.

But if Gallus could not have power, he would seize pleasure. By his early twenties, he had grown tall and broad-shouldered, with sharp cheekbones and a noble brow. Courtiers called him beautiful. Women called him dangerous. He cultivated a taste for silks and perfumes, fine wine and finer company. There was always a girl slipping out of his chamber at dawn. Always a goblet half-empty in his hand. Always a witty remark on his lips, some clever twist of a Vergilian phrase or a well-aimed jest at a provincial's expense.

As expected, in courtly gatherings, he was charming and affable. He recited poetry with the cadence of a trained orator. He debated theology with the Christian bishops who visited the palace. He memorized verses in both Latin and Greek and quoted them back with flourish. When eastern dignitaries visited, he welcomed them in their own tongue. The court poets sang his praises, comparing him to Orpheus for his voice, to Achilles for his noble profile.

But those who lived with him day to day knew better. There were fits of rage, both sudden and unprovoked. A shattered amphora when his servant brought the wrong wine. A violent backhand when a scribe misspoke a line of law. Gallus would explode, and then just as suddenly collapse into shame or laughter, as if the fury had never happened.

He would drink too much at banquets, sometimes groping senators' wives beneath the table, or rising to toast "To the dead who did not see me rot in this golden cage." Once, he struck an advisor across the face for suggesting he take a more active role in civic matters. Another time, he threatened to dismiss his entire staff, only to summon them back the next day with apologies and gifts.

Julian, his younger brother by another mother, remained nearby, also under watch. The two shared moments of camaraderie, brief escapes into philosophy or shared jokes about eunuch tutors. But Julian was quieter, more observant, and increasingly distant. Where Gallus burned like a torch, Julian smoldered like a coal. They rarely fought but rarely confided in one another either.

Gallus often found himself walking the palace gardens alone at dusk, wine cup in hand, muttering to the statues. He would gaze at the distant hills and imagine himself marching at the head of a legion, hailed as imperator by soldiers and senators alike. He imagined Rome calling his name. He imagined the thunder of hooves, the clash of battle, the triumphal procession through the Forum. Not the caged heir, but the risen phoenix.

But always, when he returned to his chamber, the guards would still be there. The door still locked. The letters he sent to his cousin Constantius II still unanswered or returned with cold formality.

He had dreams. So many dreams. Of vengeance for his father. Of rising above the shame of being passed over. Of one day sitting upon the throne of the Caesars and proving them all wrong.

As he sat on the balcony, he watched as the sea beyond Nicomedia shimmered in the summer light, the blue waves whispering against the marble colonnades of the palace like distant promises. He knew he had the bearing of a prince, the posture of a soldier, so why did they not see his worth to be more than the soul of a man in chains? How could they not see that he was no guest of the court, barely a beloved relative to the divine Emperor Constantius II, but merely a hostage awaiting sentencing but not aware of the crime for which he was being condemned.

Gallus saw the gilded cage for what it was. Every garden path was watched. Every servant's glance held suspicion. What else could he do but dream. Dreaming not like a child of grandeur and glory, but like a man convinced that destiny had simply been delayed. He knew he had to bear the burden of waiting for time to consider him worthy.

He would sit alone sometimes, in the library built by Diocletian's architects, staring at the busts of emperors past. Augustus, stoic and aloof; Trajan, the soldier-emperor; Hadrian, the philosopher-king. He traced their gazes with his own and whispered names of provinces, imagining legions marching under banners bearing his crest.

Gallus Caesar.

It had a rhythm, a cadence. It rolled off the tongue easily. One day, he told himself his cousin Constantius would summon him. Not out of love, perhaps. Never that. But out of need. The East required a strong hand, a family name, and an obedient face. And who better than the son of Julius Constantius? Who better than one of the few who survived the purge?

His thoughts grew darker then. Survived. What shame and overwhelming guilt in knowing all who you loved died, while for some inexplicable reason you were spared.

He remembered the purge well. It came like a plague, quiet and then all-consuming. That horror had carved him into two men wearing very different masks. The one man was polished, charming, a student of rhetoric and a patron of the arts. The other man was something else; shattered, suspicious, burning with unspoken fury. A mask that taught him to laugh while bleeding inside.

He could not forget the screams. Not in dreams. Not in drink.

He was twenty-five now, and when he drank, the shadows failed to disappear but only resurfaced with greater horror. He felt constantly haunted. At night, he would kneel before his father's ghost. Not literally, no statue nor shrine. But in his soul. In the chamber where he slept alone, always alone, he would lie awake, speaking to the man whose death had orphaned him.

"Father was it weakness that killed you?" he whispered once. "Or was it trust?"

He had come to believe that both were fatal, therefore he swore off both.

And so, Gallus schemed.

He kept a ledger in his head. Names of senators. Bishops. Military men. He remembered who liked him, who didn't. Who owed favors, who wanted promotion. If Constantius summoned him, he would not go as a pawn. He would go as a man prepared to rule.

His time would come. He was certain of it. One day there would come a letter from Emperor Constantius and it would say, "Let Gallus, noble son of Julius, come to Milan. Let him be raised to the dignity of Caesar and be given dominion over the Eastern provinces."

The day would come when he would be Caesar. He looked out to the sea again, imagining he could see the boat arriving bearing the messenger. He took a drink from the goblet that was never far from his hand. The scent of oleander was in the air. He thought of his father again. Of the knife in the back, the betrayal, the blood that watered the palace steps.

He smiled bitterly. He would be Caesar. He knew that day was coming. And perhaps, one day, more. Even if it meant becoming a monster to survive.

Perhaps that day would arrive with the next ship he saw on the horizon.

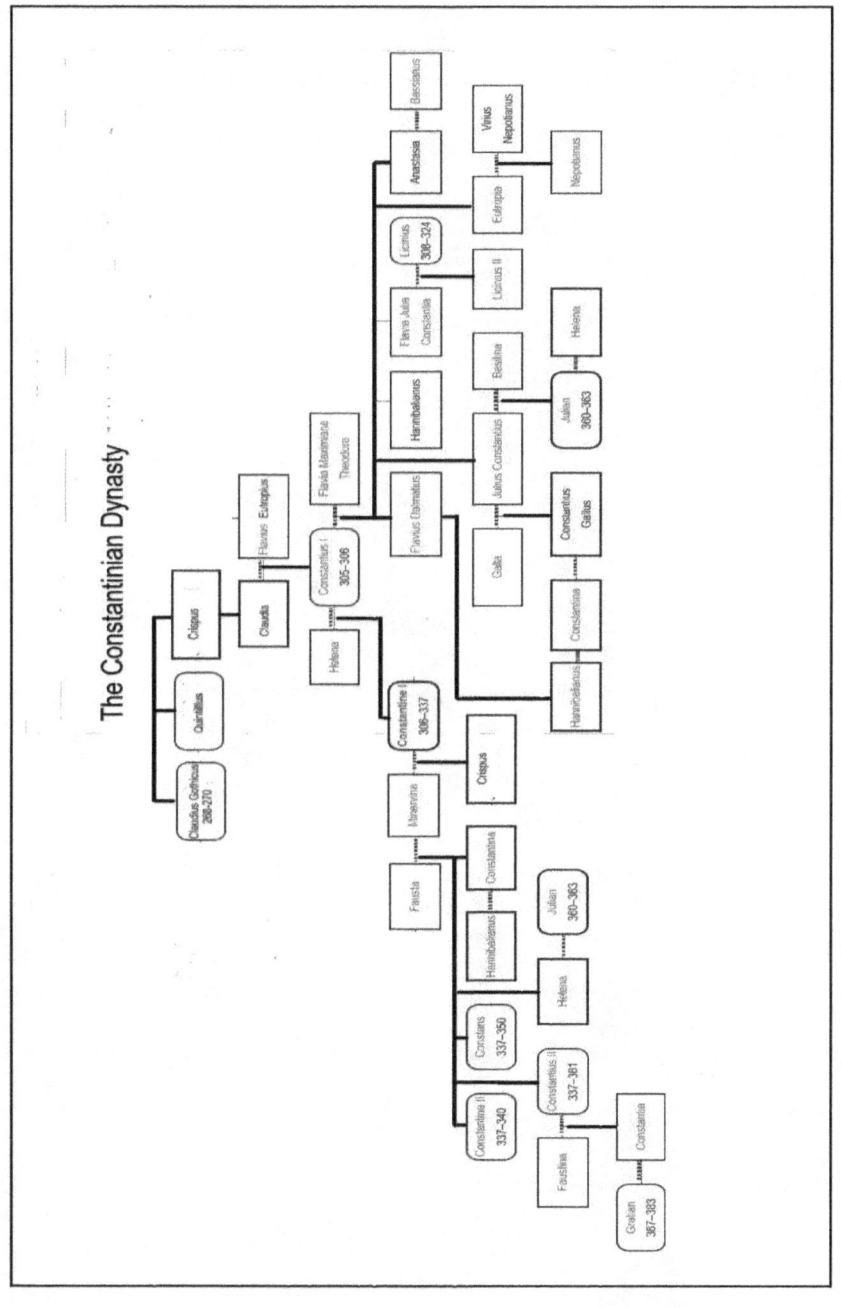

CHAPTER III: LION OF THE EAST

He stood alone in the Hall of Mirrors, beneath the great dome of Bishapur, where the light of a fading sun fractured itself on polished stone and jewel-cut glass. Shapur II, King of Kings, the Immortal Flame of Ērānshahr, gazed not at the opulence around him but at the westward horizon beyond the arches. Somewhere beyond those mountains, far across the plains, past the Tigris and the lands of the Armenians and the traitors who called themselves allies of Rome, stood Constantinople, arrogant, gilded, and rotting. He loathed that city with a hatred refined over decades, a slow-burning fire stoked by the shame of his house and the bleeding wound of Parthian pride. He had never seen Constantinople with his own eyes, but he felt as though he had known it all his life: a city of marble masks and golden lies. The Romans called it the New Rome, but to him, it was a thief-city, a thief of lands, a thief of kings, a most importantly a thief of peace.

The wind stirred the silk drapery around him. Even the desert seemed restless with indignation. He pressed his fingers against the lion seal ring on his right hand, the same ring his grandfather Narseh had once worn before he bent his back in humiliation to the dogs of Rome. The Peace of Nisibis they called it, and the very name tasted of bile. The Romans, under that spider Diocletian, had torn five provinces from Persia's side like a butcher stripping flesh. And Narseh, shamed and cornered, had knelt and signed. They said he wept according to the stories.

So much for the dignity of the Arsacids. So much for the glory of Sasan.

Shapur's own father, Hormizd II, had died too early to restore it. And so, it fell to him, to the boy crowned while still in the womb to make right the ancient wrongs and erase the shame written into stone. And now the Romans, shameless as ever, dared to shelter his brother Hormizd. His own brother! Then dare to speak of "restoring the legitimate king." A prince fattened on Greek honey and wine, now their tame dog.

He had read the reports from Antioch. Hormizd had been paraded through the court of Constantine as a darling barbarian prince, clothed in Persian silks to please the crowds and trotted out at banquets to mock the East. They fed him stinking Christian theology and whispered that he, not Shapur, should rule Ērānshahr. So be it. Let them crown him with fig leaves and Christian prayers.

Shapur turned to the map etched in silver and carnelian on the wall—a great spread of land from the Caucasus to the Indus, from the marshes of Maysan to the shores of Oman. It was beautiful but incomplete. Armenia, ever the serpent's tongue, jutted out from the heart of the empire like a spearhead turned inward. He walked closer, his boots silent on polished stone. Armenia, the wound that would not heal.

Since the days of Ardashir, the Armenians had been trouble. Too Greek to be trusted, too Persian to be ignored. They drank Zoroastrian wine and prayed in Christian churches. Half their nobles were loyal to him, the other half to Rome. But still they bled Persian sons in endless skirmishes and betrayals. The Arsacid kings there were his kin but poisonous kin, eager to side with whoever gave them the greater amount of gold.

His eyes narrowed. The last envoy from Armenia had dared to speak of Roman guarantees. Guarantees! And what did that mean, except that Caesar meant to march his legions over Persian soil once again, under the pretext of defending their precious allies?

There would be no more treaties. No more humiliations. He would drown the shame of Nisibis in blood and fire. He turned and walked down the long corridor toward the private gardens, away from the court, away from the ministers and spies and sycophants. He needed solitude. He needed air.

Outside, the world was red and gold beneath the dying sun. The orange groves were in bloom. A warm breeze carried the scent of fruit, of dust, and of burning cedarwood. Somewhere, a harp was playing. But his thoughts returned to Constantinople.

He imagined it with its domes and spires catching the light, its walls were high and thick, its streets filled with orators and liars. They worshipped a crucified god, they said. A Jew nailed to a wooden tree. Shapur sneered. What kind of empire built its temples around weakness and defeat? What kind of king called himself servant of the cross?

They were strange, these Romans, brutal and pious, cultured and corrupt. A contradiction in every breath. They wrote poetry as easily as they slit throats. They painted icons as they plotted revolutions. Constantine, that silver-tongued emperor, had declared himself a Christian and still burned his wife alive.

Shapur had no illusions about them. No awe. No envy. Only contempt.

They claimed to bring civilization, but all he had seen were broken cities and puppet kings. In Syria, he had witnessed firsthand the scars of Roman garrisons. Villages razed for refusing taxes, temples plundered and remade as churches. Children taken as hostages to be re-educated in Latin. They were a people lacking honor.

He sat by the fountain, running his fingers through the cool water, and looked to the east, toward Ctesiphon, toward the true heart of empire. He remembered what his grandfather had whispered before his death. "They are not stronger, only more cunning. One day they will make themselves to be gods out of your weakness. You must never bend, Shapur. Not to them."

And he had not. At thirty-eight, Shapur was no longer the child-emperor, the boy born under an omen. He was now a man whose name made generals tremble from Bactra to the Bosporus. He had secured the east, put down revolts in Sogdiana and tamed the Kushans. He had overseen the great canal projects and fed the people when the Tigris flooded. He had made Ērānshahr mighty again.

But none of it would matter if the western frontier remained a dagger at his throat.

No, the time for silence was over. He would answer Rome. Not with words, but with fire. He would show them once and for all they were nothing more than mere mortals that bled like everyone else.

The sound of sandals on stone pulled Shapur from his reverie. It was Aspad Gushnasp, commander of the royal cavalry, bowing low. His armor gleamed with bronze lion medallions, his beard freshly oiled, his eyes always vigilant. Behind him trailed a boy, no older than seven, with frightened eyes and golden hair.

"A prisoner, my king," said Aspad, his voice low. "From a caravan west of Arbela. The boy is Roman. Son of a tribune from the border post at Singara. His mother…"

Shapur raised a hand. "The mother is nothing. This one… let me look at him."

The boy flinched as the King of Kings approached. Shapur knelt down and stared directly into the child's eyes. Blue. Pale like shallow water. A child of the west. Shapur saw no hatred in them yet, only confusion. That would change with time, if he were allowed to live.

"Do you know who I am?" he asked softly.

The boy shook his head.

"I am Shapur, son of Hormizd, son of Narseh. The one your father's emperor calls 'barbarian'."

The child only blinked.

Shapur stood. "Take him to the House of Wisdom in Ctesiphon. Let the priests educate him. He is to wear Persian clothes, speak Persian tongue, and eat Persian bread. If he is to live, he will live as one of us."

Aspad bowed again, hiding his surprise. "No thought of requesting a ransom from the tribune, Majesty?"

"The boy will become Persian," Shapur insisted.

"And if he resists?"

"Then let the priests remind him how we will make a Roman forget."

The commander left, boy in tow. The footsteps echoed and then vanished.

Shapur returned to the fountain and gazed again at the sky, now painted purple with the first touch of night. There was a satisfaction in it, a subtle rebalancing of scales. The boy was no ransom, no threat, but a symbol: the sons of Rome could become Persian, but never the other way around. Let them learn humility. Let them feel what it was to be made alien in their own flesh. Let them know what they had done to his brother; he could do just as easily to all of them.

That last thought made him wince. The thought of Hormizd, his brother, living in the halls of Constantinople, perhaps wearing Eastern robes to impress their Greek hosts, perhaps whispering verses of Homer like a trained parrot was too much to stomach. A boy who had been too soft for court, too pretty to be feared. Now a tool of the enemy.

What did Constantine think? That he could simply install his own puppet in Ctesiphon and claim a protectorate? That the House of Sasan would crumble because one of its branches had been coaxed with honey and flattery?

He had read Roman histories. He knew how they worked. Divide and rule. Seduce with coin, then strike with steel. But this was not Syria. This was Ērānshahr. And as his grandfather instructed, he and his people would never bend.

The Roman mistake was always the same. They mistook clemency for weakness, courtesy for concession. And they never understood how deep Persian memory ran. The Greeks had come with Alexander, and they had burned Persepolis. Yet even now, centuries later, children in Istakhr still wept at the mention of that day.

Rome, for all its senators and statues, was a house of forgetting. It never learned from past lessons. Persia was a house of remembrance.

Shapur rose. He could feel it now, an ache in his chest, an old pressure returning. The weight of legacy. The burden of empire. It came for him at night sometimes, in dreams that were not dreams but the stirring of ghosts. Ardashir, his ancestor, still rode through his mind like a blazing comet, whispering not in words, but in flame: Do not let the West survive you.

Later that night, in his war room, the scribes laid out scrolls of logistics, grain stores, and cavalry deployments. Shapur waved them all away. "I do not want numbers. I want paths," he said. "I want the roads from Nisibis to Carrhae. I want the Roman fortress lines marked. I want the Armenian border posts highlighted. I want to see where their blood will run."

The generals bowed. One of them, Mithradates of Media, cleared his throat. "Majesty, there are rumors that Constantius's eldest son may be sent east, to command the legions in Armenia."

"So, they plan to make it a family affair," Shapur muttered. "Good. Let the boy come. I would rather kill an imperial heir than a provincial governor."

"Shall we prepare for preemptive raids?"

"No. Let them draw first blood. When the eagle flies across the border, we will pin its wings to the earth."

The council understood. It was not merely about warfare, it was about optics, about righteousness. If Rome could be made the aggressor, then all of Asia would see

Persia as the shield against tyranny. Even among the Greeks of Seleucia, there was dissatisfaction with Constantius's growing Christian zealotry. Pagan temples burned. Oracles silenced. A madness was brewing in the west.

Shapur would use it. He dismissed the court and returned to his private chambers.

That night, under the mosaic dome of his sanctuary, he sat with only his falcon for company. The bird, regal and sharp-eyed, watched him from its perch, still as marble.

He poured himself wine, Persian red, aged ten years. Not Roman. Never Roman.

As he drank, his thoughts grew darker, deeper. Not just about war, but about what came after.

He did not want to conquer Rome, not all of it. That was not the Sasanian destiny. But to humble it, to scar it so deeply it would never again dream of parity. This was his vision. To retake the lands of Mesopotamia. To break their Armenian alliances. To leave the Roman empire's eastern flank a weeping wound. And perhaps… if the gods willed it… to take Antioch once more.

He could already see it, Persian banners hanging from the Roman citadel, the cross torn down, Mithraic fire altars relit where once stood Christian churches. Not because he hated their god, but because their god had become an excuse for conquest. Faith, he believed, was a noble fire. But in Roman hands it was a torch of arson, burning across cultures to make way for their own imperial theology.

He would give them no more ground.

At dawn, he called for his scribes. "Prepare a message to Emperor Constantius," he said. The scribes waited, styluses poised.

Shapur spoke without notes. *"To Constantius Augustus, son of Fausta, ruler of the West: You have taken in a traitor and named him your brother. You have dared to meddle in Armenia, to build forts on Persian soil, and to raise false kings against my throne. You wear the mask of peace while sharpening your blade beneath it.*

You say Christ is your king. Then obey him and keep to your lands.

I am Shapur, son of Hormizd, son of Narseh, King of Kings of Ērānshahr, Light of the East, Chosen of Ahura Mazda. I do not kneel. I do not forget.

Withdraw your hand—or lose it."

The scribes' hands trembled as they transcribed. Shapur drank the last of his wine. The war had not yet begun.

The following days passed in restless intensity. Bishapur buzzed with quiet movement, caravans arriving under dusk, camel hooves muffled by felt wraps, couriers slipping through arches with sealed dispatches, generals conferring in whispers. The court knew better than to call it war yet but the king had changed, and all men knew it.

Shapur spent his hours walking the gardens and libraries, rarely speaking, but always thinking. Always watching.

He stopped often beneath the great bas-reliefs his artisans had carved into stone, images of his victories in the east, of Persian horsemen trampling rebels, of captives with ropes around their necks. Not out of vanity, but out of necessity. A reminder of what power was, and how fragile its memory could be. Rome made marble statues. Persia carved triumph into the mountain itself.

He studied one panel more than the others: the Triumph of Shapur at Gundeshapur. A scene where he sat mounted, a Roman commander kneeling before him. It had not yet happened. It was a future his stonemasons were ordered to carve as prophecy, not history.

The Romans built their monuments to the past. The Persians built them to intimidate the future.

Shapur's high priest, Kartir, requested an audience. The Zoroastrian magus had grown old, but not weak. His eyes burned with the same unrelenting fire he preached in the Fire Temples.

Shapur received him beneath the flame altar, where sacred fire danced behind an onyx screen. The holy place hummed with a thick silence, yet sacred and alive.

Kartir bowed low. "My king, I have read the stars. I have looked into the movements of Anāhitā's river. The omens favor you. But caution: the Roman god is wounded, not slain. And a wounded thing can still bite."

"Then let him bleed," Shapur said. "Let their bishops offer more prayers. I will give them fresh martyrs if they desire them."

Kartir's expression did not change. "I speak not of cruelty, but of clarity. The war must not be like the last. You must not merely strike, you must correct. As Ahura Mazda corrects the cosmos when it drifts from order."

Shapur looked into the fire. "And how would you have me correct it, Magus?"

Kartir stepped closer. "Break them with truth. Show their citizens how their emperor desecrates the ancient balance. Remind the east that Zoroaster gave law before Moses ever climbed his mountain. That fire burns purer than crucified flesh."

Shapur smiled faintly. Kartir, for all his devotion, was more Persian than priest. His flame was political as much as sacred. But the idea had merit.

The campaign against Rome would not only be one of swords but of symbols.

That night, Shapur called his chroniclers to his side and dictated new orders. "Create edicts in Greek and Aramaic. Let the cities of Syria and Cappadocia see them. Let it be known the Persians come not as conquerors, but as restorers of balance. Let them know we have not destroyed temples, only built them. We have not abolished gods, we have fed the sacred flame." He looked out toward the dark west. "Constantius builds crosses from law, nails men to them with taxes and creeds. We do not come to convert. We come to correct."

On the fifth night of his vigil, Shapur returned to the vault beneath the palace, the hidden chamber where only he and the royal archivists were allowed to enter. It was a room of memory, lined with scrolls and clay tablets stretching back to the time of Cyrus and Darius, of Seleucus and the fire-kings of old. The walls themselves bore inscriptions in three tongues: Old Persian, Elamite, and Aramaic.

Here was the pulse of Persia's soul. Not gold. Not armies. Not temples. History.

He lit a single oil lamp and wandered through the texts. Some were chronicles of the Achaemenids, some were treaties, or letters from Alexander, accounts of invasions and exiles. On one shelf lay a sealed scroll from the time of Narseh, his grandfather's final lament. Shapur had never read it. Tonight, he unsealed it.

The words, though brittle with time, cut deep. "I signed the treaty with eyes lowered. The gods turned their faces from me. It is a stain no flood will wash. But perhaps it will fertilize a future where my son, or his son, will avenge what I could not defend. If you read this, know that I did not forget. And do not forgive."

Shapur rolled the parchment slowly and set it back in its case. The silence in the room was absolute. His breath felt like thunder in that sanctum of stone.

By morning, the wind had changed.

Dust carried westward. An omen, the priests said.

In the main hall, Shapur addressed his generals. Fifty commanders of cavalry and heavy infantry, satraps of the provinces, emissaries from the mountain clans of the north and the desert horsemen of the south. They stood before him like statues awaiting command.

Shapur spoke not from a scroll, but from the soul. "Rome has crossed our borders again. Not only with men, but with ideas. It sends its soldiers to Armenia and its scriptures to Seleucia. It calls itself a light but it casts shadows across our lands. It offers gold to our enemies and crowns to our traitors.

They have forgotten the order of the world. Forgotten that Persia is not a kingdom, it is a pillar of the earth.

Let them come. Let Constantius send his soldiers. Let them march in steel across the Tigris. We will answer them not with pride, but with permanence."

He raised his hand.

"Begin preparations. Not for war but for remembrance. The day has come when we remind the world that east of the Euphrates, the lion still hunts."

The hall erupted in a solemn thud of armored fists against chests. Not frenzy. Discipline. Resolve.

That night, the war drums began.

Slow. Distant. Like the beat of a heart long held in check. The forges lit up. Blacksmiths worked without sleep. Horses were brought from the royal pastures. Grain wagons prepared. Banners mended.

The King of Kings stood upon the balcony of his citadel, the city below him humming with firelight and song. The chants of the priests echoed through the hills:

> "Azata vahišta ahurahe…
> The best truth is the Lord's.
> Vahištāhyā sraošā…
> Righteousness is obedience."

He looked west, toward the unseen walls of Antioch, the roads that would lead to blood. He whispered only to the wind, "I am Shapur, and I remember."

The moon had waned to a silver crescent when the summons came from Ctesiphon. Messengers rode through the mountain passes bearing Constantine's reply to Shapur's declaration. They reached Bishapur dust-choked and sunburned, escorted under torchlight into the Hall of the Lions.

The scroll bore the imperial seal of the West, a double-headed eagle stamped into red wax, flanked by a gold-threaded ribbon. Shapur broke it open with slow precision and read the Greek aloud:

"To Shapur, ruler of the land beyond the Euphrates,

I write not to threaten but to advise. Peace is the greater glory than conquest. The Christ whom you scorn instructs us to love our enemies, but also to protect the weak.
The Armenians have asked for our help, and we shall not deny it.
Your brother Hormizd lives in peace under our guardianship. He is treated as kin, not as tool.
The empire of Rome desires no war, but if it comes, we shall not be found unready."*

—Constantine Augustus

Shapur crushed the parchment into his hand. So diplomatic. So falsely humble. A Roman specialty to write threats in the language of virtue, to dress invasions in the robes of protection. "Peace," Constantine wrote. As though peace could be built on Persian subjugation. As though Rome's encroachment on Armenia was anything less than slow invasion. As though sheltering Hormizd was not a calculated move to fracture the Sasanian throne from within.

He tossed the scroll into the brazier and watched it curl and blacken. "Send a reply," he said coldly. "Three words: 'We are coming.'

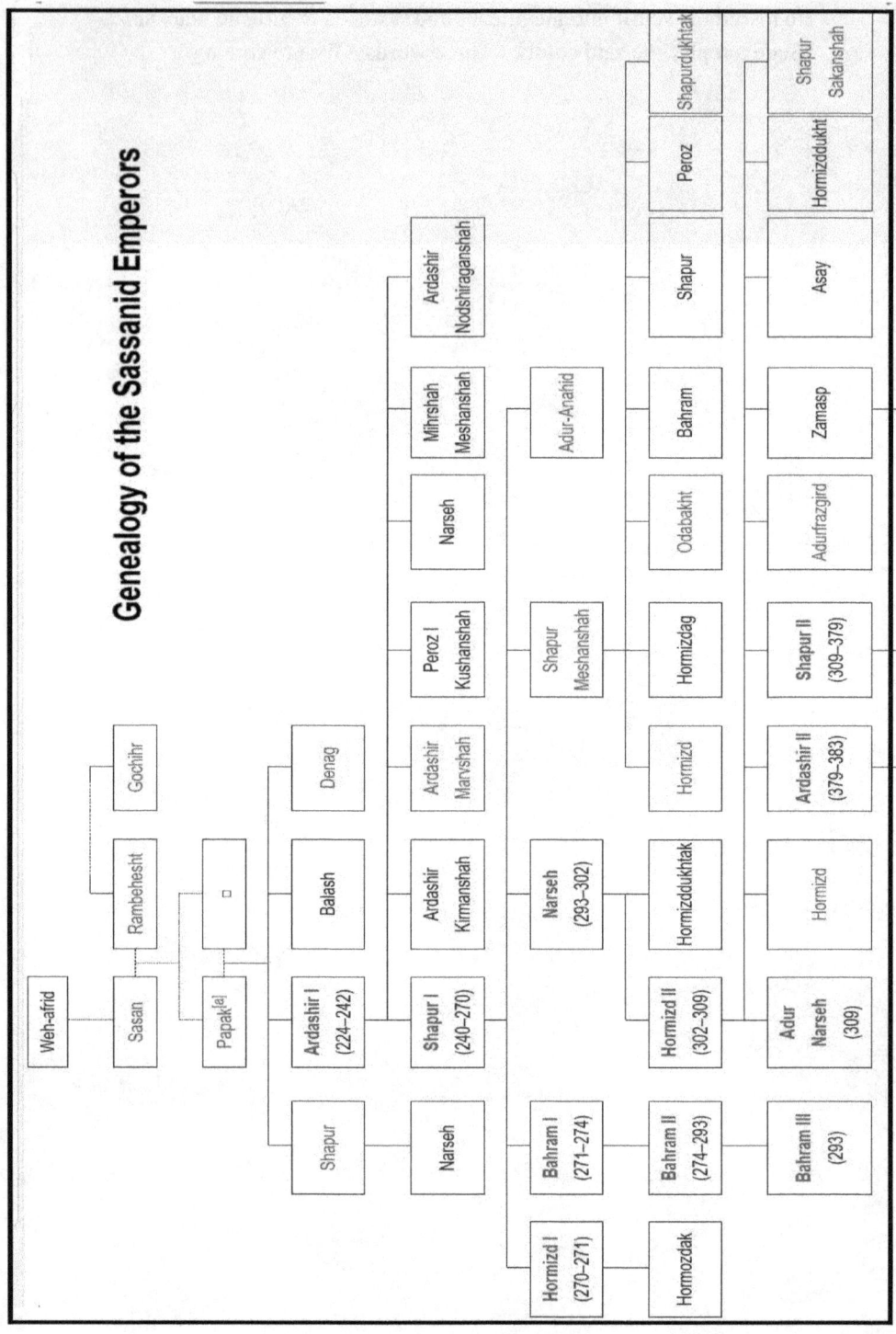

CHAPTER IV: FAMILY TIES

The halls of the Exilarch's palace in Mahoza were bathed in amber shadows, torches licking the carved stone walls with tongues of flame. The guard at the chamber door bowed stiffly as Natronai approached, his steps echoing on the mosaic floor. At thirty-three, Natronai bar Nehemiah was already a legend in the streets; a brilliant orator, a fierce patriot, and, to many, a prophet. But to others, especially in the high circles of the Jewish court, he was something far more dangerous. He was a disturbance in the natural order wishing to preserve the status quo.

The doors to the council chamber groaned open. Eleven elders, wrapped in dark robes, sat in silence around a horseshoe-shaped table of cedarwood. At its head, under a canopy of golden lions, sat Nehemiah, the Exilarch, prince of the Jews in Babylonia, heir of David, the ruler in exile.

"Come, my son," Nehemiah said, though his voice lacked any natural warmth.

Natronai bowed and took his place in the center of the chamber, under the scrutiny of a dozen sets of cold, assessing eyes.

"This is not a trial," Nehemiah said slowly, fingers steepled, "but neither is it a courtesy. Your recent sermons have troubled the hearts of the faithful. They fear you are preaching insurrection."

Natronai met his father's eyes. "I speak only what has been shown to me, Father. Nothing more, nothing less."

A long silence followed. One of the elders coughed. Another shifted uncomfortably.

"You speak of visions. Of hearing the voice of the Almighty. You tell the people you are chosen. That the hand of God has lifted you above other men."

"Because He has," Natronai said. "I did not seek it. I did not ask for this. But God came to me. He spoke to me from the wind and from fire. Who are any of us that we can defy the will of the Almighty"

Nehemiah stood, his chair scraping across the marble like a dagger against bone.

"This is blasphemy!" he roared. The walls trembled. "You profane the Holy name with your delusions. Do you think this is a game? That you can wear the mantle of prophecy like a cloak before the people, stoking their foolish hopes?"

Natronai's face was calm, but there was fire in his eyes. "Did not Moses tremble before the burning bush? Did not Isaiah fall to his knees, crying 'Woe is me'? Did not our prophets speak truth, though no one believed them?"

Nehemiah's fists slammed the table. "You are not Moses! You are not Isaiah! You are my son, and you are being led by madness."

"Is that what Johah's father insisted as well? That the voice of the Almighty was madness, a malady of his birth and he should ignore it. We all know how well that advice served him as he was punished until he relinquished and surrendered to God's will."

The elders leaned forward now, watching, some with pity, others with disgust, not knowing whether they should fear or disdain the man standing before them.

"You dishonor our house," Nehemiah continued, voice shaking with rage. "You lead the people astray. You set yourself up as a messiah, though the time is not ripe, and the Temple lies in ruins."

Natronai stepped closer to his father.

"Who are you to decide upon God's timeline, Abba? That is not my question, it is His and He holds you in contempt for challenging His authority. I did not ask to see this vision, Abba. But it just came to me, as all the others did before. An angel clothed in luminescent linen, a voice like rain upon a pane of glass, has shown me the broken world and the scroll that currently cannot be read. He placed it in my hand and said, 'Go.' Are you about to deny all that I have seen. Will you stand in this court and declare most definitely that this is not the word of God! Say it now, Father! Deny God's will!"

Nehemiah's voice dropped to a cold whisper. "You will retract your words. Before the elders, before the community. You will make it known that your visions were dreams, born of fasting or fever. You will humble yourself."

Natronai swallowed hard. His hands trembled. But his voice, when it came, was firm. "No. I will not deny the words of God! You cannot force me to do so."

The word struck the room like a blow. Gasps. A few muttered curses. Others shook in fear.

Nehemiah's eyes widened. "No?"

"No," Natronai said again. "I will not lie. I will not deny my God and heed the words of fearful men. I would rather be cast out than betray the truth of what I have seen."

"Then you will be cast out!" Nehemiah roared, pointing a shaking finger. "Out of this house, out of this city, out of our holy people! You will be nothing to me."

Something cracked in Natronai's heart, but his spine remained straight. "Then let it be so," he said softly. "Better to be a servant of God in exile than a prince in a palace of silence. May God have mercy upon your souls for what you have done this day."

Nehemiah lunged forward, grabbing his son by the tunic, dragging him inches from his face. "You arrogant boy. Do you know what you risk? The Persians already whisper of revolt. The yeshivot groan with Roman spies. The people look to us to be calm, to be stable. And you bring fire into the camp!"

Natronai's breath was hot on his father's cheek. "I merely bring the truth. Perhaps the camp needs to burn, Father. Maybe the exile has lasted too long. Maybe God is not silent. Maybe He has not forgotten us, even though you seem to have forgotten Him."

Nehemiah struck his son. The crack of the slap echoed like thunder.

Blood welled on Natronai's lip. He didn't move. He would not give his father the satisfaction of seeing his heart break.

"You will go," Nehemiah said sternly, his voice ragged with fury and grief. "You will take nothing. You are stripped of your name, your inheritance, your place in the House of David."

Natronai looked into his father's eyes and saw not a tyrant, but a broken man, desperate to preserve what order remained. Desperate to maintain everything as it had been for centuries. Afraid to accept change.

"I love you," Natronai said. "But I love God more. It is up to Him to forgive you."

Nehemiah turned away, covering his face with both hands. "Get out," he said, voice muffled by tears. "Get out before I curse you with my last breath."

"You cannot curse that which God has blessed, Abba. You should know better than that as someone who calls himself a man of God." Natronai turned and walked from the chamber, his shoulders back, though his chest ached. As he passed the elders, none met his eyes. He felt pity for them all, as he realized those claiming to be closest to Almighty God were actually the ones furthest away.

In the silence that followed, Nehemiah collapsed into his chair, trembling.

The oldest of the elders leaned forward. "He may be mad, my lord. Or he may be a prophet. Either way, I believe we may have committed the gravest of sins."

Nehemiah did not answer. He only wept.

The gates of the council chamber closed behind Natronai with a hollow, metallic thud, but the sound echoed like a funeral bell in his ears. He stood motionless in the corridor for a moment, as if rooted to the polished stone beneath his feet, staring forward without seeing. The murmur of voices behind the door had ceased. Judgment had been passed. The Exilarch, his father, had disinherited him. His name had been stricken from the rolls of his lineage. Worse still, he had been cast out of the community, excommunicated from the very people he had once hoped to redeem.

The walls of Mahoza, grand and ancient, now felt oppressive. Each brick was heavy with the weight of tradition, of generations that had held to the Law, to the continuity of exile, and to the authority of fathers over sons. His own footsteps, echoing faintly as he descended the outer steps, sounded hollow in his ears. Even the sun above seemed ashamed to shine on him. The courtyard, bustling moments ago, emptied before him like the Red Sea parting for a man no longer welcome. Not even the curious dared meet his gaze.

He walked. He didn't know where. He passed shopkeepers, elders, scribes, mothers carrying jars of water, young boys chasing stray dogs. But none of them were real. His mind was far away or perhaps buried too deep within his own thoughts.

It was only when he reached the riverbank that he paused. The canal that cut through the city flowed gently, winding its way like a quiet question through the landscape. He sat on the stone ledge and stared into the murky water.

Was it real? The question came unbidden, and it struck him harder than any accusation his father had cast. He had been so certain. He had felt the presence an overwhelming rush of holiness, of clarity that no man, no priest, no scholar could give. He had heard the voice, not with his ears, perhaps, but in the marrow of his bones, in the trembling silence between dreams. But that certainty now warred with the sting of his father's words. "You have blasphemed. You have lied in the name of the Most High." Could one who had truly heard the voice of God be rejected so utterly? Had Moses been cast out? Had Elijah been shamed?

He clenched his fists. Moses. The name came like a whisper. Not from the world around him, but from somewhere deeper. A memory? No, something closer than a single memory. More like a thought that had been waiting patiently for him to quiet the storm within. Moses. The name repeated itself, demanding to be heard. Of course. He too had been cast out. Not by Pharaoh at first, but by his own people. He had killed the Egyptian, tried to stand up for the oppressed and what had they said? "Who made you a ruler and judge over us?" Moses had fled. He had wandered into Midian, tending sheep in a forgotten corner of the world. He had married, made a quiet life. And then, only then, had the Voice come to him, emerging from an unquenchable fire.

Was this the pattern? God did not call the strong and established. He called the broken, the outcast, the wilderness-dwellers. Those who had lost everything else and so had no one left to trust but Him.

Natronai stood slowly, as if rising from the grave.

The canal trickled on, uncaring, but something within him had shifted. The pain was still there, his father's words, stinging, searing and raw. The love for his father, twisted now into a bitter vine. The ache of being abandoned, severed from community, from familiarity, from the safety of shared belief.

But under the pain… there was resolve. He could not return. He could not undo what had been said in that chamber. Nor would he even bother to try. His father had spoken in wrath, yes, but perhaps with fear, too. Natronai's visions had threatened not only his father's authority but the structure of the world their people had built in exile. A world of caution, of endurance, of waiting without expectation.

But he had been called to act. He looked up, toward the distant east. Beyond the outer city, past the plains, through the cultivated fields and dusty trade roads, rose the spires of Ctesiphon. Somewhere in that sprawling imperial city, Shapur, King of Kings, reigned over Persia. "Go to Pharaoh," the voice said. Now that same thought returned, clearer this time.

It was madness, he told himself. It was impossible. What could a Jewish exile, an excommunicated nobody, hope to achieve by speaking with the Sassanid emperor, the King of Kings? But was it more impossible than Moses standing before Pharaoh with nothing but a staff and a message? Was it more impossible than the sea opening?

He turned from the river. His steps were slow at first, then more confident. He would need to leave and cross the river into the world of the Persians. Traveling east along the Tigris until he reached Veh-Ardashir, the satellite city of the royal court. There he would wait for an audience. Somehow. He would find a way to speak to this modern day Pharaoh.

He did not know what he would say to Shapur. He did not know how he would be received, ignoring the reality that he may not be received at all. But he knew what the message was: "Let my people go." Not from physical bondage, as in Egypt, but from the bondage of fear, of forgetting the promises of God, as the suffered under Roman oppression. Rome had buried their hope beneath generations of mourning. Only Shapur could provide him with the resources to free his people, to rule the land of their ancestors once again, as a nation under God.

He walked on. Behind him, the great city of Mahoza faded into dust and silence. Before him, the long road east shimmered in the dying light of day, uncertain and treacherous. But now, Natronai understood what had been demanded of him all along.

CHAPTER V: AN ODD ALLIANCE

The Tigris shimmered like quicksilver beneath the morning sun. Natronai, son of the Exilarch of Mahoza, crossed it alone in a cedar-wood skiff, the oars creaking in rhythmic defiance of his nerves. On the western bank, the capital awaited, great and gilded, veiled in dust and pride, a city whose foundations reached deep into the soil of empires long buried.

He was thirty-three years old, not quite the forty Moses had been, but today he would face a god among men. The guards at the gate had not known what to make of him: a Jew with the bearing of a prince, robes of fine linen marked with Babylonian thread, eyes full of fire, lips speaking Farsi better than many scribes. He carried no weapon but bore the ring of the House of David, the signet passed from fathers to sons since the day the Parthians had taken in their exiled line.

They made him wait. Three days in the gardens of the outer court, with dates, water, and little else upon which to survive. Three days of incense-thick silence and pointed delays. And then, on the fourth morning, a eunuch with turquoise eyeliner summoned him through the Lion Gate. Natronai walked with deliberate calm.

The inner palace was carved from sunlight and stone. Marble lions flanked the staircases, and gilt arches framed the frescoes of battle and coronation. He passed beneath a frieze of the great King Ardashir slaying Ahriman, the demon of lies, and another showing Shapur II trampling Roman prisoners beneath the thrashing hooves of his cavalry. It was a reminder of who ruled here.

The Hall of the Hundred Columns echoed with absence. It was wide and cool, the smell of myrrh and dried blood mingling in the air. At the far end, seated atop a platform of ivory and onyx, was Shapur II, crowned, cloaked, and utterly still. Fire burned in tall braziers on either side of him, casting his face in alternating gold and shadow.

The King of Kings had been studying him in silence from the moment he entered the hall.

"So," Shapur said at last, voice like a drawn blade. "The lion of Judah crosses my river and walks into my house. Or should I say the lion cub. I have but one question. Why?"

Natronai bowed, not groveling, but with the solemnity of a man before someone of a standing beyond mere mortals.

"I come in the name of the Lord, whose voice stirs prophets and kings. I come to you, Shahanshah, not as a suppliant, but as a messenger from my God."

Shapur raised an eyebrow. "A messenger," he repeated. "A messenger from your God, so you say. I am intrigued. Go on."

Natronai's jaw tightened, but his voice remained steady. "My people suffer under the Roman yoke. In Judea, the priests have been silenced, the scrolls burned, the Temple desecrated, not with fire, but the erection of a Christian church on the site. Our land is named after our ancient enemies. Our God mocked. We are taxed, censored, watched, and crucified for simply breathing."

"And exactly what does that have to do with me? Are you accusing me of treating your people in the same manner here, in Babylon?"

"But you can help stop this," Natronai insisted.

"You are not the only ones that seek my help," Shapur said. "Constantine silences all who do not kneel to his Christ. Why would you think your cause is more imperative?"

"Then you understand that all peoples suffering under the heel of Rome are allies in pain," Natronai said. "But my people are the key."

Shapur leaned forward, fingers steepled. "Speak, son of exile. Tell me why I should care for your suffering above all others. Tell me why I should see you as more than a single ember blowing in the wind."

Natronai stepped closer, his sandals clicking softly against the polished stone. "Because I bring the entire conflagration, not a single ember. I bring you the promise of delivering a revolt that will change the world." He let that comment settle like dust after a passing storm.

"How many revolts will this be now?" Shapur questioned. "Three, four? Each time your losses have measured in the hundreds of thousands. Why would this time be any different?"

"This time is different," Natronai insisted. "There are thousands in Palestine who still remember the blood of the Maccabees. Who speak of Messiah in hushed tones. The Galilee festers with hope, the coals are still hot beneath Roman ash. There was never a descendant of David to lead these other revolts. If I rise, and if you support me, then they will follow."

"You would go to Palestine and lead this rebellion against Caesar?" Shapur asked, eyes narrowed.

"I will not only go but I will restore what Rome tried to erase," Natronai said. "A kingdom under God. A free Israel."

"And how does this advantage my empire? Why do I care if there is or isn't a free Israel? All I see is a request to aid you in gaining a kingdom for yourself."

"My lord, Lion of the East, Light of Ērānshahr," Natronai had prepared for this very moment, "what I offer is not a mere rebellion against Rome. What I offer is the crumbling of their very spine, the shattering of their hold upon the eastern provinces, and the opening of a corridor from your throne to the gates of Jerusalem and beyond."

Natronai's skill as a master orator were clearly evident.

"You ask what advantage Persia gains from a Jewish revolt. I say this: You will not merely gain territory; you will gain a buffer of loyal blood between your empire and Rome's grasping claws. A Jewish kingdom, reborn with your blessing, would serve as a loyal vassal, not out of coercion, but out of gratitude and shared hatred of the West."

He stepped forward, passion growing in his voice.

"Rome bleeds you, my lord. Every few years, they provoke war, violate treaties, or incite unrest in Armenia. They push their boundaries eastward like vines, choking what they do not own. But I say, why wait for them to strike again? Let us light the fire in Palestine before they can marshal their next assault. Let the Judeans rise not with stones and whispers, but with organized legions, armed with Persian steel, and burning with divine purpose."

It was obvious that he had caught Shapur's attention.

"And more than this: if I succeed, and I shall succeed, because the God of our fathers walks with me, then Rome's soldiers will be forced to turn inward. Syria will tremble. Arabia Petraea will see her garrisons stripped bare. Egypt may stir next. You will have not one, but a dozen fires burning in Rome's eastern holdings, and none of them lit by your hand. You may appear blameless to the world, yet the flames will clear your path."

He let that sink in for a moment.

"My lord, I will tell you this with open heart: I do not come to beg for freedom. I come to offer an alliance, a true one, built on shared history. Did not your own kings, the Achaemenids, restore our Temple and allow us to return from exile? Did we not thrive under your ancestors' justice? We remember. As Jews we remember the kindness extended to us by Persia. We have no love for the West, for Titus putting a torch to our Temple, for Hadrian's persecutions, for Constantine's crosses planted like daggers extending to the far horizon in our soil. They have tried to banish our language, erased our sages, defiled our laws. But you... you let us flourish in Babylon. And for that we are eternally grateful."

Natronai spread his arms wide.

"Help me now to lead this revolt and I shall bring you more than land. I will bring you a holy alliance. My kingdom, once born, will be your shield against the West. I will send troops when you call, grain when your cities hunger, and coin when your coffers need replenishing. More than that, I will win you the hearts of every Jew under heaven, from the Euphrates to the Nile, from Antioch to Alexandria. They will remember that it was Shapur who lifted the Messiah's hand and declared him free."

Now Natronai's voice lowered, steady but intense.

"The Romans have their Christ, forged of fables and imperial lies. But we, the House of David, still alive. I am not a dreamer, my lord. I am a descendant of kings.

And if you give me your blessing, I shall become the stone that cracks Rome's foundation."

He knelt now, while still speaking:

"Give me a few battalions. Allow my people to organize, train, and rally in your borderlands. Let the rumors spread that a son of David is rising in Palestine, not alone, but with the might of Persia behind him. The zeal of the people will do the rest. They wait only for a spark from that ember in the wind you spoke of. I am that spark."

Then, with head still bowed, he delivered the conclusion of his answer. "You have mastered the East, my lord but that is merely land. Let me deliver the hearts and minds of the people. Help me master their faith in something greater than us all. The West will not understand it. Rome cannot fight it. But Persia... Persia will profit from it for generations to come."

The chamber fell almost completely silent. Only the drip of the fountain behind Shapur's throne echoed in the stillness. Natronai remained on his knees, a vessel of conviction, awaiting the word of the King of Kings.

Shapur rose from his throne slowly. His robes trailed like smoke behind him. He descended the steps one by one, until he stood a few feet from the Jewish prince.

"You speak eloquently but do you know what you are asking? You wish for me to wager my armies on a rebellion consisting of peasants and fishermen?"

"No," Natronai replied. "I ask you to imagine what desperate people can do with pitchforks and axes, fishing nets and spears. That is all they will have at first until the first deliveries of Persian swords and shields. All I ask is for your promise that when the Romans begin to burn the lands putting down the revolt, that you come with your legions and seal the victory. When you come, it will not be as invader, but as liberator. The Hebrews will open the gates to you."

Shapur circled him now, slowly. "And what about you? Exactly what do you ask from me in return?"

"Recognition of the Kingdom. Arms and security. A safe harbor. The right to rebuild the Temple as it once was. But most of all the opportunity to be your ally. That we will be true allies celebrating in the fall of Constantinople."

Shapur stopped behind him.

"You speak like a prophet."

Natronai did not turn. "I am," he said. "But I am also a tactician. And I know Rome's weakness. It is no longer a city of iron, but of contradiction. A Christian emperor commanding pagan legions. Greek cities ruled by Latin laws. Even the senators despise the house of Constantine. All that remains is the push."

Shapur said nothing for a long while. Then he moved back to his throne, ascending like a lion returning to its rock. "Let me remind you again that the last time your people rebelled, Rome slaughtered them by half. They burned your cities and sowed salt into your earth."

"And still we live," Natronai replied. "But more importantly, we remember and that will spur us to victory."

A smile ghosted across Shapur's face. It was not mockery, but something colder: calculation. " It is apparent that you hate Rome more than I do."

"No," said Natronai. "I only hate what Rome does to the soul. That is far worse than hate."

Shapur tapped the armrest of his throne once, twice, thrice. His gaze never left Natronai. The brazier flames danced on the walls, casting long shadows behind the columns, like giants listening to the words of men.

"You hate what Rome does to the soul," Shapur murmured. "And yet you would trade the spiritual yoke of exile for the earthly sword of my empire?"

"We will serve God first," Natronai replied calmly. "And ally with the King of Kings as long as our goals are aligned. I do not ask for thrones or temples. Only the freedom to rebuild what was ours, what is ours, and what will always be ours."

Shapur chuckled softly, without mirth. "I have met prophets before. Most smell of sandalwood and honey. You smell of ash and conviction."

Natronai said nothing.

"Are you willing to die for this?"

"Yes."

Shapur's face hardened. "Thus far you have lived a soft life. Raised in a palace. A prince within your own city. Servants awaiting upon your every need. Do you honestly believe you would be willing to kill for this dream of yours?"

Natronai did not hesitate in answering. "If God demands it I would release a river of blood upon the earth."

Shapur rose again, now walking slowly back toward him, the hem of his cloak sweeping over the floor.

"You propose a rebellion within Rome's borders. A holy war. You would light a fire in Palestine, and hope it spreads to Syria, to Egypt, to the very gates of Antioch. All while my legions are occupied in the mountains, watching the eagle bleed. We would only come to your aid when it would be possible to come, whenever that may be. No sooner."

Natronai nodded once. "We will continue to fight until you are able to come and deliver the death blow to the Romans."

"And you trust your people are ready for this war?"

"They are desperate," said Natronai. "The rabbis preach caution, but the youth whisper of vengeance. The Zealot blood runs again in the veins of the shepherds and scribes. We are a vineyard pressed by foreign boots. The grapes are nearly ready to burst."

"You speak as if you have been there and both seen and heard things, yet until today, I presume, you have never been out of Mahoza."

"Only because God has shown me these things in my dreams and visions and I know them to be true."

"Do not think me blind to what transpires in Mahoza. There has been talk of these visions that you claim to experience. I know this in the same way that I know you were excommunicated by your own father several days ago because you insisted that these visions were true."

"My father is a man paralyzed into inactivity by his own fears," Natronai replied.

Shapur smiled. "I am well aware of men like that. They are the making of obedient vassals but little else. I certainly do not doubt your dreams and visions. True kings will experience them and they are what drives us to becoming legends within our own time. I feel sorry for all those that rule and have never experienced them." Shapur folded his hands behind his back and turned his gaze outside one of the window, where the sun now bled across the horizon like a crimson ribbon. "You know," he said, "your father is not the only princeling that I know of that refused to believe that the gods speak to those whom they consider worthy."

"You speak of Hormizd," Natronai said, without flinching.

That earned him a glance. "Yes," Shapur said, surprised by Natronai's mention of his brother. "I doubt anyone else would have guessed that I was referring to my brother. He's gone soft with Greek wine and Christian sentiment. They parade him about like a domesticated wolf cub. He never believed in the visions that I experienced. And now…" he turned to face Natronai, "they use him as a sword against me. Just as I might use you."

Natronai smiled, just faintly. "Then we understand one another."

Shapur stepped forward again, now face to face within a couple of feet of the Jewish prince. "You want to restore Israel. I want to destroy Constantinople's legitimacy. But let us not deceive ourselves, our alliance is one of necessity, not love."

"True alliances always are," Natronai replied.

Shapur appraised him again. Natronai's face was proud but unbending. There was no fanatic's foam at his lips. No wildness. Just steel. Cold, god-forged steel.

"You are a dangerous man," the Shahanshah said.

"I was born in a drowning pool," Natronai replied. "Danger is how we breathe."

There it was again: not defiance, but depth.

After a long silence, Shapur spoke again, his voice low, deliberate. "You understand what this would require."

"I do."

"You must have emissaries in every town in Judea, in Galilee, in the Decapolis. You must be ready to sabotage roads, attack supply trains, intercept couriers, and turn tax revolts into a holy war."

"I am well aware."

"You must not break too early. If you rise too quickly before my eastern forces are positioned, Rome will crush you, and I will gain nothing but your bones."

"I know the rhythms of prophecy, Majesty. I will strike when the heavens open and not a moment before. I will know when to expect your reinforcements to arrive and we will hold on until then."

Shapur raised a brow. "Do they really speak of Messiah among your people?"

Natronai's voice became quiet. "Not in my father's house. He has forbidden it. And certainly not among the Sanhedrin in Palestine as they fear it would mean the end of their holding on to the reins of power but as for the common people, they never stopped."

"And do they think it is you?"

"No," Natronai responded truthfully, "but they will follow me based on my heritage until he comes if there is to be another. I may only be a forerunner, a voice crying in the wilderness. Or perhaps I am the one they have been waiting for. Only in victory will we be able to tell."

Shapur smiled. "Even your language has the flair of poetry."

"Truth demands poetry," Natronai said. "It must pierce the flesh like a blade dressed in silk."

They stood in silence again.

Outside, the wind rose over the river. Bells chimed in the Temple of Anahita. A hawk circled the parapets. Perhaps it was a sign.

Shapur exhaled deeply and moved to a side alcove where a tall bronze map stood mounted on stone. His hand traced the lines of the Fertile Crescent, the Euphrates, the coast of Phoenicia, and the crumpled valleys of Judea.

"You would begin where?" the Emperor asked calmly.

"Caesarea," Natronai stated. "It is a city filled with Rome's pride; amphitheaters, palaces, garrisons, but also filled with Jewish artisans and Samaritans who feel equally crushed. From there, the fire will spread. To Tiberias. To Sepphoris. To the hills where the Zealots reside in quiet anticipation."

Shapur shook his head. "You are overlooking the fact that the Roman governor resides in that city with several cohorts at his disposal. They Romans have the advantage to respond with speed because they are already there. But also, with cruelty against the citizenry. You will be undone before you have even begun. That is not the way to start a successful rebellion."

"Where would you suggest?" Natronai asked, eager to learn from a superior strategist.

"I suggest you set your first target lower," Shapur recommended. "You must raise your army first from the outlying towns and the villages. Places the Romans do not care about and where they likely do not have ears. Do not think about a fortified city like Caesarea until you have distracted them enough that they send most of their forces to the north. In these small towns, some will have posted Roman garrisons. Wet your teeth on several garrisons before attempting a larger prize."

Natronai nodded his head. "A wise suggestion Majesty and one I will definitely heed."

"Once the Romans become embroiled in my own war in the mountains of Armenia, their forces bogged down, I will send you men to end your war." He turned back. "And when the land is broken, then the Roman legions will be scattered…"

"That is when I shake the foundations of Constantinople by taking over Caesarea and capturing the governor." Natronai raised his chin.

"Exactly," Shapur grinned as he returned to his throne, his mind already moving like a general's, anticipating routes, sabotage, Roman countermeasures, rebel supply lines. It was not a prophet standing before him, it was a piece on a chess board and he was the grand master. "Very well," he concluded. "You will have my support. But discreetly at first, so as not to raise Roman suspicions. Gold, arms, and letters of passage for your agents. I will instruct the satrap of Adiabene to grant you safe travel and access to my scribes. The best of my palace guards will accompany you. His name is Ashurbanipol and he will serve you bravely He will also keep an eye on protecting my investment,"

Natronai bowed. "You are most gracious, Majesty."

"You will also receive a Persian escort when the time comes for you to leave. A small caravan that will resemble merchants but consisting of expert fighters. Not large enough to interest Rome, but visible enough to embolden your faithful."

"My many thanks, Majesty."

But Shapur held up a hand. "At no time will you speak in my name unless I command it. If your revolt fails before I can send you reinforcements, I will deny any knowledge of you. If it succeeds, I will claim you as an ally. Is that understood?"

Natronai nodded once. "Perfectly, Majesty."

Shapur studied him for a long moment, then reached into the folds of his robe and removed a signet ring shaped like a lion devouring a serpent. "Take this. It bears no name. But it will open doors in my empire that most would not dare to knock upon."

Natronai accepted it with both hands.

"And may your God," Shapur said with an arched brow, "be as loyal as your tongue."

After the audience concluded, Natronai was not escorted out of the palace. Instead, a servant in plain robes led him through a side corridor behind the throne room, a narrow, unadorned stone passage lit by oil lamps in niches. It smelled of frankincense, sweat, and the passing of ages. He did not ask where they were going.

Eventually they reached a plain iron door. The servant opened it and bowed to him. Inside was a long chamber with a mosaic floor, scroll racks from floor to ceiling, and a single table at its center. A man sat at the table already, waiting: grey-bearded, robed in black, with the jeweled belt of a priest but the posture of a bureaucrat. His eyes were ink-dark and unreadable.

"This is Veh-Shapur," said the servant before bowing himself out. "The Shahanshah's Minister of Secret Matters."

Natronai stepped forward. "So. Even prophets must be vetted."

Veh-Shapur gestured to the seat across from him. "Even prophets," he said mildly, "cast shadows."

Veh-Shapur questioned him without expression, moving seamlessly between Aramaic, Middle Persian, Greek, and even Hebrew. He asked for names of any acquaintances Natronai might have in Palestine, whether the Essenes had truly died out, whether the Samaritans could be bribed, and which Roman citizens Natronai thought were most prone to bribery or blackmail.

When Natronai answered, Veh-Shapur recorded nothing. His memory, it seemed, was his scroll.

At one point, the minister narrowed his gaze and asked, "And what if Rome offers you a crown? What if Constantius himself offers to restore Jerusalem and rebuild the Temple in your name?"

Natronai didn't flinch. "I would spit on it."

Veh-Shapur tilted his head. "You are ambitious."

"No," Natronai said. "I am chosen. Rome cannot give me anything that God hasn't already promised."

The silence between them stretched what seemed an eternity.

Then Veh-Shapur leaned back. "You are dangerous."

"So, I've already been told. It is the reason I have been excommunicated."

He folded his hands. "Shapur has decided to invest in your cause. But his generosity has fine edges. You will receive what you need: coin, arms, messengers, A small escort, but not as soldiers. At least not openly."

"I understand."

Veh-Shapur gave a slow nod. "I believe you do."

That night, Natronai was given a guest chamber in one of the old royal wings, stone-walled and humble, but furnished with cypress-framed couches, copper mirrors, and thick rugs woven in Sogdian patterns. Servants left him apricots, cold lamb, wine, and scrolls of Zoroastrian hymns, perhaps to see if he would read them.

He touched nothing. Instead, he stood alone by the narrow window, watching the moon rise over the rooftops of Ctesiphon. Somewhere far beyond, over desert and plain, Judea lay sleeping under Roman stars. He whispered a prayer not to be heard, but to be remembered. "Adonai, give me wisdom. Not the wisdom of priests or kings, but the wisdom of Joseph in Pharaoh's court. That I might survive among lions until the dream is fulfilled."

The next morning, Shapur summoned him again. This time it was not to the throne hall, but to the royal stables.

They walked alone between rows of the Shah's horses: black stallions bred in the eastern provinces, trained for war from birth. Each bore embroidered harnesses, bronze ornaments, and saddles wrapped in ox hide. Shapur moved among them like a father among sons.

"These creatures," he said, stroking one gently behind the ear, "know war better than most men. They don't argue. They don't hesitate. They listen to the wind."

Natronai kept pace beside him.

"They're beautiful," he said.

"They're truthful," Shapur corrected him. "There's no deception in muscle or bone. That's why I come here. When the palace fills with flatterers, these are the only ones that remind me I am still mortal."

He stopped walking and turned. "Why did your father not come to try and dissuade you from this madness?"

Natronai blinked. "The Exilarch would never be allowed into Ctesiphon without first being summoned."

"But you were."

"I crossed the river without asking."

Shapur studied him again, this time less as a king measuring a pawn, and more like a soldier sizing up a comrade. There was a flicker of respect now, behind the iron in his eyes.

"I will tell you why I think he did not come," Shapur continued. "Because secretly he hopes he was wrong and you are the messenger of your god that will deliver your people from Roman oppression."

"Or, as he said in his final words to me, I am no longer his son and he no longer cares whether I live or die."

Shapur shook his head. "Never believe that it is possible for a father to no longer love a son. Trust me when I say he will always care deeply for you."

"You do not know my father," Natronai replied.

"Do you know what they call me in the west?" Shapur asked.

"The Beast of the East. The Second Xerxes. The Scourge."

Shapur smirked. "Good. I like it when my enemies are afraid and call me names that terrify them. But do you know what they call you in Ctesiphon?"

Natronai's expression did not change. "I did not know that I was known in this city. I'm guessing a heretic. A madman. A rabble-rouser. Perhaps some mistake me for a Messiah?"

"Not yet. That is how I know your father cares for you, If he didn't, I would have heard you called many names by now. He has purposely protected you."

"Am I to feel regret now that you have told me this?" Natronai questioned.

"No," Shapur shook his head. "I only wanted you to begin this mission without anger clouding your judgement. From this day forward you must be focused on only one objective."

They looked at one another for a long moment. Then Shapur gestured toward the stables. "Choose one."

"A horse?"

"A partner. You'll need one to ride west, won't you?"

Natronai hesitated. Then stepped into the row. After a few moments, he stopped before a lean grey stallion, smaller than the others, but restless-eyed, with a scar on its neck.

Shapur raised an eyebrow. "That one?"

"Yes."

"Why?"

"Because it is different from all of the others. It's seen something. And survived."

Shapur nodded once. "Then we are alike."

They spent an hour together afterward, pouring over maps in the royal command tent outside the city walls. Shapur unrolled a massive leather atlas marked in red and gold ink, detailing every mountain pass, caravan route, fortress, and aqueduct between the Zagros and the Jordan Valley.

"You will go first to Edessa," Shapur said. "There is a man there named Yazdin awaiting you. A merchant. But he has more swords than silks. He will help move supplies into Syria."

"From there I go to Damascus?"

"No," said Shapur. "You let Damascus rot. That city is loyal to Byzantium. But the Decapolis, Gadara, Pella, Gerasa, these places are neglected. Ready to rise if touched by fire. I will give you names of people to talk to. They may help you once your revolt begins but I cannot guarantee it."

Natronai's finger traced the map downward. "And from the east?"

"You'll have support from the Mesopotamian frontier. Arms will flow through Adiabene and across the Euphrates at night. But you must be like smoke. Visible enough to inspire but invisible enough to survive. You raise the men and I will see that Adiabene will provide them with swords."

Natronai nodded. "And the final objective?"

Shapur's voice was iron. "Jerusalem. Nothing says defeat to the Romans as an independent Jerusalem under Jewish rule once again."

Outside, the wind kicked up sand and the banners of Persia, lions, bulls, and phoenixes whipped like living flame against the desert sun.

Inside, two men, an emperor and a rebel spoke in measured tones of fire, siege, rebellion, and providence.

And far to the west, in Constantinople, no one yet stirred. But the storm was coming.

On the morning of Natronai's departure, the sky was veiled in crimson haze. The Tigris looked like blood. Natronai dressed in the plain robes of a merchant's garb, dyed in indigo, with no insignia of rank or lineage. His beard was trimmed, his face unmarked. To the world, he was no one. But in the hidden pouch beneath his tunic, he carried two scrolls and one ring.

The first scroll was a sealed letter bearing Shapur's cipher, to be delivered to Yazdin in Edessa. It gave Natronai access to Shapur's covert network across the western frontier; smugglers, spies, and assassins bound by silence and silver.

The second was older: a copy of the scroll of Isaiah, worn thin by time and thumbprints, passed to him from his father through Shapur, with a single whispered command: "Remind them who you are." Perhaps Shapur had been right about the Exilarch's love for his rebellious son.

The ring was cold to the touch. It bore no name, only a symbol: a beast devouring a serpent but as Shapur described, it had the power to open locked doors.

Natronai mounted the grey stallion he'd chosen in the royal stables. The animal stood as still as stone. Beneath his saddle, concealed in the lining, were gold coins, two small knives, and a vial of venom, Shapur's parting gift, "for when words fail."

The Shahanshah did not come to see him off. He had already gone north to review troops near the Armenian border, or perhaps to commune with his own doubts.

But Veh-Shapur was there. The old minister stood by the garden gate, his expression unreadable. "You know what's at stake," he said simply.

"I do."

"Don't trust any city with Greek walls."

"I don't."

"And listen to Ashurbanipol. He may not speak much but when he does it will be for your own good."

Veh-Shapur handed him a final parchment, thin as skin, sealed in wax with no mark. "This is a letter from the Shah to his agents in Syria. Break the seal only when you have no other path and death is staring you in the face."

Natronai tucked it into his belt. "Understood."

The old man stepped closer, then laid a hand briefly on Natronai's shoulder. "You are either a prophet," he said, "or a madman."

"Perhaps they are one and the same," Natronai said.

He rode out accompanied by his entourage without fanfare.

CHAPTER VI: THE RISE OF CAESAR

Nicomedia, the Eastern City of Marble and Shadows, slept under a veil of spring mist when the imperial courier from Rome arrived. It was the hour before dawn, when the city clutched its last breath of silence before the clamor of markets and magistrates roared to life. In the eastern quarter, nestled within the palace of Galerius Gaius Vettius Aquilinus, known to his household and few companions simply as Gallus, stirred in his private quarters, still hungover from the previous night's wine and poetry.

The knock at the door came sharp and unexpected.

"My lord Gallus," said a breathless servant, barely able to catch his breath between words. "A courier from the West. He bears the imperial seal."

That sobered him more quickly than cold water. Gallus sat upright, his auburn curls falling in disarray across his face, and his mind began to race. He stood, pulled his cloak over his shoulders, and stepped out into the candle-lit atrium where the courier waited, a tall man in the polished leather and gold-threaded sash of the agens in rebus.

The courier bowed. "By order of Augustus Constantius, I bear news of utmost urgency."

Gallus's eyes narrowed, searching the man's expression for hints of his fate. The wax seal bore the Chi-Rho of the imperial house. It was now obvious the letter had been sent by his cousin, the Emperor. It could go either way. Either the Emperor was freeing him from his imprisonment in the Nicomedian palace or he was providing advance notice of his execution. He broke it and read.

He fell slightly backwards, barely catching his balance as he read the notice.

"To my cousin, Gallus, in whom I place confidence as both kinsman and servant of the Lord: By this letter you are named Caesar of the East, under the supreme authority of the Augustus. You are to report at once to Antioch, and prepare to defend Armenia against the forces of Shapur. A campaign is imminent. Also, you are to root out any signs of unrest in Syria Palestina. We have reason to believe a seditionist of Davidic descent is gathering followers. Any such movement must be extinguished swiftly. The stability of Christendom demands it."

He blinked and read the letter again. As he did so, he read aloud, "Named Caesar of the East."

A sharp breath escaped through his lips. His pulse thundered in his ears.

"Leave me," he commanded. "All of you."

When the room was clear, Gallus paced about like a lion unchained. It had finally come. The dream he dared not utter aloud, not even in his sleep. The murmur he had long ago buried under layers of courtly charm and drunken pretense. He'd been orphaned in blood, the son of Julius Constantius, but he had survived by being quiet, by learning the games of men more powerful than him, by seducing noblewomen and flattering tutors. But deep inside, he had always believed he was meant to rise. Now, the purple was within reach.

He poured himself a cup of wine, something aged and spiced, and toasted the empty chamber.

"To Caesar Gallus," he whispered. Then louder: "Caesar Gallus!"

He laughed, a rich and disbelieving sound. He had been caged in Nicomedia like a prince under parole, surrounded by spies, denied any real command, allowed to hunt but not lead, bed but not marry. Now? He would ride east as Caesar, second only to Constantius himself. Crowds would part before him, legions would bow, governors would fall prostrate. He would command. He would punish.

Summoning his steward with a clap the man ran into the room holding another scrolled parchment.

"Summon my household. We leave for Antioch within three days."

"My lord?"

"Do you not hear, fool? I am Caesar now! You will address me as such!"

"Caesar, another imperial letter just arrived." The servant held out the scrolled parchment for Gallus to grasp.

A sudden shiver of fear ran up and down his spine, the thought that the Emperor may have already changed his mind. Nervously, he broke the seal and began to unroll the document. His hands trembled, not with fear, but with the raw, white-hot irritation of a man who believed he had already been unleashed once, only to find the collar drawn tighter. He stretched out the parchment and began reading.

The scroll smelled of oil and cedar, the emperor's precise script flowing like an accusation: "In order to make you a more effective Caesar… my beloved sister Constantina shall be sent to Antioch, whereupon you shall take her as wife."

Gallus read it twice, then a third time, his pulse pounding. A laugh, harsh and humorless, escaped his lips. Marriage? To Constantina? He flung the letter onto the marble table and began contemplation on how he could possibly escape such an arrangement. He knew her reputation well enough, the widow of Hannibalianus, a woman whispered about often in hushed tones. Proud, imperious, a creature of the palace with blood colder than snow on the Thracian hills. And she was his cousin, for

Jupiter's sake! This was not a marriage; it was a chain, a political yoke meant to bind him hand and foot to the will of Constantius.

Gallus clenched his fists until his knuckles blanched. "So, this is how the Emperor seeks to tame me," he muttered under his breath. "He crowns me with one hand and shackles me with the other."

Yet as the fire in his gut raged, another voice whispered. A voice that was soft, sly, serpentine. Think, Gallus. Think as a Caesar, not as a common fool. Marriage to Constantina was no humiliation. It provides even more proximity to the purple, a blood tie reforged in the very heart of imperial power. If something unfortunate was to happen to Constantius, who else would be next in line to be emperor? The answer was obvious. With her beside him, doors would open that no sword could batter down. The daughter of Constantine's line. What more potent emblem of legitimacy could a Caesar brandish before the world?

He sank into the ivory-backed chair, fingers drumming the armrest. Yes, Constantina was said to be fierce, perhaps even cruel. So what? Cruelty was a virtue in an empire populated by wolves. And if she brought her own ambitions to Antioch, then perhaps... perhaps their ambitions could march side by side. "This could be an opportunity," he muttered under his breath.

Gallus's lips curved in a slow, predatory smile. "So be it, Constantius," he spat. "Send me your lioness. Let her think she comes to tame me. In time, she will learn that Gallus is no lapdog to heel at another's command."

He rose, calmer now, the first wild storm within him quelled by the cold arithmetic of ambition. To wed Constantina was to drink deeply from the chalice of destiny. And if the wine tasted of vinegar, well, Gallus had long ago taught himself to savor bitter draughts.

He repeated his last command to the steward. "Summon my household. We leave for Antioch within three days. And have them start preparing for my wedding as soon as we arrive."

The steward paled and bowed low.

In the morning, Gallus summoned Eusebius, his chamberlain and informant. The man was pale, thin, viperish. Gallus trusted him because he trusted no one. But he recognized Eusebius for what he was, the Emperor's rat, and he wondered why he had not seen him at all the previous day.

"You must have heard, I've been made Caesar," Gallus said, sipping watered wine and watching the chamberlain's reaction carefully.

Eusebius's eyes narrowed. "That is... astonishing."

Gallus tossed him the scroll. "Not so much. I am surprised you weren't already aware. I thought you knew everything that happened within these palace walls."

The eunuch read quickly, lips twitching. "Not everything Caesar, but I do try. I see that you're to take up command in Antioch. And govern from there."

"I know."

"You'll have the command of the Syrian and Egyptian legions. The garrisons of Judaea. The grain ships of Alexandria."

"Yes. I am aware of that too."

"And the wrath of the people when famine comes, or the armies fail," Eusebius smiled wickedly.

Gallus leaned back. "You probably see already why I called you."

Eusebius lowered the scroll. "You need a man to take charge and see that everything gets done."

"I need loyalty. I need to know if you are that man that will be loyal to a fault."

"You only receive that kind of loyalty through blood," Eusebius answered in a somewhat taunting tone.

"I will be marrying Constantina, in case you weren't aware of that either, so I think that provides me with the blood at least from one side. The question is whether or not I have your loyalty?"4

"All these years in Nicomedia and you still feel need to ask me that question."

Gallus didn't answer.

Three days later, as his caravan passed through the outer gates of Nicomedia, Gallus looked out over the hills. The sun struck his new insignia with fire: a golden brooch shaped like the chi-rho, beneath which dangled the laurel of Caesar.

By imperial edict, a detachment of the Comitatenses had been dispatched to escort him. Their centurion, a lean Illyrian named Lupicinus, saluted him with stiff precision.

Gallus returned it, wondering what secret orders this buffoon had received from Constantius, that he was not to know about.

The journey to Antioch was swift. Imperial messengers had cleared the roads, and Gallus traveled in splendor. At every waystation, bishops offered greetings, provincial officials bowed, and the gossip of the East buzzed with his name. Gallus drank it in. In every town square, he found a way to stand where he would be seen, the golden belt of Caesar glittering, the imperial letter displayed like a talisman.

But it was in Antioch that his transformation found its fullest expression.

The gates of Antioch, that old queen of cities, opened in a swirl of banners and incense. Bishop Theophilus greeted him at the gates with a golden crucifix and a choir of boys singing Te Deum.

Gallus dismounted slowly, letting the crowd drink in the vision of the new Caesar: youthful, cloaked in purple-trimmed white, his green eyes flashing with delight.

He addressed the crowd with theatrical humility. "I come not to burden Antioch, but to serve her. By the will of the Augustus, I defend the East against the enemies of Rome and Christ."

The crowd roared its approval.

Later, in the palace of Daphne, Gallus reclined amid a newly appointed court, surrounded by gold-threaded cushions and eunuchs bearing platters of spiced lamb. Constantina, his soon-to-be wife and the emperor's sister, was to join him soon. For now, he ruled alone. And that suited him.

But amid the laughter and the music, his mind turned to the second part of the emperor's letter. "A seditionist of Davidic descent."

Gallus summoned his advisor, Domitian, a grim-faced Syrian convert. "What do we know of the Jews in Palestina?"

"They have not forgotten Jerusalem," Domitian said, grimly. "Even after Hadrian made it a Roman colony, they still speak of a return. They call themselves children of the promise."

Gallus leaned back, sipping wine. "And this would-be king they believe in?"

"A legend, my lord. They call him their messiah, but no one can say when or if he will come."

"But don't they already have this one they call Prince of Hillel, claiming to be of the royal line," Gallus questioned.

""Rumors, my lord. Nothing but unsubstantiated rumors."

Gallus was not yet satisfied. "Is that all they have?"

"There are other stories, Domitian continued. "Some say there is such a man preaching in the hills, near Galilee. Others claim that one of their royal family from Babylon is intending to come to Palestina."

"Well, is he?" Gallus demanded to know.

"Is he what?" Domitian was confused.

"Is one of that Babylonian family heading west as we speak," Gallus explained.

"I don't know, my lord. I have heard nothing of a man descended from King David but such a man would declare that Christ was not the final king."

Gallus's smile froze. This was dangerous talk. "The Emperor obviously thinks there is some truth to this man. Bring me names. Bring me their writings. Anyone claiming to be descended from David must be made an example of. We will not suffer a second Christ."

Domitian bowed. "Shall we involve the bishops?"

Gallus considered it. "Only discreetly. Christianity thrives on martyrdom. Judaism might do the same. Better to erase any potential threat quietly. Let their secrets vanish in the desert."

Domitian bowed. "Yes, Caesar."

CHAPTER VII: WEDDING BELLS

Over the weeks that followed, Gallus became the star of Antioch. Theaters put on plays extolling his virtue. Coins were minted with his profile. Bishops came from as far as Edessa and Tyre to kiss his ring. And he began reshaping the East. He increased the military levy in Osrhoene. He reinforced fortresses in Melitene and Amida. He met with envoys from Armenia and sent emissaries to King Arsaces to strengthen the fragile alliance against Shapur. But nothing delighted the city more than the preparations for Ceasar's wedding.

The city writhed like a living jewel beneath the late Syrian sun. From the balcony of the Imperial Palace, Gallus looked down upon Antioch and felt, for the first time since the imperial courier brought news of his elevation, that he truly wore the purple. The Orontes shimmered in the distance like molten bronze, its bends glittering through groves of cypress and myrtle. Beyond, the Daphne hills rose in gentle waves, their temples crowned with golden tiles that flamed in the afternoon light. But it was the city itself that held him captive: a chaos of motion and music, banners and blossoms, perfumes thick enough to taste on the wind.

Every street had become a garlanded river of humanity. Laurel wreaths hung from colonnades, and from the balconies of merchant houses spilled silks of Tyrian purple, saffron, and vermilion. Boys clambered upon statues of Augustus and Trajan, flinging petals into the throngs below. Brass trumpets blared, their calls braided with the high-pitched wail of Syrian pipes. Somewhere far off, drums pounded like a thousand racing hearts.

And all of this delirium of color and sound was for her. Gallus's jaw tightened. Not for him, though he was Caesar of the East, master of Syria, Arabia, and Egypt. No, the people had gone mad for the emperor's sister, Constantine's own blood, the woman destined to be his bride.

Constantina. The name struck him like a hammer, heavy with expectation. He gripped the balcony rail until the bronze bit into his palms. Let them cheer her, he told himself. Let them see a goddess riding down from heaven to bless their city. For when she is mine, when the diadem rests upon both our brows, they will then cheer for me twice as loud.

He turned from the view, his cloak of imperial purple sweeping behind him like a storm cloud. In the polished bronze mirrors of the reception hall, he caught his reflection: tall, broad-shouldered, the square jaw of a soldier offset by the curling dark gold of his hair. He was handsome and he knew it, though the poets of Antioch whispered of his aggressiveness when wine ran too freely. But aggression, Gallus thought, was a Roman virtue when tempered by strength and the features of a god.

His attendants swarmed about him like bees to a rose. One adjusted the fibula on his shoulder, another dusted his boots with powdered pumice until they gleamed. Gallus waved them away with an impatient flick. "Enough. Am I a man or a marble statue? Leave me now."

They scattered, bowing low. Alone, Gallus moved to the map-strewn table. The East was his now; its deserts, its caravan cities, its teeming ports where spices from India mingled with silk from Cathay. Antioch, jewel of the Orient, lay at his feet like a courtesan of legendary beauty. And soon… soon, Constantina would too.

A smile spread across his lips, thin and sharp. When the letter came commanding him to wed her, he was initially upset, but the fury had cooled, hammered into something harder, something finer. If Constantius thought to bind him by blood, then so be it. The chain would become his sword to wield. For Gallus knew the power of symbols, and nothing shone brighter than the daughter of Constantine the Great. With Constantina at his side, Antioch would blaze like a second Rome, and Gallus would be its sun.

Beyond the palace, the city roared with a long, rising thunder that sent the pigeons wheeling from the rooftops in silver clouds. Gallus strode back to the balcony. Down the marble-paved colonnade of the main street came the first ranks of the procession: soldiers in armor gilded like fire, their spears catching the sun in blinding arcs. Behind them lumbered elephants, caparisoned in cloth-of-gold, their tusks tipped with silver. Musicians followed, the crash of cymbals and brazen horns drowning out the sea of voices.

And then he saw her. Distant yet unmistakable. A litter wrought of ivory, borne on the shoulders of eight Ethiopian slaves whose skins glistened like obsidian in the light. The curtains of the litter billowed with every breath of wind, and through the gauze shimmered a vision in gold and emerald, a face pale as marble framed by coils of black hair.

Gallus felt something twist in his chest. He understood it to be desire, but also a flicker of unease. She moved like a goddess, and gods were never easy to tame.

The litter swayed gently, like a ship borne on a perfumed tide. Beyond the veil of silk that veiled her, Constantina could hear the city roaring, like some great beast roused from slumber. Antioch. The jewel of the East, the city of laughter and vice, now laid bare at her feet. She could almost taste the incense in the air, heavy with frankincense and myrrh, twining with the musk of sweating bodies pressed against the colonnades.

They were all there; merchants in white chitons clutching their laurel wreaths, Syrian women draped in peacock-colored veils, children perched on their fathers' shoulders. And their eyes, thousands upon thousands of eyes, fixed upon her litter as though upon a holy thing. She could feel their hunger like heat on her skin. Not for her beauty, though beauty she knew she had plenty of, in the way a blade has an edge, but for what she represented: Constantine's blood, Rome's divine lineage, the power that could raise cities or grind them into dust.

Let them look, she thought, a smile curving her crimson lips. Let them see the lioness sent to tame their Caesar. She sat erect, a column of poise, her robe flowing like molten sunlight over the cushions. Gold thread caught the glare of the Syrian sun, casting shards of brilliance that dazzled even her own eyes. Around her throat coiled a collar of emeralds so deep they seemed to drink the light. From her ears dangled pearls the size of doves' eggs, gifts from some Eastern king long since dust.

On her head rested no diadem, at least not yet. Her brother, Constantius, had sent it ahead, to be placed upon her brow during the wedding ritual. A wise precaution, for the diadem was more than metal; it was a blade, honed to draw blood from those who coveted it. And Constantina had learned early that in the House of Constantine, blood flowed as freely as wine.

As the litter jolted over the marble paving, she parted the silken curtains and looked upon the city that would soon be hers. Antioch glittered like a fallen constellation: its colonnaded avenues ablaze with garlands, its porticoes draped in cloth-of-gold, its fountains spilling wine instead of water in honor of the day. From the hippodrome to the Orontes, every stone seemed steeped in celebration.

As her gaze swept the streets, she felt the stir of an older instinct, sharp as the scent of iron beneath the perfume: danger. It always lurked at the edges of splendor. She had seen too many triumphal processions end in blood. Constantine, the world-maker, had died and left his brood to devour one another like wolves. She had survived not by innocence, but by teeth and talons. Now she was to wed Gallus. Her cousin. Her leash but also her prey.

Constantina's fingers tightened on the ivory armrest of the litter as she thought of him. She had never seen him grown, not since childhood games in the gardens of Constantinople when he was a flaxen-haired boy with laughter too loud and temper too quick. They said he had grown into a man of imposing frame, a soldier's strength, a lover of games and wine. They also said he had a cruel streak, as sudden and sharp as the lash of a whip. She did not fear cruelty. Cruelty she understood well.

What she did not understand and which she could never allow was submission. If Constantius thought to make her a gift to Gallus, bound to Caesar with a silken cord, then her brother was a greater fool than she believed. She was no coin to be spent in a game of men. She would rule beside Gallus or over him, whichever the fates decided.

The crowd surged, a great shout rising like the roar of a cataract. Trumpets blared, and from somewhere near the palace, brazen gongs thundered their welcome. Constantina let the curtain fall and reclined once more among the cushions, her smile like frost upon her lips.

"Shout loudly Antioch," she gloated to herself. "Gild your streets and burn your incense. For today you greet a bride but tomorrow, you shall bow before a queen."

The litter halted. Outside, voices barked commands; the tramp of feet and clatter of arms rang loud against the paving. A shadow fell across the gauze, and Constantina felt the tremor of something akin to fear, but not quite, quicken in her breast.

He was there. Gallus. Waiting to claim her.

She drew one slow breath, steady as the draw of a bowstring, and whispered to the empty air, "Let us see, cousin, which of us wears the crown."

The bronze doors of the Imperial Palace yawned wide, and sunlight spilled upon the marble steps like molten gold. Gallus stood at their head, framed by a double rank of guards in polished cuirasses, their spears a forest of silver points. Behind him loomed the great colonnade, its capitals wound with ivy, its pavement strewn with roses.

His heart beat like a drum against his ribs, though none would know it from his face. He wore the calm mask of command, the imperious tilt of the chin, the eyes like blue-green ice beneath the diadem that clasped his golden-brown hair. The purple cloak spilled from his shoulders, heavy with threads of gold, its hem crusted with pearls. A sword hung at his side, its hilt a fire of jewels. The sight of Antioch itself, pouring into the great square below, shouting his name, crying Ave Caesar! until the heavens rang filled him with a sense of power.

Gallus's breath tightened.

Slowly, with the poise of a queen, she parted the veil.

The sunlight struck her, and for a heartbeat he thought the gods had sent some flame-born spirit to walk among men. Her robe shimmered like molten gold, falling in folds that clung and drifted by turns. A collar of emeralds coiled about her throat, green as spring in the deep forests of the North. Her hair, black as obsidian. was bound in a coronet of twisted gold, and from its shadow her eyes looked out: great dark eyes that held a depth like midnight waters.

She met his gaze. Across the gulf of trumpets and banners and shouting throngs, she looked at him and in that instant Gallus felt the ground tilt beneath his feet. Not for beauty alone, though beauty she had. It was the will behind it, the force that seemed to coil like a serpent in those eyes.

He stepped forward, down the marble steps, each stride ringing like iron on stone. Guards dropped to their knees as he passed, but Gallus saw only her. The litter halted at the foot of the steps; the slaves bent, and slowly, like a goddess descending from Olympus, Constantina emerged.

She was tall, taller than he remembered and her presence struck him like a spear. No shrinking maiden this, no docile bride plucked for show. She stood upon the sun-drenched marble as though upon an altar, her chin high, her gaze leveled like an arrow.

Gallus smiled. Smooth as oil, edged as steel.

"Constantina," he said, his voice carrying over the hush that fell like a drawn curtain. "The East has long awaited its empress." He had practiced that line over and over until it sounded like poetry.

Her lips curved, scarlet as blood upon snow. "Has it?" she murmured. And the soft tone was mocking but perilously sweet, stirring both heat and wrath in his veins.

Gallus bent and kissed her hand. It was cool, hard as carved ivory. When he raised his head, their eyes locked and for a breath, for a single, searing heartbeat, the square was silent.

And then the world broke in thunder. Trumpets blared, drums roared, and Antioch screamed its joy to the sky as the Caesar and the Emperor's sister stood side by side, like twin stars blazing in the noonday sun.

The Octagonal Church shimmered like a jewel box torn open to the sun. Light struck the walls of porphyry and serpentine marble until they glowed like embers; lamps swayed on chains of gilded bronze, their flames mirrored in a thousand polished surfaces. And through the haze of incense, the vault soared like heaven itself, heavy with the thunder of hymns.

Constantina advanced with measured steps, her sandals brushing the blue-and-gold mosaics as if she walked upon the sea. All eyes drank her in; the bishops and generals, the senators with their sharp, appraising gaze. She felt them cling to her every movement, the silk of her veil whispering against her cheek, the weight of the jewels at her throat, the pearls that trembled in her ears. But Constantina's thoughts were not on them. They were on the man who waited by the altar, rigid with power in his purple mantle, his golden shaded hair catching the shafts of light like a crown of flame.

Gallus. Her cousin. Her captor. Her key.

As she looked at him the thought that he was taller than she remembered crossed her mind. Broad of chest, his jaw cut in the hard lines of a soldier. His eyes, a deep aquamarine, bright, and keen, burning with something that might have been pride, or hunger, or both. He looked at her as men look upon a city they mean to conquer.

Try, cousin, she thought, the chill of amusement brushing her lips. Try and see what it costs you.

They met at the altar. His hand closed upon hers, hot and heavy, as though to imprint his will into her flesh. She yielded outwardly but inwardly she was stone, her resolve coiling tighter than the emerald collar at her throat.

The bishop droned through the prayers, the choir soared, and Constantina bowed her head, a vision of meek obedience wrought in gold and silk. But behind the lowered lashes her mind moved like a drawn blade. She spoke the vows in a voice soft as flowing water, and the church trembled with joy, but each word in her breast was an oath of iron: she would not bend, not break, not vanish into the shadow of any man, not even one who wore the purple.

The crowns descended. She felt the rubies bite her brow like drops of fire, and for an instant the weight thrilled her. Power. Naked, glittering, perilous. They placed the twin circlet upon Gallus, and the crowd roared, but Constantina smiled, cool and remote, thinking to herself that it is not the man who rules, but the will that masters him.

The chalice came, sapphires catching the blaze of lamps. Gallus drank, his throat working, his gaze locked on hers. Then the cup touched her lips, cool, bittersweet, a mingling of honey and steel, and she drank, slow, deliberate, her eyes never leaving his.

The doors flung wide. Trumpets blared. The world crashed in like a wave of gold and scarlet, a storm of voices crying their names. Gallus tightened his grasp, lifting her arm high, and Constantina smiled that smile of marble queens, her heart cold as the snows of Thrace.

Let them cheer, she thought as the incense and light roared about her. Today a bride. Tomorrow, their ruler.

Night fell upon Antioch, but the darkness was flooded in light. From the palace poured rivers of brilliance from thousands of torches blazing like a forest of fire, their glow mirrored in the marble colonnades and the polished bronze doors. The air quivered with the clangor of cymbals, the shriek of pipes, the roar of drums.

Gallus entered the triclinium to a thunder of acclaim. The hall was a sea of splendor, its pillars wrapped in silk, ceilings hung with garlands heavy with roses and jasmine, the floors strewn with myrtle and violets that crushed sweet beneath the sandals. Tables of ivory groaned beneath the weight of wonders: peacocks glazed in honey, their tails gilded and spread like suns; boars stuffed with figs and almonds; stags wreathed in flowers; fishes bright as rainbows lying on beds of fennel. From golden ewers poured wine dark as garnets, foaming in crystal cups.

Gallus stood at the head, Constantina at his side, their thrones raised upon a dais draped in Tyrian purple and sown with stars of gold.

He looked upon her, and his blood burned. She sat like Juno enthroned, her veil fallen, her hair a torrent of night, her eyes pools of black flame. She smiled but not at him, not truly, but at the world, at the throng prostrate in their adoration. And Gallus thought: Let her smile. Let her bask. Soon she will learn who is the master in this house.

He raised his cup, and the hall shook with acclamation. "To the glory of Rome!" he thundered, his voice rolling like iron. "To the House of Constantine and to my bride, the light of the East!"

The roar was like a cataract. Cups clashed, wine spilled like rivers of blood. Gallus drank deep, the fire of the Falernian searing his veins, and laughed. A great, golden laugh that rang to the vaults. This was power. This was his empire. This was the purple dream made flesh.

Constantina smiled as he toasted her, her lips curved like a bow, her lashes veiling eyes that glittered harder than the gems on her breast. The light of a thousand lamps danced upon the wine, the gilded dishes, the throngs of courtiers who bent their spines until they seemed to break. It was a scene torn from the tales of Persia; a feast of kings, a carnival of flame and jewels.

And yet, beneath the music and the laughter, Constantina heard another sound: the silent hiss of envy, the murmur of daggers drawn in dreams. She had lived too long among wolves not to scent their breath. Some smiled and fawned and pressed her hand; others watched from behind their cups, their eyes calculating, cold.

Gallus roared, drunk with triumph and wine, his great hand striking the board so that the goblets leaped. She watched him from the corner of her eye, the flush upon his cheek, the hunger in his glance, the pride that swelled in his throat like a drumbeat. A man of passions, quick to rise, quick to blaze, and quick, perhaps, to fall.

She let her fingers trail upon the arm of the throne, the emeralds winking like serpents in the light, and thought: If he thinks of me as his prize, his ornament, his silken chain, then he shall find this chain has teeth.

The feast spilled out into the gardens of Daphne, where cypress and myrtle whispered in the night wind and fountains leapt in columns of silver under the Syrian moon. Torches flared along the marble paths, their flames mirrored in pools strewn with lilies. Everywhere was a sea of motion with dancers whirling in veils of flame, jugglers tossing hoops of fire, acrobats vaulting through rings that hissed and spat sparks. The air throbbed with pipes and cymbals, the pulse of drums like the beating of a giant heart.

Gallus strode among it like a god of victory, the purple mantle streaming from his shoulders, his arms flung wide as Antioch roared its worship. Cups foamed, laughter shattered the night like golden glass, and the gardens were a tide of jewels and white limbs and flashing torches.

Then came the thunder. Gallus lifted his head as the first roar shook the air with a deep, guttural bellow like the cry of a wounded titan. From the far end of the gardens, beyond the marble balustrades, a pillar of fire spouted into the sky, curling into a blossom of emerald and gold. A thousand voices screamed as more followed. Scarlet roses of flame bursting in the darkness, rivers of fire streaming down like rain from the vault of heaven. Greek fire hissed in bronze tubes, flung high to scatter in crimson showers, painting the night in blood and glory.

Gallus laughed, his arms upraised, his hair a halo of light in the infernal glare. Let Rome see! Let the world see! Gallus reigns in Antioch, and the stars themselves fall at his command!

He turned to her then, his bride, his prize. She stood on the terrace above the fountains, the firestorm burning in her eyes, her robe streaming like molten gold, her arms bare and pale as ivory. For an instant Gallus felt the breath catch in his throat, for she seemed not woman but some goddess of old. Bellona, perhaps, or Nemesis, born of flame and night.

He mounted the steps two at a time, seized her hand, and lifted it high so the fire crowned them both in light. The crowd roared like a sea, and Gallus smiled. A wolfish smile, exultant, drunk on power, on wine, but most of all on her.

"Come," he murmured in her ear, his breath hot as the torches. "Come, wife. Let Antioch dream of us and let us make that dream flesh."

The night burned. Fire blossomed above the gardens, cascades of scarlet and green that bathed the marble in blood and emerald. The roar of the crowd was a storm in Constantia's ears, the heat of torches a furnace on her skin. And Gallus seemed to be everywhere all at once; his laughter, his voice, his great hand crushing hers in a grip that bruised like iron.

She smiled as he led her through the throng, her face a mask of radiance, her lips curved in that perfect arc the sculptors strove to carve. She smiled, though her thoughts were cold as moonlit steel. He thought this was his triumph, that these fires crowned him king of the East, that this night sealed his dominion over her.

"Let him think so," she thought. For every blaze must burn itself to ash, and men who soar too near the sun find their wings charred to dust.

They passed beneath arches of roses, through halls of marble and porphyry that glimmered in the torchlight like veins of living flame, until at last they stood before the doors of the inner chamber. Doors of cedar bound in bronze, carved with vines and beasts that seemed to writhe in the flickering glow. Gallus thrust them wide.

The chamber breathed heat and perfume, aloes and roses and the musky tang of Eastern oils. Lamps of crystal hung like captured stars, spilling honeyed light upon the floor where silks lay strewn like pools of molten color. A couch of ivory towered at the center, its cushions heaped in a riot of purple and gold.

Gallus turned, and for the first time since the day began, the mask slipped. The laughter died, the roar stilled, and in its place came a hunger raw as a wolf's.

"Constantina," he said, her name a growl in his throat. He came toward her, the lamps kindling fire in his hair, his eyes blue as steel drawn from the forge.

She did not move. She stood like a column of light, her veil fallen, her robe flowing in molten folds, her hands clasped loosely before her as though in prayer. Only her eyes stirred with black flames that flickered as his shadow fell across her.

He caught her wrists, gently at first, then with a force that bit. "Mine," he said, the word thick with wine and triumph. "By Rome, by the blood of Constantine, by the will of the gods, you are mine."

She smiled. Slow, soft, cold as the kiss of snow. "Yours," she whispered but in her voice was a music he did not hear, a note of mockery so thin it might have been the hiss of silk on marble.

His mouth crushed hers. His arms were bands of iron, dragging her against the furnace of his body. She yielded outwardly, utterly but inwardly she lay coiled, silent as a serpent in the heart of a rose.

Let him think he conquered. Let him dream himself lord of her body, master of her soul. The dream would be sweet and brief. For in this game, the prize was not flesh but power, and the hand that ruled would not be his.

When at last the lamps guttered and the night closed like a velvet shroud, only the whisper of silk and the low thunder of his breath broke the stillness. And in that darkness, Constantina smiled, her eyes open and black as the abyss.

For this was no marriage of hearts, but of empires. And in the shadow of the diadem, love was but a mask for war. And war was something that Gallus eagerly awaited to experience. As the East was preparing for war, Gallus delighted in its preparation. He trained with his legions personally, riding along the Orontes River with his gilded helmet flashing in the sun, barking commands with theatrical authority. Soldiers cheered him on. Officers flattered him. He began to believe the imperial mantle had always been meant for him.

At the same time he kept a finger on the pulse of Judea. Reports came from Caesarea, from Tyre, even from the Jewish communities in Mesopotamia. The name of the seditionist was more than a myth now. It had become a whisper: Natronai. A man born of both royal and priestly stock, son of a prominent Exilarch in Babylon. Preaching for a return to Zion. Calling himself a messenger of God.

"He must be found and stopped," Gallus said to Domitian. "Before Passover. The Jews will gather then. If he appears, it could ignite a revolt."

He sent word to the Syrian governor to double the guards in the Decapolis. Spy on the synagogues. Monitor the roads from Mesopotamia. "No one claiming descent from David is to be allowed to speak publicly," he decreed. "Anyone refusing to acknowledge Christ as King shall be punished as a heretic and traitor."

But something deeper stirred in Gallus that made him worry. A memory from his childhood. A rabbi in Nicomedia who had once told him stories of David and Solomon. How the Jews waited for a king to restore their kingdom. It wasn't a matter of 'if' but 'when'. And when that 'when' would finally occur, nothing would be able to stop them. He had been only a boy then. But the tale had lingered.

"If they believe in their blood so much," Gallus murmured one night, "then let them bleed for it."

By summer, all was in readiness for the war to take place in Armenia. The legions were deployed. Intelligence flowed. Shapur had stirred in the East but had not yet crossed the border. "What was he possibly waiting for?" Gallus wondered, restless, for his first campaign.

"We will not wait for the Persians to act. We strike first," he instructed Domitian.

"But what about the matter in Palestine?" his aide questioned.

Gallus's eyes glittered. "Let their lion come. The trap has already been set."

CHAPTER VIII: THE JOURNEY

The roads west of Ctesiphon were empty under the weight of heat and silence. The land rolled out in dusty brown plains and half-buried ruins, temples fallen to time, bones poking from the sand like old warnings.

Natronai passed them with eyes half-closed, repeating the Shema beneath his breath. "Hear, O Israel: the Lord is our God, the Lord is One."

Every few miles, they encountered travelers; a caravan of Nabatean traders heading east, a Persian scout on foot, an old woman gathering medicinal herbs. None bothered to give them a second glance, to which Natronai sighed with relief that their disguise as merchants was effective. Nevertheless, he watched everything, counting river crossings, measuring the wind, listening for birds, looking for anything suspicious and threatening. At night, they made no open fires, knowing that the roads west were populated with bands of robbers.

They reached Adiabene in six days. There, in the shadow of the mountains, he met a woman who spoke no names but handed him a satchel lined with iron-points and folded maps. She spoke cryptically, saying, "May the wind hide you." Then she vanished. Natronai was left scratching his head, questioning how could the wind hide anything? He never bothered to ask anyone else in his troop, dismissing it as nonsense.

The second day out of Adiabene passed beneath a sun that gave no quarter, bronzing the stones and bleaching the wind-scoured path. Natronai, riding in the center of the caravan, wore a linen headwrap pulled low over his eyes, his fine garments cloaked in thick layer of dust. Around him, twenty men moved with the deliberate sluggishness of traders but in reality they were the hand-picked warriors by Ashurbanipol, each one picked for unmatchable skill and discretion.

The caravan carts bumped along the ragged path, their axles creaking with carefully distributed weight. No silks or spices filled their interiors, only rations, arms, and a handful of scrolls sealed with a manufactured signet of an imaginary trading house. The façade was immaculate, or so they believed.

But obviously not everyone was fooled. A plume of dust appeared on the northern rise, not more than a quarter mile ahead. As it neared, the silhouettes of mounted men, lean, sinewy Arabs upon wiry horses looking determined to intercept the caravan. Natronai could recognize none of the riders of the sands with piercing eyes as sharp as falcons. Natronai's gaze narrowed. He counted at least twenty.

Ashurbanipol rode up beside him, ready to protect his charge. The grizzled general said nothing at first, just grunted and spat into the dust.

"I know them," he murmured. "Banu Sim'an. Raiders. Sons of the wild hills above Hatra. Filth that robs the road and vanishes into the stone."

"Do they outnumber us?" Natronai asked.

"Does it matter?" Ashurbanipol's smirk was sharp and dry. "They think we're peddlers. They will learn otherwise very quickly."

The leader of the raiders trotted forward, all charm and poison. He was wrapped in black and red robes, a thin curved blade bouncing at his side, his beard braided with copper wire. He raised a hand in mock greeting.

"Peace upon you, honored travelers," he called out, his voice oily with practiced politeness. "The road to Nineveh is long and treacherous. Perhaps we may share words and wine, if you have any."

Ashurbanipol slowed his horse but made no gesture of welcome. "We are poor men with little to trade. Silk and copper we seek, but none to spare."

The Arab laughed, a practiced, careless thing. "No one travels this road without treasure. I smell Tyrian dye, and that horse" he nodded at Natronai's grey steed "was bred in Media. Come, come, friends. Let us speak calmly as brothers."

Around them, his men fanned out. Some on foot, others circling slowly on horseback, drawing the perimeter tighter with every heartbeat. One leaned too close to a mule, feigning curiosity; another glanced beneath the canvas tarp of one of the carts.

Natronai looked left, then right. They were surrounded.

The raider leader began speaking again, idle nothings about sandstorms and false caliphs, but Ashurbanipol was no longer listening. He had seen the signal: a raised eyebrow from one of the caravan men, a barely perceptible flick of a hand.

With a sudden, shrill series of whistles, not dissimilar from the cry of desert kites, Ashurbanipol broke the mask of being helpless.

What happened next occurred in a heartbeat.

The "merchants" tossed off their robes and cloaks, revealing mail beneath, glinting in the high sun. Short swords and recurved bows appeared like magic from beneath the carts. The camels roared and bucked as their handlers armed themselves with curved scimitars.

Ashurbanipol himself swung from his saddle, landing hard on the earth, his great war axe already in hand.

The bandits reeled back, startled, but their leader was quick. "Kill them!" he screamed, his voice cracking. The desert was immediately filled with chaos.

Steel rang in the desert air. One of Ashurbanipol's archers loosed an arrow before his foot even touched the ground, striking a raider through the throat. Another dashed forward and split a bandit's leg at the knee before he could draw his dagger.

The battlefield was tight, violent. Swords met at close range, too close for elaborate maneuvers. The clangor of iron was deafening. Sand kicked up by horses created brief moments of blindness, where death emerged from the murk like a beast.

Natronai, unarmored but not unarmed, drew the short sword at his waist. It was a weapon he'd been trained with since a child, back in Mahoza, but never in true combat. His heart hammered. He saw a rider barreling toward him, a cruel blade raised.

But Ashurbanipol was faster. With a roar, he hurled his axe, spinning, end over end until it struck the rider full in the chest. The man collapsed in the dust, dead before he hit the ground.

"You stay alive, my prince! Leave the fighting to us!" Ashurbanipol bellowed, retrieving his axe from the fallen foe.

It was not a long battle. Once the raiders realized their prey was a phalanx in disguise, their bravado drained. Half broke and ran into the rocky highlands, pursued by a handful of Ashurbanipol's riders. The rest were cut down or captured.

Within fifteen minutes, the road was quiet again, broken only by the groans of the wounded and the cries of dying animals.

Ashurbanipol wiped blood from his cheek; it wasn't his. He then stood beside Natronai. "They thought us weak. Most men do when they see merchants," he said, eyes scanning the horizon for survivors. "But you do not ride with weak men."

Natronai looked at the bodies scattered across the sand, their dark blood steaming in the heat. It was his first real taste of the road. Of what leadership in these wild lands would cost.

"Spare the leader," Natronai said. "I want to ask him questions."

Ashurbanipol grunted his disapproval but complied.

The raider chieftain had taken a gash across his thigh and lay groaning beside a boulder, teeth gritted in pain. Two of the caravan guards dragged him to his knees before Natronai.

"You knew who we were," Natronai said calmly. "You did not come here to rob us, you came with one directive, to kill us. Did someone send you?"

Standing beside Natronai, Ashurbanipol placed a hand on his shoulder. "My Prince, they are robbers. This is what they do. Why would you think otherwise?"

"He didn't flinch when you threw off your robes, giving up your disguise. "Most robbers would have given the order to run at that point knowing we would probably not give chase. Instead, he gave the order to attack."

Ashurbanipol nodded, indicating he agreed with his logic. He slammed his fist into the side of the leader's head.

The man spat blood.

"Who do you ride for?" Ashurbanipol demanded an answer now that he realized they had not been selected at random.

"We ride for no one."

"That's a lie," Ashurbanipol growled.

The raider said nothing.

Natronai crouched in front of him. "Your life hangs on a thread. My friend is not very happy with you right now and I'm not certain how much longer I can restrain him. If you tell me the truth, I may give you food and water and let you take your chances wandering through the desert."

The man looked up, defiant, but his eyes wavered. The resolve began to bleed from them.

"There was a whisper," he said at last. "A rider came to our camp near Nisibis. Told us to watch for a caravan of cloaked Persians heading east. Said they were not what they appear but fat with silver. They must all die. He paid us half in advance with gold."

Natronai frowned. "Then who sent the rider?"

"Didn't say. But his cloak bore the eagle of the Legion."

Ashurbanipol's face darkened. "Romans."

Natronai stood slowly. His pulse pounded. "Or someone pretending to be. Either way, they knew our route and suspected our purpose."

The heat was beginning to ebb. Late afternoon shadows stretched across the scorched plain like reaching fingers. The blood of the fallen had dried in black flakes across the stones, and the smell of it, a mix of iron and death, hung low in the air.

Ashurbanipol dragged the wounded Arab captain beneath the shade of a tilted acacia tree. The man's leg was bound, but not well, just enough to prevent him from dying too quickly. He had a lean, vulture-like face, and despite the pain etched deep into his brow, his eyes still burned with stubborn hatred. Natronai stood over him, a hand resting on the hilt of his sword, not out of threat, but steadying himself. The young man's heart still beat hard in his chest from the chaos of the ambush. Yet now that the danger had passed, a different urgency settled on him, one of suspicion.

He had trusted the route out of Adiabene was secret. Someone had betrayed him.

Ashurbanipol crouched beside the prisoner. "You gave us part of the truth already," he said gruffly. "Now give us the rest."

The raider sneered. "I told you all I know. A rider, a foreigner, came to us with gold coin and word. Said a caravan would come, poorly guarded, cloaked as merchants. Told us the route. That's it."

"Describe him more carefully," Natronai insisted.

"Roman. Or so he dressed. Tall. His tongue was polished, like an envoy. But his eyes were strange. Green, but empty. I've known soldiers, and I've known spies. This one smelled like something between the two."

Ashurbanipol snorted. "Could be a deserter."

"Could be," the prisoner rasped, "but no deserter brings a pouch of solid aurei stamped with the sigil of Antioch's mint."

Natronai and Ashurbanipol exchanged a glance.

Antioch. The name carried weight. The imperial city of the East. Constantius' jewel in Syria.

Natronai stepped closer. "Do you know what house he was staying with?"

"No name. Only a rumor that he'd come north from Harran, and that he had business with men who wear no uniform but carry Roman steel."

A silence fell.

Ashurbanipol finally rose, wiping his brow with the back of his hand. "What do you want done with him?"

"Feed him. Bind his wounds properly. And leave him to the mercy of the desert."

"You want to spare the life of this carrion?"

"For now," Natronai said. "We made a promise and we will keep it."

Ashurbanipol gave a grunt of assent and signaled two of his men. The prisoner was dragged away, howling as his leg was jostled, but no longer defiant, just beaten.

Natronai walked to the edge of the cliff, where the hills dropped away to the basin below. His cloak flapped lightly in the wind. Ashurbanipol joined him after a moment, silent.

"I can think of only a few who knew our route," Natronai said, eyes narrowed against the sun. "My father. You. The scribes at the Exilarch's office. And the old woman we met in Adiabene."

"You think your father would betray you?"

Natronai said nothing. After a long moment, he answered, "No. Not yet. Not unless he's grown more desperate."

Ashurbanipol folded his arms. "I can assure you that no scribe of the King of Kings would dare to be a Roman spy."

"Which leaves the old woman. She said something strange to me when we left. She told me that I should hope the wind would conceal us."

"That is strange," Ashurbanipol agreed.

"If the wind had been blowing the sand in the desert then it would have been almost impossible for the robbers to find us. I think she said it because she knew there were men looking for us. I think she is a double agent."

Ashurbanipol grunted. "When I have the chance I will send word back to Adiabene and have her arrested."

"It is only a suspicion," Natronai argued.

"But a logical one," Ashurbanipol replied.

"But there is another matter we need to focus on. If the coin came from Antioch, we must assume one of three possibilities."

"Go on."

"First, someone in the Roman administration knows who we are and fears our journey. They want me dead before we reach our destination."

"That would mean someone in Constantius' inner circle," Ashurbanipol pointed out. "Perhaps even Gallus," Ashurbanipol added darkly. "Your fame spreads among the Jews of Mesopotamia. Not everyone in Antioch likes the idea of a Jewish prince claiming Messianic lineage. Stories of your mad claim may have reached his ears in Antioch."

Natronai rubbed his temple. "That would mean they have been following my movements for quite some time. They would need spies in both Mahoza and Ctesiphon."

"That is not unreasonable," Ashurbanipol assured him. "Do you not think that we don't have our own spies in Antioch and Constantinople. We even have them in Rome itself."

"Second," Natronai went on, "Antioch may have been warned by rival factions within the Yeshivas."

"Your Rabbis?" Ashurbanipol scoffed. "They can barely agree to anything among themselves from what I've been told."

"True but there is a line of communication between the Yeshivas in Babylon and those in Palestine. It wasn't as if I hadn't been mentioning I was coming to liberate Jerusalem as a son of David. The coming of a messiah would be a threat to those in positions of power in Palestine. The tongues of Rabbis are sharp, but some have long arms and wealthy friends in dark places such as Antioch. Word of my 'conversations with God' may have spread farther than you think."

"And the third possibility?"

Natronai hesitated, knowing his response would not be liked by Ashurbanipol. "Persian agents."

Ashurbanipol looked up sharply. "I already said that no scribe would dare to defy Shapur.

"But if one of his ministers or generals believed I was a Roman pawn, or perhaps even something worse, afraid that I might also stir a rebellion among the Jews in Babylon, that person would feel justified to defy Shapur's orders."

"If that was true," Ashurbanipol explained, "I would have killed you before you even crossed the Tigris."

That reasoning hung in the air like a blade.

"Well then, I'm glad you decided that I wasn't a Roman pawn," Natronai said smiling at the man that was ordered to be his protector.

Both knew it was true that someone had sent word to Antioch. Natronai's rise, quiet though it was, would certainly not have gone unnoticed. A son of the Exilarch, seen speaking in visions, drawing followers in secret among the academies, speaking of a coming redemption, that would be enough to draw the ire of scholars, the fear of Rome, and the wrath of Persia all at once.

Natronai deferred back to his companion. "So, what would you advise?"

Ashurbanipol stared out at the long path stretching east. "I say we leave no trail. Change the route again. No more letters. No messengers. From now on, your words go no farther than your own mouth, and only to ears you can trust."

Natronai nodded. "We move at dawn."

That night, the caravan camped deep in a dry ravine, off the road and sheltered by the crescent walls of rock. Guards were doubled. Fires were few and small. Natronai remained awake long into the night, watching the stars, listening to the desert wind whisper over the cliffs.

He thought about his father and the words they had exchanged in Mahoza. "You walk the line between prophecy and delusion."

Could this possibly have been his father's doing? Or was this a move by the Romans, who had spies in Ctesiphon and now viewed him as a possible rebel? Or were the Persian authorities acting preemptively, afraid of any influence he might have over their emperor?

Or... all three?

What frightened Natronai most was that he could not rule any of them out. Although he told himself his father was incapable of doing such a thing. His brothers...they could be a different story. The trap had been too deliberate, too well-placed. This was not a simple robbery. It had been an assassination attempt and it meant he was now walking toward danger. He was already deep into it. He looked out to the horizon, where the rocky cliffs cast long shadows across the road ahead. Somewhere, someone out there had tried to arrange his death. The message was clear. From now on they would remain alert and careful.

CHAPTER IX: TRAITOR

By the second day, the hills gave way to Roman terrain as evidenced by old boundary stones marked with Latin abbreviations, half-erased by sand and time. The air changed as well, less dry, heavier with salt and shadow. The Roman grip, though weak, could still be felt in the way the villages had been erected; planned, squared, and most of all nervous.

They heard the Latin being spoken. They saw Roman patrols in the distance; equestrians wearing dusty crests, watching every stranger with tired suspicion. Natronai kept his head down as he prayed quietly that they would not be noticed.

The city of Edessa shimmered beneath a curtain of late summer heat. Its ochre walls and colonnades rose from the red plain like a desert mirage, baked in the sun, guarded by arched gates and Roman sentries who barely lifted their eyes as the multitude of caravans passed through.

Natronai's disguised retinue entered the city at midday, cloaked as linen traders and potters returning from the interior. Ashurbanipol, ever watchful, rode at the rear, eyes sweeping from rooftop to alley. The ambush two days before had left him raw, his nerves on edge.

They followed the winding roads through the eastern quarter until they reached a narrow colonnaded street near the silk market, fragrant with dye vats, reeking of mulberry leaves and human sweat. There, half-hidden between a leather workshop and a grain dealer, stood a humble silk shop with green curtains fluttering like weary flags.

Ashurbanipol dismounted with a grunt. "This is it?"

Natronai nodded. "Yazdin's instructions had been accurate."

The shop's wooden door creaked open at their approach. A plump man in his fifties stepped out, his face oily with sweat and charm. He wore a lavender robe too fine for his surroundings, and a smile that never reached his eyes.

"Peace, friends! Peace upon the sons of Abraham and their faithful swords!" he cried, arms open as if welcoming long-lost cousins. "I am Yazdin of Edessa, at your humble service!"

Ashurbanipol frowned. "You talk too much."

Yazdin blinked, but his grin remained plastered on. "In Edessa, talk is cheaper than bread but far more nourishing for the soul. Come, come, you must be tired, dusty, and ready for answers." Without waiting, he beckoned them through the shop, past silk bolts and threads of golden weave. Behind a hanging tapestry was a narrow stair leading downward. It smelled of earth and salt, and the air grew cooler with every step. At the base of the stairs was a heavy oak door. Yazdin produced a key from inside his sleeve.

Beyond it was a cellar chamber lit by oil lamps and lined with shelves filled with old crates and straw bundles. But a false wall of stacked amphorae swung open at Yazdin's touch, revealing a second, hidden room beyond.

Eight people stood waiting in the hidden room. Five men, two women, and Yazdin's younger cousin, a thin boy with darting eyes that never seemed to rest. Each wore travel garb beneath their cloaks, and around them lay weapons; bows, javelins, daggers and scrolls sealed with wax. They stood when Natronai entered.

"My lord," said a dark-bearded man in his thirties, bowing. "I am Raba ben Nathan. These are the guardians assigned to aid your crossing into Osrhoene and across the Euphrates."

Ashurbanipol's hand never left the hilt of his sword. He didn't like it. Eight people, eight wagging tongues who knew the road, the mission, and their destination. Eight too many.

Natronai thanked them with due formality, but Ashurbanipol lingered at the rear of the room, studying them, particularly one couple standing apart from the rest. The man, thin-lipped and balding, held his wife's hand too tightly. She was veiled, quiet, with downcast eyes. Something about them pricked at the old general's instincts.

Later, when food and watered wine were served in the upper chambers, Ashurbanipol made his move.

He turned to Yazdin and said, "Let's play a game. A lesson from the East."

Yazdin blinked. "A game? Of what sort?"

Ashurbanipol raised a brow. "A test of silence. In the courts of Parthia, when there is suspicion among allies, the accused are separated and questioned alone. If their stories match, they are cleared. If not…"

He left the sentence unfinished.

The room fell silent.

"Let's not be ridiculous," Yazdin attempted to make light of any insinuation regarding their collective loyalty to the mission. "I can personally vouch for everyone in this room. I have known them for years."

"Then you have nothing to worry about," Ashurbanipol concluded.

Natronai gave a small nod. "Proceed."

Ashurbanipol had the eight people taken into the adjacent room one at a time. He kept the questioning simple, extremely simple. There were just three questions. "When did you learn of the mission?" he asked first. Next was, "Where do we cross the Euphrates?" and finally, "What is the name of the Arab clan we encountered on the road from Adiabene?" He knew any traitor would either know too much or try too hard to know less.

Each man and woman was questioned in turn. Most gave vague answers, as expected. Yazdin had been smart enough not to share all the details with his associates. They'd only been told the next destination was Nisibis, then onward to the east.

But when the thin-lipped man entered, he answered the third question, "Banu Sim'an," without hesitation.

Ashurbanipol's eyes narrowed. "How did you know their name?" he asked coldly.

The man froze momentarily. "I…I heard it mentioned downstairs."

"No one said it."

The man swallowed. "Yazdin, I think told me. Perhaps I misheard…"

Ashurbanipol stood, his voice rising now. "Wrong again. Yazdin never knew the tribe's name."

The man paled.

Ashurbanipol leaned in close. "Let me guess. You delivered word to one of your Roman handlers. He in turn mentioned to you the name of the Arabs that usually did his dirty work, while we were still in Adiabene. Or maybe even earlier. A simple rider, a coin for a courier. You thought no one would trace it."

The man bolted for the door.

But Ashurbanipol was quicker. With a movement like a striking cat, he hurled a dagger from beneath his robe. It struck the traitor in the thigh, dropping him to the floor with a scream. Within seconds, his wife charged into the room, wailing behind her veil.

Natronai approached moments later.

Ashurbanipol addressed him calmly. "We found our traitor."

The man wept as he was dragged upright. "I did it for my wife! They had my wife's brother! He's a hostage in Antioch! I had no other choice!"

Ashurbanipol turned to Natronai. "Even now, he lies. There is no brother. Only coin. They offer him gold, and this man readily takes it. Who knows how many others he has betrayed over the years?"

Natronai looked to the woman, who had collapsed on her knees, face hidden and still wailing. Whether she wept in grief or shame, he could not tell.

"Strip them both and search for any weapons," Natronai instructed. "Bind them and keep them locked in this room. They will not be continuing with us."

Yazdin, pale and shaken, tried to speak, but Ashurbanipol silenced him with a glance.

After the traitors were bound, Ashurbanipol looked around at the remaining six. "If any of you believe loyalty can be purchased, let this be your warning. This road you will find is not paved with mercy."

Natronai stepped forward and placed a hand on the old general's shoulder.

"You were right," he said quietly. "I owe you my life once again. We might have walked into another ambush."

Ashurbanipol simply grunted. "No man lives long by trusting everyone."

He turned and walked to the corner, inspecting the remaining crates. But his eyes never stopped watching the remaining six.

That night, as the others slept, Natronai stood outside the shop under a moonlit archway, staring at the city walls beyond which new dangers waited. He had come seeking allies, but the deeper he traveled, the more he found shadows wearing friendly faces. The betrayal had not broken his resolve but it had changed something inside him. It was obvious there would be no safe harbors, not now. Not in Edessa. Not even among those who prayed to the same God. If he was to survive the journey to Palestina, he would have to become harder, colder, more like Ashurbanipol.

And perhaps... that was the price of becoming a messiah. Could a man who claimed to hear the words of God, ever walk side by side and be understood by the common man.

They departed Edessa at dawn beneath a reddened sky, the scent of mulberry trees behind them and the rifted land of the northern desert ahead. Ashurbanipol advised that they leave their horses behind with Yazdin and purchase donkeys instead, knowing that the Roman sentries they would encounter from now on were not accustomed to seeing merchants mounted on well-bred horses. The city faded in the dust, and with it the memory of betrayal. Ashurbanipol rode at the front, hardened and alert as ever, but Natronai noticed that the old soldier had not slept the night before. He didn't need to ask why.

The path around Damascus followed the old Roman roads that still held their shape beneath centuries of sun. If there was one thing that Rome knew how to build well, it was their roads. With each passing mile, the landscape softened. At first it was olive groves, then fields of barley and chickpeas, the green patches tucked into dry folds of land like old cloth stitched into worn garments.

The six companions who remained after Edessa traveled in silence, now watchful, loyal, and perhaps most importantly aware of what they did not know. Ashurbanipol had seen to that. But what they did know was certainly invaluable.

"This port master will turn blind for a price," one of them identified safe passage across the river.

"This centurion has a Judean wife," another pointed to the Roman at an inspection point that would let them pass without even looking into their wagons.

"This aqueduct feeds Antioch. A crack here would flood the market." As another passed on useful information that would spread panic and confusion once the rebellion had begun.

All of them were aware of the places where Natronai could draw recruits into his army. "These towns still remember the Temple. Give them a voice," or "this village still pays honor to their fallen during the Bar Kochba war, two hundred years ago."

And in every sentence, Natronai saw it coming closer: not just the rebellion, but the kingdom of Israel, rising once again from the ashes like the fabled phoenix.

Natronai slept little. He traveled constantly; Migdala, Gadara, Caesarea Philippi. From ruins and wells, from scrolls and songs, the movement rose. No sooner did he mention his name in a town, news of the 'Son of David' spread like wildfire. The men called it teshuvah, the return. The women called it revenge. The elders called it madness. And the young? They called it hope. But Natronai was not ready to gather the people into an army; not yet. First he had to assess the mood and temperament of the population, gauging their reaction to his presence before he began any effort to recruit.

For nearly two weeks they passed through the countryside unhindered. No brigands, no Roman patrols, no curious informants. Much of that had to do with the knowledge of the six companions they acquired in Edessa. Somehow they seemed to know someone in every place they passed through. Villagers gave them bread and shade without questions. Traders on the road nodded and moved on, after willingly giving them supplies. At night, Natronai would sit apart from the others, watching the sky. There were no visions, no voices from the clouds, but something inside him had begun to shift.

In Hazor, they passed through the city unchallenged. The guards at the eastern gate took one look at Ashurbanipol's glare and turned away. Their lodging was arranged by a contact from Yazdin's network, a discreet old Jew who ran a dye shop and spoke in whispers. He had little to offer but a clean cellar and dates sweet as honey.

It was there, beneath the beams of a stone house older than Rome itself, that Natronai found himself standing at the small window that overlooked the alley below. A shaft of dusty light fell across his face as a bee crawled along the sill. And suddenly without warning, there was no doubt, he knew. Not a word. Not a voice. But a certainty, as clear as a blade drawn in moonlight: You are the vessel. You are the spark. The kingdom is yours for the taking as long as you remain true to the cause and do not become distracted. The sense of it frightened him. It did not come from his own mind. Nor from madness. But something outside. Something that watched him as he watched the world.

The next morning, he did not tell the others. He didn't need to. They could already tell that something about him had changed. He was more confident, more self-assured in the decisions he made.

They left Hazor three days later, skirting Galilee's eastern edge, and following the Jordan Valley southward. They reached Gadara just before the first fall rains. The city, carved into limestone hills and wrapped in Greek colonnades, was a quiet town at the end of empire, where Roman laws were regarded with little passion.

It was in Gadara that Natronai began to dream vividly. Not wild prophecies, not apocalyptic symbols, but instead memories that he had forgotten long ago. His grandfather's voice in Mahoza. A song sung by his mother when he was a little child. The smell of Torah parchment freshly inked. The voice of his eldest brother, asking why the world was so cruel. He awoke from each dream calmer, but something else had changed.

Even Ashurbanipol noticed. "You've stopped asking questions," he said one morning as they saddled their mules.

Natronai smiled faintly. "Because the answers are no longer what I need."

Ashurbanipol scoffed. "You're speaking like a sage. Or a madman. Either way we must always seek answers."

"Only if we still have questions," Natronai responded. There was no mockery in his tone, only serenity.

From Gadara they followed the shoreline to the widest point of the Sea of Galilee. It was a clear afternoon, and the lake first shimmered in the sunlight, blue and vast, cradled by hills. A thousand songs had been sung of its waters, and more sermons than could be counted. It was a place where voices had once called fishermen to leave their nets. A place haunted by zealots, prophets, and echoes.

As they approached the shore, something inside Natronai broke wide open. It was not emotion, nor the awakening of an epiphany. It was a stillness, a holy quietness as if the entire world had slipped away. A strange sensation that spread from his chest to his fingertips, then own his spine into his toes. The lake was utterly still, as if the wind feared to touch it. Its surface like polished glass. Natronai walked alone to the edge, his shoes slipping on the mossy stones, until he removed them.

Ashurbanipol watched from behind, arms crossed, saying nothing.

Natronai stepped into the water.

It was cold, alive, ancient, but most of all, sentient.

He went no farther than his knees, but stood there for a long time, eyes closed, arms at his sides.

The others did not approach. They sensed what he was feeling. Or perhaps they feared it.

When he finally returned to shore, he spoke directly to Ashurbanipol. "I know now why I was born."

Ashurbanipol did not ask. He simply nodded and said, "Then walk carefully. Because someone else knew too, a long time ago and now the Romans bow down to him after making him a god. I'm afraid of what you'll become if the find there's another Jew having the same experience."

That evening, Natronai sat at a fire beneath olive trees, listening to the night insects and distant waves. He did not speak. He did not need to.

The others around him, his guards, his escorts, his companions, they too felt something different about him now. As if they had been joined by another presence. Something or someone had merged itself into his being, creating a metamorphosis as he went from caterpillar to butterfly.

Whatever the source of this presence, Natronai had crossed from scholar to pilgrim, from exile to witness, and now he was ready to face and accept the challenge he had prepared for his entire life. . And though the journey ahead would be perilous, for the first time he felt that he was not alone. He had become aware of the spirit that now walked beside him. And when he finally slept, it was not dreams that came to him but peace. For the first time in his life, his dreams had fallen silent and in that silence he could clearly hear the voice of God.

It was now three months since he left Ctesiphon, His journey had taken him to this very moment. Natronai stood alone on a cliff above Lake Tiberias. The wind tore through his cloak. Below, smoke from a Roman garrison stationed far away blurred the horizon. A line of olive trees marked the ancient road toward Jerusalem.

He removed the Isaiah scroll from his belt and unrolled it slowly. He began to read the words of Isaiah. "Comfort ye, comfort ye, my people, saith your God. Speak ye comfortably to Jerusalem, and cry unto her, that her warfare is accomplished, that her iniquity is pardoned: for she hath received of the Lord's hand double for all her sins."

As he continued to read, his words were carried on the wind.

Suddenly they began to appear. Behind him, a dozen men from the nearby village, waited and listened in silence. Before long a crowd of shepherds, scribes and stonecutters surrounded him. Every one of them armed with staffs, pitchforks and hammers.

Natronai turned, acknowledging their presence. "It begins."

And in the halls of Constantinople, over two thousand miles away, in the tower of his private chapel, Emperor Constantius awoke from a dream of fire and brimstone and could not explain why his heart was pounding furiously.

CHAPTER X: THE PRINCE AND THE PROPHET

Sepphoris shimmered on the hilltop like a half-remembered dream, with its white stone buildings that were sun-washed and wind-worn, their rooftops crowding together like an unending river of tiles. Beneath the city's gaze, the Galilean valley spread wide and fertile, dotted with olive groves and countless fig trees. But the air in the city itself was anything but quiet.

In the agora, near the western gate, one voice thundered like a prophet of old. "You bow to Rome and call it peace!" shouted the man standing atop the marble steps, tall and broad-shouldered, his linen cloak billowing like Elijah's mantle. "You accept paying the tax of the idolaters, the decrees of swine-eaters, and dare to call it halakhah? This is not the law! This is punishment for being who and what we are!"

The crowd pressed in, not to riot, but to listen. Market-sellers paused with dates half-measured. Fishermen leaned on their baskets. Even Roman guards stationed along the edges didn't interrupt. They had grown accustomed to the Jews protesting. They would complain endlessly but in the end they would pay the levied Jew Tax. That's all that mattered.

"The Rabbis say the covenant must adapt. That the circumcision of infants may be delayed, lest the Greeks and Romans be displeased. That one may partner with idolaters in the market, for the sake of survival. I say no! Who gave these men the right to alter the laws of Moses. Certainly not I, and I am one of them. I say enough! The time of listening to the rabbinical Sanhedrin must end if they continue on this path of assimilation."

Gasps of horror and murmurs of dissatisfaction rose simultaneously from the crowd. Those remembering the old ways were more than happy to do away with the rabbinical councils, while the rest feared what they would become without the rabbis to guide and protect them.

The speaker lifted his arms, calling for silence.

"The house of Hillel has sold our inheritance for Roman comfort. But the Lord sees! The Lord waits! And the Lord will deliver."

Someone from the edge shouted: "Then who will lead us? Certainly not you. You are just one of them seeking your own venue to power."

The man smiled grimly, and then pointed skyward. "You are right, I am not worthy. But I have never claimed to be. God will raise a son of David. Not in Tiberias. For the claims of descent by the house of Hillel are false and without merit. A fabrication of convenience but without any evidence. He will come, not from halls lined in silver. But like Moses, from the desert in exile, in silence, and raining down in fire."

It was the first time that Natronai heard of this speaker that the people were already calling the Lord's messenger. Standing alongside Ashurbanipol, they were cloaked in their merchant garments with faces shadowed beneath heavy cowls, listening intently from just outside the circle of heat this rabbi's words had ignited. Natronai recognized it immediately. This was no ordinary teacher. This was a flame that could ignite a wildfire.

Natronai turned to one of the nearby vendors, a grey-bearded man chewing a sprig of mint. "Who is he?"

The man squinted. "Don't you know? That's Isaac. Son of Ben Eleazar the potter. Studied in Tiberias, under the tutelage of those same rabbis he's now condemning but he was never cowed by Judah the Prince. He caught on quickly to what those parasites in Tiberias were all about. Lives here now. Speaks like he's Elijah himself."

Natronai nodded slowly. "And the people? Do they actually pay attention to him?"

"You ask me, I think most would die for him."

"And what about you?" Natronai asked pointedly.

"What about me?" the merchant feigned not understanding the question.

"If a war was to break out against Rome, would you be prepared to die for him."

The merchant looked at Natronai suspiciously, thinking that he may be spying for the Romans. "I have a successful business to operate," he avoided answering directly. "It would take the true son of David returning before I'd even consider it," the merchant laughed, thinking such an event impossible.

"Good, then I will hold you to your promise."

Before the merchant could respond, Natronai had already turned and was walking away from the stall, accompanied by his large, brooding companion.

"We must meet this Isaac ben Eleazar," he confided to Ashurbanipol. "He will be instrumental in our assembling of an army."

"I'll admit he can talk," the Persian general conceded that the man may be of some use, "But do you really think he can deliver?"

"I know my people," Natronai replied, "and I can read their faces. The merchant was right. Most of those listening would follow him to the ends of the earth if he requested it of them."

"But that would undermine your own authority," Ashurbanipol questioned the wisdom of having the orator join their cause.

"If you studied our history, my friend, you would know that Moses always had a spokesperson at his side that could explain the details to the people. At first it was Aaron but later it became Joshua. This man will be my Aaron."

They waited until the crowd had dispersed later that afternoon and they sought him out. They found Isaac seated in the shade of a sycamore outside the beth midrash that his father had built for the city. He sat with knees drawn beneath him, scroll open, voice gentle as he taught three barefoot children from the Psalms. A humble setting for a man who earlier that day shook the marketplace to its foundation with an epic speech.

They approached silently, trying not to disturb the lesson but it was too late.

Isaac looked up once and paused. "You are far from Babylon, my prince," he said to them.

"You knew I was not from here?"

Isaac smiled thinking the answer to the question was obvious. "The Tiberians bend their shoulders when they walk. The exiles of Mahoza walk like bowed iron. And your companion, even beneath his hood is mistakenly a Persian."

"But how did you know I was of one of the two families calling themselves the Princes of Israel?" Natronai knelt beside the man.

"I know because I was told you would be coming."

Natronai coiled backwards, wondering if somehow this was a trap.

"Don't be worried," Isaac assured him. "You are not the only one that receives visions."

"I am Natronai," he said. "Son of the Exilarch, Nehemiah."

Isaac's brow twitched. But he did not rise or even attempt to bow.

"You're actually early," he said simply.

Natronai blinked. "Early?"

Isaac closed the scroll and dismissed the children. "As I just said, I was told of your coming. I've been waiting for you. Just not so soon."

They sat together under that tree long after the sun had slipped behind the hills, while Ashurbanipol stood guard a short distance away.

They conversed for a long time. There was no pomp, no ceremony. Only two men, one with the lineage of kings, the other with the fire of prophecy, speaking of scripture, empire, and destiny.

"I do not wish to be king," Natronai confessed. "Only to restore justice. The Temple. The people. The Messiah's job is to deliver, not necessarily to rule."

Isaac nodded. "Which is why you must be one. We Jews have become like the other nations. The same way we needed Saul to become king over a thousand years ago, the situation is no different now. Left to our own devices, we will agree on nothing. A king offers a singular voice on the matter and it will be done. Two Jews discussing a matter will result in three solutions, none of which will be acted upon,"

Natronai could not help but to laugh. "And you? How do you see your role in all of this"

"I am merely the voice," Isaac said, "but you are the answer."

They shared figs and shared a moment of silence.

Isaac then spoke again, his voice low and dangerous. "Judah of Hillel preached patience. But now his son Hillel II sits and dines with Roman magistrates. He has grown to enjoy his life of comfort. He declares that Israel must wait for Messiah, as a bride waits in mourning for the groom that has passed away. He practically denies that there ever will be a Messiah and for that reason the people must rely on his family. But I say: the bride must wake and see that the groom is nearer than she dared to believe. Do you swear to me that the family of the Exilarch are descendants of the House of David?"

"Yes, I swear it." Natronai's voice was level and did not fluctuate.

"Prove it."

Natronai pulled the signet ring from his inner robe—gold, worn, inscribed with the lion devouring the serpent. He placed it in Isaac's hand. "That is the Emperor Shapur's ring. He provided it to me to show everyone that I have his support."

"But it does not say that you are who you claim to be," Isaac dismissed the ring as if it didn't exist. "The people will need proof."

"I have only the Isaiah scroll that my father gave me."

"Let me see it," Isaac urged him to hand it over.

Natronai retrieved the scroll from his bag and held it out, repeating the message that had been passed through Shapur. "He said it will tell them who I am."

Isaac eagerly took the scroll, handling it carefully as he could tell immediately that it was ancient. Unrolling it partially, he held it up against the sun and laughed excitedly. "Welcome son of David."

"You believe me now?" Natronai didn't understand.

"Obviously, you have not paid attention to your own family traditions," Isaac scolded him.

"Perhaps not," Natronai acknowledged. "What are you referring to?"

"This scroll which you are carrying about so casually, do you have any idea how old it is?"

"It's ancient apparently," was all that Natronai knew.

"Try over eight hundred years. The legends say that when Ezra decided to read the entire Tanach to the people, he had no copies from the prophets within his own collection, so he had to borrow the scrolls from the Temple that had returned to Judea when Zerubbabel was appointed as governor. These were all copies from within Zerubbabel's personal collection, or in other words, from the royal family's library. In order to ensure that Ezra returned every scroll that he had been lent, Zerubbabel's documents were all marked with a special ink along the edges that can only be seen when exposed to the rays of the sun. That is what I was looking for and that is what I found."

"What did it say?" Natronai was curious.

"Just what you would expect it to say. 'Property of the House of David.' Property which was returned to the Temple but was carried back to Babylon before Titus burned down the Temple. That is why it was in the possession of your family."

"I had not heard the story before," Natronai admitted.

"Which could only mean two things. Either the scroll does belong to you or you stole it, but I believe the former is more likely than the latter." Isaac grinned broadly.

The rabbi cradled the scroll without trembling. "Now let the people see it."

The hour had grown late. Isaac had invited Natronai's caravan to spend the night in the courtyard of the school he operated in the heart of Sepphoris. Smoke curled from the oil lamps hanging low in the study hall of the beit midrash. Scrolls lined the cedar shelves like silent witnesses. Outside, in the courtyard, Natronai's small platoon of men were already asleep, the night completely silent save for the wind brushing against the shutters. Inside, Isaac unrolled a worn scroll in front of Natronai and Ashurbanipol. The scroll had nothing to do with Scripture, it was about genealogy.

"Here," he said, jabbing a finger at a name. "Hillel II of the house of Hillel. That's who is in charge of Tiberias now. He claims descent from David, through Hillel the Elder. And yes, Hillel was a sage. A light in his time, we all know that but there is no proof he descended from a royal line." He turned sharply toward Natronai. "But wisdom is not inheritance. And faith is not blood."

Natronai said nothing. He listened as one does when the spirit tightens in the chest.

Isaac continued. "Their claim is built on three pillars: Hillel's descent from David, his acceptance by the Sanhedrin, and their custodianship of the oral law. But all three are cracked." He paced now, the hem of his robe sweeping the tiles. "First, regarding descent. The elder Hillel came from Babylon; we know that to be true, but the Babylonian records from his generation are fragmentary. The chain was never sealed. There is no uninterrupted line as there is with your family," he turned to Natronai, eyes intense, "your house has kept its records under Persian oversight, with scrolls sealed and guarded for centuries. How is it possible that we do not see any linkage between your family and that of Hillel's if his claim was true?"

"We only recorded the Exilarchate," Natronai said quietly.

"Yes," Isaac said, voice rising. "But you also only intermarried within your own family or with that of the Kohenim. At some point there would have had to have been a marriage to the line of Hillel but there isn't any. The true line of David, recognized even by Rome's enemies, remains hidden in plain sight in Babylon, while the Hillelites, fat with Roman subsidies, pretend their tenuous link gives them authority."

He rolled up the scroll and set it down with force.

"Second pillar concerns legitimacy. The Hillelites claim authority because the Sanhedrin remains in their control. But what is the Sanhedrin now? Nothing but a Roman registry office dressed in Jewish clothes for the purpose of tax collection. I've seen it with my own eyes, Natronai. I've sat behind the court lattice and watched Roman soldiers escorting scribes into deliberations. I've heard them debate taxes with more care than Torah."

Natronai frowned. "I'd heard rumors but I never imagined it was that bad."

Isaac's voice dropped to a dangerous calm. "They sit in Tiberias. On lands given by Rome. In buildings restored by imperial funds. They preach that survival depends on submission. They permit Roman festivals so long as the menorah is not removed. And they ban sermons like mine."

"Ban?"

"They declared me posek sheker. A liar in halakhic matters."

Natronai's eyes hardened.

"They say rebellion is blasphemy. But what is more blasphemous than bowing to idols in the name of peace?"

Isaac pulled another scroll. This one was thinner, less formal. They were his personal notes. He read from them. "'Better to live under Edom than to die under Jerusalem's illusion.' That is what Rabbi Gamaliel the Fourth said to the procurator in Scythopolis."

"Gamaliel?" Natronai asked. "Also a descendant of Hillel?"

Isaac nodded grimly. "Father of Hillel II who now sits in the chair. They smile and quote the Psalms. But they dine in palaces built by Rome. I've seen their wine. Sicilian. Their robes? Dyed in Tyrian purple. Their students mock prophecy. Their scribes edit the Mishnah with Roman commentary."

He read another of his notes, letting the parchment crinkle in the quiet.

"They are not guardians. They are collaborators."

Natronai stood, moved to the open window, and stared out toward the west, where the faintest glimmer of stars stretched over the hills. He said nothing for a time. Then spoke softly, "My father warned me of them. He said that the Sanhedrin was dead in all but name. That their Torah was gutted."

Isaac joined him by the window. "They fear the coming of the Messiah more than Caesar. Because the Messiah does not negotiate."

"Then what must we do?"

Isaac turned to him, voice no longer gentle. "Expose them. Reveal to the people that the house of Hillel no longer defends the covenant. That their bloodline is cracked. That their rulings are tainted. That their silence is complicity. Only your bloodline runs pure and has the blessing of the Almighty."

"And what will the Sanhedrin do in response?" Natronai asked the obvious question.

"They will call it lashon hara. Slander. They will cry for unity. Plead that now is not the time."

"And if we divide the people by doing so?"

Isaac stepped closer.

"It is better to divide the people and serve the remnant faithful, than try to unite them all in comfortable exile. The one thing you must never do is show any leniency toward the House of Hillel. Any dealings with them will contaminate you and it will cost you the faith of the people. They will abandon you as quickly as God does."

Natronai met his gaze. "Of this you are certain? There is no way possible to bring the House of Hillel over to our cause? Better to fight the Romans united than fractured."

Isaac didn't blink. "I have heard the whisper of God in the corners of this land. He is not silent. He is waiting. Waiting for you but one wrong decision and He will abandon you as He did with so many other kings during our history. Believe me when I say if you have anything to do with the House of Hillel it will cause your downfall."

Natronai reached into his robe and withdrew the lion signet, given to him by Shapur and placed it upon his middle finger. "Then let us do it. In public. Let the people see the true line. Let them hear the truth from your mouth. And let them decide whom they will follow; Rome's rabbis or God's appointed."

Isaac was ready with his next move. "I will declare it next Sabbath," he said. "Before the whole city. We will not whisper anymore. We will speak jointly to the people and our liberation will begin here in Sepphoris. Such is the will of God!"

"So be it!" Natronai agreed.

CHAPTER XI: THE CORONATION

The sun had only just begun to crest the low Galilean hills when the people of Sepphoris rose from their beds. The air, warm already with the scent of ripening fig trees and baked dust, was charged with anticipation. A rumor had run like a spark through the northern towns, from Nazareth to Cana, from Magdala to Jotapata: Rabbi Isaak ben Eliezer would be speaking this Sabbath, not merely on the law, but on deliverance.

They came on foot, in carts, atop donkeys. Men with flint in their eyes, women clutching children, old men leaning on their staffs. The streets of Sepphoris were filled to bursting. Every rooftop was occupied; every window crowded with faces. The market stalls were abandoned. Even the Roman sentries stationed on the outskirts dared not approach the gathering due to its overwhelming size. They watched uneasily from a distance; fingers curled near hilts.

Within the synagogue itself, a grand stone structure at the heart of the city, adorned with olivewood carvings and golden menorahs, the air was thick with tension and the rising heat. The pillars vibrated not from sound, but from expectation. At the center, standing beside the ark of the Torah, dressed in white robes woven in Babylon and fringed with blue, stood Isaak ben Eliezer, lean, black-bearded, with eyes burning like coals.

As the main synagogue of Sepphoris, filled to bursting, as pilgrims and townsfolk pressed shoulder-to-shoulder came to hear of the coming of the Messiah, Isaac ascended the bimah as he had done every other sabbath. Word had spread like fire through the Galilee that the rabbi who denounces Rome would be speaking again but this time, he would not be alone. Elders stood on tiptoe. Children sat in rafters and the Roman informants listened from every vantage point they could gain.

He waited until the last murmurs died down.

And then he spoke. "Brothers. Sisters. Children of Abraham.

We gather here in the holy name of the God of our forefathers, the God of Abraham, of Isaac, and of Jacob. The God who brought us out of Egypt with a mighty hand and an outstretched arm. The God who gave us His covenant at Sinai. The God who promised David an everlasting throne, and who promised through the prophets redemption.

But look around you. Do we see Zion in glory? Do we see a land flowing rich with milk and honey?

No. Instead, we see the eagle banners of Rome stretch out across our homeland. We see our Temple mount defiled and we are forbidden to even set foot upon it. We see taxes that bleed the poor, crosses that line the roads, soldiers who mock our Sabbath, and tyrants in Caesarea who sit on David's throne by the will of Caesar, not by the will of HaShem.

Where is our comfort? Where is our Deliverer?

I say to you, rejoice, for he has come!"

Afterwards. he read no psalm. He sang no prayer. Instead, he held up the signet of Shapur in one hand and the Scroll of Zerubbabel in the other.

"This is the ring of the Exile. A gift from the Emperor Shapur to the man bearing the true bloodline of Jesse and David, hidden not by cowardice, but preserved in faith in Babylon. And this is the Scroll of Isaiah, the scroll possessed by Zerubbabel and read before the people by Ezra when we restored the Temple and rebuilt our nation. It too has come from Babylon to signal to all of us that the Lion of Judah has returned and it is time to rebuild the Kingdom of Israel.

The house of Hillel falsely claims the throne, but they do not bear this seal and they do not possess this scroll. They dine with Caesar. They are the empire's whores doing their bidding willingly, while betraying all of us for silver and gold. This man, Natronai ben Nehemiah, is the son of the covenant, the chosen of God and he has come to deliver us from this evil."

A collective gasp. Some cried out in protest, fearing the wrath of the Romans and the House of Hillel. Others fell to their knees, giving thanks to the Almighty.

"We do not reject Torah," Isaac continued. "We reject its corruption. We do not rebel against God but instead we return to Him."

He turned to face his guest who sat to his right side. "

"This man who sits by me is Natronai ben Nehemiah, a true descendant of King David, born of the House of Exilarchs, steeped in Torah since birth, blessed with visions and fire, and sent by God not to preach only, but to free the children of Israel!

Like Moses, he has been rejected by his own kin.

Like Joseph, he has been cast down before he will be lifted up.

Like David, he has fled into the wilderness with his life in danger.

And like the Servant of Isaiah, he has borne the griefs of our nation.

And now, the time of waiting is over.

Natronai is not king. Not yet. But he is the signpost. And I say to you, if the covenant is to live, it must pass through him."

The people erupted into wild cheers and applause. After tonight, the city would never be the same.

"My brothers," Isaac continued, "you know me. You know my teaching. And you will now know what is written in this scroll."

He unrolled the Isaiah scroll and read aloud, his voice trembling with power.

"Listen to the prophet Isaiah, from Isaiah 61:

*'The Spirit of the Lord God is upon me,
because the Lord has anointed me to bring good news to the afflicted;
He has sent me to bind up the brokenhearted,
to proclaim liberty to the captives
and freedom to the prisoners.'*

"The Redeemer shall come to Zion, and unto them that turn from transgression in Jacob, saith the Lord."

Then he turned once again, gesturing to the man to his side.

"This is our Patricius of David, the aristocrat of exile, the prince of our people, the one we have prayed for, Natronai ben Nehemiah. A man not crowned by Rome or anointed by compromise but one who is born of the root of Jesse. Who else but the Patricius has stood before kings and not bowed? Who else but him has walked barefoot into Galilee to declare, The Kingdom is at hand? Who else dares proclaim the Jubilee of the Lord in the face of Roman spears? I say to you no one has come before him in such a manner and now that you know the signs you have heard the testimonies, you will know the truth. Those sick of heart will now be healed. Those that have been blind these many years to the lies from Tiberias will now see. And the hearts of the people, your hearts will burn with hope again!"

A thunderous roar emerged from those assembled, reverberating with an intensity that the Roman sentries watching carefully from a distance shook with fear.

Isaac knew he now had their full attention and undying loyalty. Remember what the prophet Zechariah said:

*'Behold, your king is coming to you;
righteous and having salvation is he,
humble and mounted on a donkey.'
And he shall break the bow of Ephraim! He shall cast down the chariots of Rome!
He shall gather the scattered ones of Israel and pour out the Spirit upon the dry bones!
He has come! He has come!*

"I say to you, yes he has come!"

There were more gasps from the congregation. Others openly wept.

"He does not come to rule over you by the sword, but to restore the covenant of God, your true King. He does not claim what is not his. But I say to you this my brothers and sisters, the Lord has given him to us and we shall not turn him away."

Isaac knew it was time to seal the pact. "I ask you, are you not weary of oppression?"

In a unified voice the congregation shouted, "YES!"

"Are you not thirsting for justice?"

This time even louder they responded, "YES!"

"Will you sit idly while the Covenant is trampled underfoot? Or will you rise?"

"We will rise!" they all screamed passionately.

"Will you take your place in the story of our people , that same story that began with Abraham, that crossed the Red Sea, that crowned David and that now calls upon you, the men and women of Galilee, to be remembered in the Book of Redemption?"

"Yes we will," they were wild with enthusiasm.

"There is no more time to wait. The days of Daniel are upon us. The fourth beast devours the earth but the Ancient of Days is seated. And the Son of Man comes in the clouds! Rise, oh Israel. Take heart, Judah. Stand, sons of Zebulun and daughters of Naphtali. For the Lord has remembered His people. And the Messiah walks among us!"

The synagogue trembled immediately not with noise, but with the stillness of inspired greatness. The kind of awe-struck stillness that descends when the soul knows it is in the presence of something divine and eternal. The people had roared when Isaac ben Eliezer spoke, but now they waited, breathless. He had raised their eyes toward the heavens, but now all eyes turned forward, to the man standing humbly beside him, half-shrouded by the carved wooden ark, his head bowed as if in prayer.

Once more Rabbi Isaac's voice rang out, but now softer and more reverent. "Brothers and sisters, the moment has come. You have heard my words, but now you will hear the voice of the one anointed. Anointed not by oil, but by suffering. Anointed not by men, but by the Spirit of the Living God. Behold the Patricius, the true heir of David, the rod from the stem of Jesse. I give you...Natronai ben Nehemiah."

A hush fell over the entire community. Even the doves nesting in the synagogue beams ceased their cooing.

Natronai stepped forward, holding nothing but the ring that Isaac passed to him. His robe was simple, linen, coarse, and travel-worn. Dust clung to his sandals. His hair was dark and unkempt; his beard streaked with the gold of the Galilean sun. But his eyes as most recalled later burned like the Sinai set afire. People who met his eyes swore that they forgot the world, forgot their aches and debts and griefs. In his eyes lived something both ancient and beyond time.

He mounted the bimah in silence. And then he spoke, not loudly, not theatrically, but in a voice rich as flowing wine and piercing as steel. "I am no king, I wear no crown of gold," he began. " I am no prophet. I come not from the palaces of Jerusalem, but from the remnant of her ashes. I come not with scrolls of power, but with a fire in my bones. A fire kindled by Almighty God. My people…do you not see? The time of waiting is now over. You have prayed long enough. You have wept beside dry wells and buried your sons beneath foreign coins long enough. You have lived as slaves in the Land of Promise long enough.

The Lord has heard your cry.

He has heard the broken songs of your harvest.

He has seen the fear in your daughters' eyes.

He has counted the lashes on your backs and the taxes in your purses.

And now, He has remembered His covenant. Just as He spoke to Isaiah, so too He speaks now:

'Can a woman forget her nursing child, or show no compassion for the child of her womb? Though she may forget, I will not forget you. Behold, I have engraved you on the palms of My hands…'

I swear to you, the hand of the Lord is upon me. Not for my sake. Not to make me great. But for you. For this nation. For this people whom He calls His bride.

You look at me and ask, 'Am I the Messiah?' I tell you this, I am what God has made me to be. He is the potter and I am his clay. I did not choose this path. I did not seek this yoke. But when the voice came to me, not in fire, not in thunder, but in a whisper that shattered stone, I knew that I could not turn away.

I walked the wilderness of Mahoza, I knelt in the blood of my forefathers. I stood before kings who wore iron crowns and their words were ash to me. I saw angels descend in dreams and heard the groans of our fathers and their fathers under Roman chains. And I said, 'Hineni. Here I am, Lord. Send me.'

And now I say to you, Sepphoris, Nazareth, Tiberias, Magdala, and all the other cities, towns and villages…Rise.

Not with anger, but with purpose. Not for vengeance, but for liberty. For the day of the Lord has come. And those who sit in darkness shall see a great light.

I will lead you but not to riches.

I will lead you but not to glory as the world sees glory.

I will lead you through fire, through trial, through the sword…but I swear before the throne of the Almighty, when we reach the other side of that fire, we will find freedom. Zion shall shake off her dust. The Temple shall rise again. And your children shall sit beneath their vines and fig trees, unafraid.

The Lord says, 'Believe in Me!'

Do you feel His words burning in your chest as I do? Then come with me. Not as soldiers of war but as sons and daughters of the Covenant. And I will serve you as God's humble servant so long as Israel lives. For the Kingdom of Heaven is at hand and you are its firstborn!"

Natronai open his arms, embracing the crowd.

As he did, something moved through the crowd like a divine wind. It rippled through their bones, shook their bodies, loosening the chains from their hearts. The people bowed their heads and then without warning they surged forward. Not to worship, but to follow. Weeping. Singing. Falling to their knees. Men who had never prayed aloud shouted psalms. Women laid their scarves at his feet. Boys ran to fetch cousins, fathers, uncles that may have been standing outside to come see the deliverer.

Then, from the outer courtyard, someone cried out: "Baruch Haba B'Shem Adonai!" "Blessed is he who comes in the name of the Lord!"

Another voice shouted, "Long live the Son of David!"

And the people erupted in songs, in cheers, in chants that echoed off stone and stirred the very dust. Cries of Hosanna! swept through the crowds.

And so it began. Not as a rebellion of politics or ambition, but as a holy firestorm. A war of the spirit. A pure movement of destiny.

As Natronai, the Patricius, stepped down from the bimah, he did so not as the son of the Babylonian exilarch, but as the long awaited Jewish Messiah.

CHAPTER XII: THE NEW COVENANT

The weeks that followed forged a bond deeper than politics. Isaac taught by day. Natronai organized by night. Scrolls were copied. Messengers sent. Secret meetings convened in undisclosed caves and private olive presses. Arms were smuggled in from Persia, just as Shapur had promised. Prayers were whispered openly and louder than before, sending a clear message to Rome.

Meanwhile, during the next few nights, Sepphoris remained quiet, cloaked in a silence laden with the tension of a people waiting for that one specific spark to incite an inferno. Word by now had spread throughout Galilee that Natronai, son of the Royal House, was the long awaited Messiah.

On one particular night, while drafting their document in the upper room of the grain merchant's house, something deeper and reverent took shape. Natronai sat cross-legged on a low stool, his linen robe cinched tightly, curls of dark hair clinging to his temples. His face was drawn but resolute. Across from him, Isaac ben Eliezer, rested a heavy parchment scroll on the cedar table. He was older, with the first streaks of silver in his black beard and a voice that could silence crowds, but tonight, he was scribe, taking down Natronai's dictation.

"You cannot say such things as merely a proclamation," Isaac said, dipping his quill into ink. "Words of significance must be written down, otherwise people will forget. And that which is written must be as resounding as the Torah and trumpet its meaning throughout the population. Every word must carry justice and the sword."

Natronai nodded. "I agree. We must lock the people into a covenant, just like at Sinai. The words must light a flame lit in the souls of our people. But where do I begin?"

For days they had debated the structure. Isaac had suggested they begin with law: something tangible to reform the corrupt synagogue authorities, something holy to reclaim the priesthood from Rome's collaborators. Natronai had countered that it must begin with liturgy, by providing a new prayer to awaken hearts dulled by despair.

But both agreed that it must end with rebellion. Together, they wrote a manifesto; part law, part liturgy, part rebellion and they called it The Covenant of Fire. The oil lamps flickered in the upper chambers of many the houses in Sepphoris over many nights, Isaac ensuring that they didn't stay longer than one night in any one house. The flames from the lamps cast long, swaying shadows on the plastered and stuccoed walls and just in the same manner that the lamps burned through the hours of darkness, they began their book with fire.

"These are the words of Natronai ben Nehemiah, Prince of Israel from the House of David, as spoken to him by Yahweh, Our Lord and God and King of the universe."

"Hear, O Israel: The Lord your God is a consuming fire, a jealous God. And He shall not hold guiltless the one who kneels before tyrants or bends the neck to the yoke of foreign masters."

So began the Covenant of Fire, not with comfort, but with confrontation. The opening lines evoking Moses' ascent on Sinai but reimagined it for a generation under Rome's heel. In these verses, God was not distant and silent, but incensed, demanding loyalty not only in ritual but in resistance.

"We must remind them," Isaac whispered as he etched the words, "that to worship God is also to cast down idols."

Natronai's voice sharpened. "We will remind them that Caesar is the last and greatest idol of them all."

They crafted a liturgical formula to be read aloud in synagogues, in homes, and in rebel camps.

"Blessed are You, O Lord our God, King of the universe, who teaches our hands to war and our fingers to battle."

"Blessed are You, Shield of Abraham, who remembers the covenant and awakens the slumbering lion of Judah."

It was familiar enough to feel ancient, yet radical enough to ignite something long dormant. These were not passive blessings. They were invocations for war.

Isaac took up a new section of the parchment and began to write again. "These must not be laws of domination, like Rome's edicts," he said. "But neither can they be the soft words of exiled rabbis content with silence."

What emerged was a hybrid. A Tanach book of resistance. The laws balanced between moral clarity and military necessity.

"No man shall raise a sword against his brother, the weak, or the harmless, but only against the oppressor."

"Let no tax be paid to Caesar, nor to the procurator, nor to Hillel's line. The treasury of the Lord shall be rebuilt in the hills."

"If a leader among you grows fat with bribes or bows to Rome, let him be cast out and his name blotted from the assembly.

"The Sabbath shall not be broken except in battle or deliverance."

Natronai insisted on including a controversial clause.

"If a priest or elder shall betray the people to the Romans, let his beard be cut and burned, and both his hands be broken. Let him walk the streets as a warning to all who barter Zion for silver."

Isaac hesitated at first. "It is harsh," he said.

"But necessary," Natronai replied. "The Temple was not destroyed by the legions alone, it was destroyed by the Sadducees who sold it stone by stone. And as half my blood is the House of Aaron, I bear that guilt just as much, and I will see that it is not repeated."

"You've just put all the elders in Tiberias, including the House of Hillel on notice," Isaac reminded him.

"Only if they do not support God's righteous cause. They will be given the opportunity to make the right choice. Even though we do not wish to commune with them, we will still need their support in order to unite all the people."

Isaac was still weary. "Just remember that you said these are the words of God as spoken to you..."

"They are," Natronai replied immediately.

"Then they are not to be mitigated. You must carry them out as has been instructed, otherwise you risk not only losing the Lord's blessing but the support of the people as well. You are aware of that?"

"I will do as I have been instructed. There can be no exceptions."

Having said that, Isaac wrote down Natronai's decree regarding the betrayal by a priest or elder onto the parchment.

They called these the Statutes of the Redeemed, and in the margins, they left blank spaces, lines for local judges to write their own halakhot, or laws of enforcement under the authority of the Covenant. Unlike the Talmud of the Tiberian rabbis, Natronai argued there has never been an oral tradition, nothing more than a fabrication of these rabbis to glorify their own name, and therefore the statutes of his laws would be interpreted and decided upon b each judge that enforces them. Some may interpret it harsher than others but it was up to the individual judge to use the law to devise the punishment that best suited the degree of the crime.

But of all the sections in their Covenant of fire, the most rousing part of the book was its liturgical songs, compiled and composed jointly by Isaac and Natronai. They called them 'Shirei Ha'Olim', Songs of the Ascenders, evoking both the warriors who would ascend and liberate the holy hill in war and the pilgrims to Jerusalem that would come afterwards. One of the hymns said it was to be sung accompanied by hand drum and flute, and it was destined to become a rallying cry.

> "O daughters of Zion, put on your red veils,
> The Bridegroom comes, but He comes with blood.
> He rides not a donkey, but a lion's flank,
> And His eyes are beacons from God."

Another song was based on Psalm 2 but rewritten.

> "Why do the nations rage, and the Gentiles plot in vain?
> The Lord shall laugh from the heavens, and say:
> I have set My King upon the ruins of Rome."

There were songs and hymns written to be taught to children or sung by the warriors before raiding Roman garrisons. There were prayers to be shouted by battalions. and laments to be sung by the townspeople, reminding them how long they have been in exile within their own land, meant to break the hearts of those too hardened by centuries of grief that they could feel no longer.

The final section of the Covenant of Fire was Natronai's idea alone. It was presented as a chilling register of Rome's crimes against Israel. He called it the Sefer HaPekudah, the Scroll of the Reckoning. It was intended that on each line, a scribe would later write the names of a Roman officials, tax collectors, informants, and turncoat Jews that received divine punishment. It was part litany, part hit list and part recording of those that finally received Jewish justice.

"I will not let these men die in comfort," Natronai vowed. "Let them know they are written in the Book and one day they will receive their just reward by our hands."

Isaac struggled with it. "You walk a dangerous road. If the Romans get hold of the book with names filled in then they will bring charges against whomever filled in the names."

Natronai could not help but laugh at Isaac's concern. "And why should we be concerned about that?" he questioned. "We are going to war. All of us will be charged with treason under Roman law, regardless of who signs a list. Any Jew that wouldn't be charged by the Romans we can safely assume would be a collaborator and that would mean we would levy charges against them. Was it not God who said, 'I will avenge, and I will repay?' From this moment on, we are the enemies of Rome and it is my wish that my name is first on their list of enemies, so that the people would rally around me."

A silence fell between them. It took a moment to recognize that once committee to the rebellion, every Jew in the land would be branded as a criminal. Old men, the infirmed, women, even children would all become fair game for Roman retribution.

Finally, Isaac nodded. "Then let the scroll be sealed with fire. We will win or we will die, but either way we will be free of Rome."

At the end of the text, they added a final declaration. Every copied scroll would be signed by every commander, elder, and rabbi who joined the movement and possessed a copy. In that way it would be a personnel binding of loyalty and fealty to both the rebellion and God. The declaration to be made prior to signing was quite straightforward.

"We make this covenant not only with those present today, but with our sons and daughters, and with the Lord of Hosts who sees all things. If we falter, may fire consume us. If we are faithful, may fire protect us. This is the Covenant of Fire."

Both Natronai and Isaac dipped their pens into scarlet ink and signed the original copy of the parchment, the color red being an echo of the blood on doorposts in Egypt. A sign of deliverance, and of judgment.

When they finally finished, the sky outside had grown pale with the promise of dawn. Isaac's hand trembled from writing, but his eyes were lit with something fierce. It wasn't that he was hesitant or had second thoughts, but he spoke only to reinforce his own conviction that they were committed to the cause. "You realize," he said softly, "that when this book goes out, there will be no turning back. Rome will call it sedition. Hillel will call it madness. Even your brothers in Babylon may disavow us."

Natronai stood and lifted the scroll. "Let them. I did not come to Palestina to make peace with tyrants. I came to set fire to the decaying wood. Now summon your students and have them start making copies. I want every synagogue in Judea and Galilee to have its own copy of the Covenant of Fire within the month."

And as the sun broke over Sepphoris, the Covenant of Fire was placed in a wooden chest, wrapped in linen, and carried to the Galilean hills, where it would pass from hand to hand between Isaac's students until there would be enough copies to ignite a nation.

Within days it was already spreading to Tiberias, to Pella, and down into the Judean hills. From there it crossed the Jezreel Valley, reaching the caves near Mount Tabor. There were now thirty copies circulating that had been written by devoted scribes. Each was treated like Torah, kissed before opening, and unrolled with reverence when it arrived. .

In a village near Nain, a group of farmers had the covenant read to them by their local priest beneath the cool shadow of olive trees:

"Let no man say, 'I am but a vine dresser,' or, 'I am too old for war.'
The Lord called Moses from the burning bush, and he was eighty.
The Lord called David from the field, and he was but a boy."

The farmers immediately dropped their tools. The next day, they forged spearpoints from ploughshares and wrapped their arms in strips of linen dyed with pomegranate juice which had become the sign of the Redeemed.

In Magdala, it was sung. In Tiberias, it was memorized. In Bethsaida, a crowd of youths tore down the imperial standard from the tax station and burned it, singing:

"He has remembered His covenant forever,
the word He commanded for a thousand generations."

Within weeks, the leaders of the northern assemblies, the elders, zealots, rabbis, even former Zadokites met in secret near Mount Arbel. Natronai stood before them, with Isaac at his side, and unfurled his copy of the Covenant of Fire.

When he spoke, it was not a plea but a challenge. "We are not simply rebelling against Rome," Natronai said. "We are rebelling against every false priest who has defiled the name of God. Every man who sold righteousness for coin. Every Levite who chants psalms while ignoring the blood in our streets."

One of the elders, Yehoshua of Kfar Kana, rose. "You would risk the wrath of the eagle for a scroll and some songs?"

"I would risk the wrath of Ghenna itself," Natronai answered, "to restore the Kingdom of God in Zion."

Silence followed and then came a murmur of assent.

Isaac unrolled a second parchment. "This is what I have called the Sefer haMetzarim, the Book of the Besieged. Every community that signs does so saying that it has willingly entered into the Covenant of Fire. Every community that refuses shall be regarded as under cherem, banished from the protection of God and man. Our forces will not come to defend it when they find themselves attacked by Rome. You all will have the opportunity to make the right choice. "

One by one, village leaders pressed their seal upon the parchment.

After signing each was handed what Isaac referred to as an appendix. He called it the Sefer Nistarim, or "Book of the Hidden" in which he laid out detailed plans for insurgency. The book contained guidelines for building hidden caches of weapons in synagogue basements and mikvaot. Instructions for messaging through coded liturgical phrases. Even a new calendar, synchronized with the lunar cycle, to time attacks with festivals and full moons. It was something that Isaac had been working on long before the arrival of Natronai, but only now he had the justification for distributing it.

The rebellion had a constitution and now it had teeth.

CHAPTER XIII: THE SANHEDRIN

They had always been cautious men. Businessmen, politicians, scholars and scribes, jurists and grammarians. Descendants of families having inherited wealth and power, giants who now walked in fear. When word spread through the halls of the Sanhedrin in Tiberias that the son of the Exilarch had crossed into Roman Palestine, which provided their first threat, it had now become far worse, as he had been hailed in Sepphoris as the heir to the throne of David. Their reaction was not one of awe, it was terror.

With the Temple still in ruins and the priesthood in disarray, Isaac proposed what many in Tiberias considered blasphemous, as he declared their Jewish court illegitimate and setup a temporary Sanhedrin in Sepphoris, made up of twelve elders from the Galilee, two from Judea, and three kohanim known for their piety, along with five Levites. Though not sitting directly on this newly established court, Natronai served in the role of witness and to affirm the Covenant, pronouncing halakhic judgment when needed. It was this new Sanhedrin that at its first assembly, gathered in the ruins of the old synagogue atop Mount Meron, that ratified the Covenant of Fire.

At the same time, they also composed a final declaration that was to be read in every town where the Covenant was being proclaimed and accepted.

"From this day forward, we do not recognize the authority of the Roman governor, nor of the authority of the House of Hillel and the unsanctified assembly that to date has laid claim to being this land's legal authority. We are a people reborn in fire. We are the Children of God. We are Israel. And our King is coming."

Behind closed doors, in a marble chamber lined with scrolls and silence, the Nasi Hillel II, patriarch of the House of Hillel, sat pale-faced, flanked by whispering advisors. He had called for an emergency session of the Tiberias Sanhedrin to discuss the matter of this upstart Messiah.

"This cannot stand," one council member murmured. "If the people believe he is of David, we lose everything."

"He is of David," said another quietly. "His line is older than yours, Hillel. It is documented."

Hillel II slammed the table. "What are you implying?" he questioned angrily. "Who here dares to question my birthright? Remember this, his lineage is not recognized by Rome but mine is. It is Rome that rules here, and they say my family is the only one authorized to rule. And know this well, without Rome, we are dust."

He sat patiently at the head of the semicircular chamber, his thin fingers pressed together beneath his beard, his eyes hollowed by nights of lost sleep, waiting for someone, anyone to speak up. Finally, he could not wait any longer. "Now speak," Hillel said, raising his eyes at last. "Let no one hold back. Let no fear of shame keep truth from our ears. The hour is too grave."

The murmurs began before the words formed fully. Then came the flood of responses. "It is rebellion, plain and unvarnished," said Gamaliel ben Shimon, his voice tight with emotion. "They've declared a rival Sanhedrin and did so openly! In Sepphoris no less! And what's worse, they've begun issuing rulings…rulings that contradict our own! We must tell Rome immediately and they will put an end to it."

"They say they have twenty-two elders," added Rabbi Yeshaiah, "with Natronai ben Nehemiah presiding over halakhic matters. And this Natronai, they call him Patricius. That's not a title of our fathers. That's Roman. That makes this a political matter that directly challenges Rome. They must come and put an end to it immediately."

"You are only partially right. It is far more than political," muttered another. "It's messianic. They call him the 'Deliverer.' That name alone is enough to stir the people."

"They only believe that because he is of the House of David," said Rabbi Eliezer bar Perachya, his voice soft but unshaken. "There are whispers among the Galilean villages. They say he will restore the Kingdom. That he has the favor of Shapur of Persia. That he speaks with the voice of prophecy. Perhaps we should first check this out to see if it is all true?"

Hillel's jaw clenched. He knew all this already, of course. The letters had come in over the last week in increasing numbers from rabbis in Arbel, from emissaries in Nazareth, even from synagogues in Yodfat and Cana. There were stories of miracles, speeches, marches, gatherings by torchlight. But it wasn't only stories. He knew of the Constitution of Fire. That changed everything. It was law. It was structure. Natronai and Isaac had announced a restored lunar reckoning declaring the calendar that Hillel had been working on to be flawed and therefore void. Everything they had done thus far, he considered to be an act of betrayal, not to Rome, but to him personally.

"The people are deserting us," said Rabbi Judah ben Meir. "This is not just a sect. This is a movement. Sepphoris is packed. Hundreds of men arriving daily. They come singing psalms, dressed in white, proclaiming deliverance. The man is raising an army. This time Rome will utterly destroy us."

"Then let us send word to Rome," said Gamaliel. "Let the Emperor see this for what it is. Sedition. Rebellion. Let him know that we have no part in this and need Rome to protect us from what this Natronai will do."

"Rome?" Hillel said, more to himself than to the others. He stood slowly. "Rome has no interest in a provincial messiah unless we can show that this army has already launched an attack against Roman interests."

"He is gathering arms," snapped another elder. "Isn't that enough for them to see that he is a threat."

"Do they think that men follow a would-be King of David's line just to hear sermons?" asked Rabbi Teraphon.

"They don't know what to think," Hillel answered. "They only think of a Messiah in terms of Jesus. They have no other perception. Unless they see dead Romans, none of their garrisons are going to send a single word to Caesar."

"But we can let them know that there are already rumors that he has armed companies, hiding in caves like Bar Kokhba's men did before him."

That name fell like a thunderclap. Even the lamps seemed to flicker at the mention of Bar Kochba..

"If he proves to be another Bar Kokhba," said Rabbi Perachya, "we must not delay. We must warn the authorities before it is too late."

"Rome does not need warning," Hillel said with sudden sharpness. "Rome needs direction. If we bring this before the Emperor without precision, without indicating specific locations of these hidden companies of men, we risk his thinking that we are stoking the fire rather than quenching it. You think the swords of Rome have dulled? No. If we appear to be hiding any information, Rome may choose to consider us collaborating with the rebels and they will cleanse the land of us all."

He let the weight of his words settle.

"And yet," Hillel continued, softer now, "we cannot ignore this. The man is not merely a preacher. He is shrewd. He has Isaac ben Eliezer, once one of our own, giving halakhic weight to every decree. And from what I've been told, he has the hearts of the people. That is more dangerous than spears."

Rabbi Yeshaiah stood. "Then what is our course?"

Hillel paced slowly. He looked not just tired now, but much older. "We must send word, but not merely to the Emperor. First, to the Prefect of Caesarea. Let him monitor Sepphoris closely. Let him place loyal eyes in the assemblies. If arms are being gathered, they will be found."

He turned to another elder. " And to Antioch. Gallus must be made aware, if he is not already. Let the imperial courier be prepared. But our message must be crafted carefully. We cannot accuse a son of David and think that the people will overlook what would be perceived as treasonous. You know what happened the last time the people thought we handed over a Messiah to a Roman governor."

"Then what do we say?" asked Rabbi Judah.

"We say what we must but do not focus on the man," Hillel said coldly. "That there is a growing sect, that has established their own legal and political council, usurping our authority that was given only to us by Rome. That they are issuing decrees without Roman approval. That their doctrines oppose the established and approved Sanhedrin."

"And when Rome acts?" one asked quietly.

"Then Natronai will naturally fall beneath Rome's hammer through his connections to this rival Sanhedrin. We will not be guilty of directly turning him over to Rome."

"And if he is truly who he claims to be?" one of the Rabbis asked the inconceivable.

"If that is the case, God will not abandon his chosen one… let us see if Heaven spares him."

The room fell still again. At that moment, only the wind outside could be heard, brushing through the palms along the Galilean hills.

Rabbi Gamaliel finally spoke. "And what of the people? If we are seen to be inviting the Romans upon our own brethren…even if it is made clear that our only concern was this rival Sanhedrin."

"We are not inviting anything," Hillel dismissed the concern. "We are preserving Torah. We are preserving the Sanhedrin. We are preserving Israel from another bloodbath. That is our mandate, to protect our people."

At last, Hillel looked toward the chamber doors. "We must prepare the dispatches. One for Caesarea. One for Antioch. I will write them myself. Let them go out tonight."

"And Sepphoris?" asked Rabbi Perachya.

Hillel's gaze darkened. "Send no one there. Not yet. Let them believe we are frozen in fear. Let them declare another law, and another. Every word they speak will become a charge against them."

He turned back to the council, eyes burning now with the fury of a patriarch whose house had been challenged. "We were entrusted with the authority of Moses, of Ezra, of Rabban Gamaliel before me. We will not surrender it to a dreamer in white robes. Not while I draw breath."

And with that, the meeting adjourned. The elders filed out slowly, each carrying his own burden of doubt, dread, or resolve. Outside, the night air had turned cool, and the stars above Tiberias shimmered faintly.

Once the last members of the council had left, Reb Hillel II set about writing the letter to the Emperor.

"To the Emperor Constantius, Defender of the Peace, Protector of Syria and Palestina:

We, the lawful representatives of the Jewish nation, write to warn of a dangerous figure who has entered your province. He claims descent from the line of David and seeks to inspire sedition among the people. His name is Natronai, son of the Exilarch of Mahoza, and he has allied with radical elements among the Galileans. He claims to be the true Messiah and if he should be successful in his mission then it would cast doubt upon your Messiah, the one you say is the son of God, Jesus Christ. Though I do not share your faith, I need you to know that we, your loyal citizens of Palestina, have no desire to crush it either.

As loyal subjects of the Empire, I can assure you that we do not support this rebellion. The House of Hillel remains committed to order and peace under Roman law.

Hillel II, Prince of Israel"

It said everything that Hillel had assured his council members he would not mention and said nothing of the matter that he promised he would confine his comments to. In his own heart he knew that Constantine would probably care nothing about there being a second Sanhedrin. Letting the Jews fight among themselves had always been Roman policy. But a threat to the emperor's religious beliefs, knowing that Constantius was fanatical about his faith, he knew it would result in an immediate response. And that response he knew would rid him of his concerns regarding Natronai ben Nehemiah, once and for all.

CHAPTER XIV: THE EARS OF ROME

In Constantinople, Hillel's letter arrived at the imperial palace under seal. It was read aloud by the chamberlain in the evening court, as Emperor Constantius II stood overlooking the Bosphorus, cloaked in purple and as silent as stone. He said nothing for the longest time.

Finally, he turned to his general, Flavius Arbitio, and snorted. "They're frightened."

"Who, Excellency?" his chamberlain was confused.

"This self-proclaimed prince of Israel and this court he presides over, of course."

"Of this... son of David he speaks of?" The chamberlain still desperately tried to grasp the context of the emperor's response.

"No," Constantius corrected him, "of their own people. This is not a plea for restoring order and justice. It is a plea for protection. Protection from their own blood. He wants me to come and save their worthless lives."

He paced once, eyes distant as he glanced into the future. "This rabbi, Isaac, and this prince from Babylon, they've struck a nerve. I can't just dismiss it. The last thing I need is to experience Hadrian's folly and have a second Bar Kokhba. I need you general to take care of this."

Arbitio stiffened. "Shall we send the legions in from Syria?"

"You mean do what my cousin should already be handling?"

"If I may speak in his defense, Majesty, he is engaging the Persians in Armenia. That is requiring his immediate attention." Arbitio was aware that most of the Syrian legions had been moved to the north.

"If he is to be Caesar, then he must be able to deal with enemies on more than one front. I won't accept his excuses. We will deal with this matter ourselves and then I'll deal with Gallus's incompetence."

"Then I will sail with my best legion and deal with this matter personally," Arbitio offered. "The sooner we sail, the sooner we can put an end to any rebellion before it has a chance to fester and affect the region."

"Go prepare them," Constantius said coldly. "But first I want spies. Reports. Names. Let the Jews betray each other for a few weeks. Then we send in the sword."

But fate, as ever, was not idle and within days of instructing Arbitio to prepare to invade Palestina, word came galloping from the West. Magnentius, Roman general of Gaul, promised to liberate the population from the tyrannical hands of the

Constantine family and was proclaimed as Emperor of the Western Empire by his troops.

The messenger kneeling before Constantius did not look up, but he could feel the hot panting breath on the back of his neck.

"Anything more you wish to tell me?" It was obvious that Constantius was not pleased with the message thus far.

"He was proclaimed by the legions in Augustodunum. Already the Rhine frontier is his. And Italy wavers, Majesty."

Constantius turned pale. "Are you saying that Rome supports him? Be precise when you talk to me!"

"Yes, Majesty. Magnentius has gained the favor of the senators in Rome."

Magnentius was a man of low birth but immense charisma, a commander of the cavalry who had once bowed to the imperial family but was now crowned by his soldiers and embraced by senatorial elites desperate for a return to the old gods and old glories. He wasn't even a tolerant Nicene Christian but instead, Magnentius courted the pagan gods, winning over the disaffected, the families with old money, and more of a concern, a host of vengeful generals.

Constantius dismissed everyone present in the council chamber and then retired to sit alone in his private well into the night, staring at a mosaic of Christ Pantokrator, his golden eyes staring down in silence.

He prayed aloud. "Why must I fight Rome more than Persia? Why Lord have you given me this crown, only to send challenge after challenger to try and rip it from my head? I have served you faithfully. I have made you supreme, the one and only true God of the Empire Tell me what I should do Lord Jesus to rid myself of enemies lurking around every corner. Forgive your humble servant for any sins I have made against you and pardon me for any trespass I will make in the future. I pray of Thee, show me mercy and kindness for the rest of my days Amen."

By morning, the decision had been made. Constantinus had received the answer he had prayed for. Palestina could wait but he could not ignore it entirely. He summoned a scribe and dictated a letter with precision:

To my beloved cousin Gallus, in Antioch,
In light of recent developments in the West, I cannot respond to a rising emergency in the Eastern provinces and must entrust it to stronger hands. I need you to put down a rising threat in Galilee and Judea, that may have escaped your attention thus far. You are to bring order. Stamp out the sedition in Palestina. The matter of some so-called Davidic prince that has appeared in the province is now yours. This Natronai, the Exilarch's son, must be dealt with immediately."
You are the Caesar in the East, now prove it.

Constantius sealed it with the imperial sigil, added a pouch of coin, and instructed the scribe to hand it off to the fastest rider in the stables.

At his palace in Antioch, Gallus rose, smoothing his robe, and stepped into the atrium where he was told a courier had just arrived from Constantinople. Upon entering, he saw that a young officer of the imperial post, cloaked in dust, boots caked with road mud, and his face burned by Anatolian sun was awaiting his arrival and then knelt immediately.

"From the Emperor, Caesar," he said with head bowed.

Gallus's stomach tightened, wondering what Constantinus might want now.

He took the scroll. The seal was genuine. Unbroken.

He dismissed the man with a wave, returned to his chamber, and broke the wax. To my beloved cousin Gallus, in Antioch, it began. He read it once. Then again. Then a third time. He did not move for a long while. He read the scroll again. Each word glowed like fire. *'Stamp out the sedition in Palestina.'* Was the emperor not aware that he was dealing with the Persian infiltration into Armenia right now? So far it had just been minor skirmishes but it could break out into total war at any moment.

'This Natronai, the Exilarch's son, must be dealt with immediately.' He cursed under his breath. Did Constantinus really think he had no knowledge of what was going on in Palestina. He was tempted to write back a letter to the Emperor saying that not only was he already aware of this Jewish interloper from Baghdad but already had operators in the field trying to stop him for months but then thought it best not to reply. Constantinus would take his acknowledgement and his inability to stop him for months as evidence of failure. It was clear he already thought that he was incompetent.

"The Jews. Always the Jews. Why is it they have been every Caesar's bane," Gallus asked himself. Even as a boy he had heard the whispers about rebellions, messiahs, blood in the streets of Jerusalem. They were a never ending problem. Why had Constantius chosen him for this? Was it a test? A trap? Or worse. An excuse to have him fail and then feel justified for removing him from his position and then either face exile or execution. After all, this was the way of the House of Constantine.

Later, he met with his tutor, an aging philosopher named Callinicus of Rhodes, who had once taught him logic and theology by the edge of the sea. Gallus liked the man because he did not flatter.

"Have you heard?" Gallus asked, pacing. "The Emperor demands I remove some minor agitator that thinks he can get the province of Palestina to rise up against the might of the Empire."

"I have," Callinicus replied.

"Well?"

The old man shrugged. "You were always meant for the East."

Gallus stopped. "Exactly what is that supposed to mean?"

"The East has always been a hotbed for insurrection. It is now and will be so in the future as well. It takes someone with the resolve to put out each fire as it erupts, knowing that the fires will never stop." Callinicus's face looked grim, suggesting it was a hopeless challenge but one which would be accepted by someone like Gallus.

Do you think I'll survive it?" Gallus was more curious than concerned.

"No one survives the East," Callinicus said. "They endure it. Or they are devoured by it."

Gallus gave a bitter smile. "If so, then I'm to deal with this so-called son of a line of long, dead kings.. This Natronai."

"Is he the real thing or just another whisper in the wind? The Jews have had their share of false liberators over the years,"

"Oh, yes. Definitely real enough to frighten Rome's allies. Otherwise, how would my cousin even know of his existence? Real enough to ignite Galilee from what I've heard."

Callinicus nodded. "Then make him a martyr or make him a bitter memory. It's within your power to do either."

Gallus's eyes burned. "Or make him a symbol of my ascension to a loftier position."

"Aye," Callinicus agreed. "But do not forget Icarus sought loftier heights as well."

He woke before dawn, the activity in his mind not letting him sleep. As much as he resented the idea, he knew he had to respond to Constantius's letter, even if it was just to acknowledge receiving it.

'To my cousin Constantius Augustus, by the grace of God, Emperor of Rome. I, Gallus Caesar, accept the burden you place upon me. I shall take up my charge to pacify the East in all areas of conflict. I shall see order restored in the East. And I shall deal with the Jewish threat swiftly and without hesitation.
I remain your faithful servant.

He signed it with a crimson seal: a phoenix rising from flame. It was a subtle message. I may serve, it said but I too am reborn.

In the weeks that followed, Gallus moved with a speed that astonished everyone at his court. He studied maps of the East, reviewed troop reports from Palestine, and ordered fresh arms from the smiths of Bithynia. He held private councils with generals, Jewish informants, and dissident clerics. He asked about Natronai. About the rabbi Isaac. About Sepphoris. About the Sanhedrin. About loyalties in Caesarea, Gaza, Tyre.

He learned that some Jewish leaders feared Natronai, and others worshiped him. That Roman officials in Palestina could be bought, but not cheaply.

He issued a public proclamation in both Greek and Latin that he circulated throughout the territories that informed the public that Caesar Gallus, by decree of the Emperor Constantius, intends to restore justice in the East. Peace shall be kept. Rebels shall be punished. And the law of Rome shall shine again in the lands of Syria and Judea.

It was the first notification observed by Natronai and his followers that they had seriously caught the Roman's attention. Thus far they had free reign to do as they pleased throughout Galilee without any serious consequences. Things might be different from now on and they would need to be prepared.

Publicly, Gallus appeared to have everything under control, but privately, his thoughts were more complex. He was haunted by his own Christianity, wondering if the God of the Jews was the same God that he worshipped. If so, on who's side would God choose to fight. As pagans, the Romans that fought under Vespasian or Hadrian didn't need to concern themselves with the God of the Jews but that was different now. Both the Romans and the Jews now shared the Old Testament in common and each believed they had the blessing and protection of the one true God.

Gallus called again on Callinicus. The old philosopher brought with him a parchment map of Jerusalem, that he pulled from the library archives. Gallus laid it out on his desk.

"The Temple Mount," he murmured. "The city walls. The Mount of Olives. All of it still alive in their dreams."

Callinicus nodded. "And in ours, as well. We now share the same history."

Gallus looked up. "I wonder what it would mean to walk there. Not as Caesar, but as conqueror. Do you think the Lord would forgive me?"

The old man said nothing.

Gallus ran his hand over the map.

"Do you think God still listens to prayers from that place?"

Callinicus tilted his head. "That depends on who's praying. If you let the Jews take the city and begin praying on the Temple mount, there is no telling what may happen."

"Then we must make certain that never happens. Jerusalem is too precious to let it fall into their hands. I must keep them confined to the north, in Galilee."

"How do you propose to do that?" Callinicus was curious.

"By letting the hounds of Hell loose so that they fear setting a foot outside their hiding places."

The meaning was not immediately recognized by his tutor. "The hounds of Hell?"

"Perhaps I should have said only one hound," Gallus smiled wickedly.

CHAPTER XV: THE COMING STORM

The winds over the Sea of Galilee had shifted but they were not with rain but with whispers. Riders had come from the coast. A merchant from Caesarea had passed through the Jezreel valley and brought tales. Roman letters had been intercepted near Bet She'an. And by week's end, a courier loyal to the rebels arrived at the gates of Sepphoris with a single sentence carved in wax: Rome rides.

Natronai read it in silence as he stood on the roof of the house Isaac had claimed as their makeshift war room. Below, the hills rolled green and gold. From the east came the morning sun. From the west, the coming storm.

Inside the house, Rabbi Simon bar Isaac of Sepphoris was already laying scrolls flat across the cedar table. They consisted of troop maps, census rolls, reports from sympathizers in Tiberias, Caesarea, Pella, and Jericho. Every scrap of information they had of where Roman forces were stationed.

"Even if his troops have left Antioch," Isaac said without looking up. "I doubt they'll cross into Galilee before next month. They'll want to run reconnaissance of the territory before making any significant moves. And even if they move quickly after that, we still have three weeks, four at most, before the legions cross into the province."

Natronai nodded. "Do we know how many?"

"Four legions, perhaps five. Plus auxiliaries."

"You mean Syrians or Greeks, right?"

"Both," Isaac replied. "And Arabs. Nabataean horsemen loyal to Rome. Mercenaries."

"You're suggesting over twenty-five thousand men. And how many can we raise?" Natronai asked, somewhat shaken by the enemy numbers.

Isaac raised his eyes. "Depends. If we're lucky, ten thousand. Maybe fifteen."

"But half of them would be untrained."

"Yes," Isaac admitted. "But zealousness compensates for a lot. We know the terrain better than they ever will. I'll manage the correspondence between Galilean factions and map out all the supply routes through the Upper Jordan Valley. We'll hit and run, never engaging their full strength directly.

Isaac's provided a more methodical approach to Patricius's impetuous raids, ensuring early victories against fortified customs posts and small garrisons posted along the major thoroughfares. Whereas Natronai rallied his forces with glorious visions of a free Jerusalem, Isaac framed their armed struggle as a commandment from God to fight when imperial edicts directly contravened Torah law, such as the attempted prohibition of circumcision, the banning Sabbath rest, and the coercing of religious conversion by the Romans. Remaining passive and praying for deliverance by God alone was not an option. The teachings by the Tiberian Council of Hillel II that Jewish suffering was by divine decree would no longer be accepted. Isaac's own council in Sepphoris refuted such thinking by quoting halakhic precedents such as the principle of pikuach nefesh, on the preservation of life, that insisted when a life is threatened then violent resistance was ordained, and when ordered by a legitimate council such as his own, then it would be sanctified.

Weeks before the expected arrival of Gallus's first troops, on a particularly warm and sunny afternoon, they gathered the local commanders of their rebel army. These captains of their forces consisted of Zealot descendants, tribal chiefs, and even a few disillusioned Roman auxiliaries who had either converted to Judaism or married Galilean women. They met at an old olive press outside Sepphoris, its ancient stones cool, moss-lined, and bearing silent witnesses to the revolution.

"Gallus's men will come first through Caesarea on the coast," Natronai declared. "He'll want to make a show of authority to the procurator, showing him who's in charge. We'll let him do so. The longer the Romans remain in that city, parading around, the better for us. Therefore, we don't meet him there."

Isaac stood beside him, pointing to a map.

"Instead, we bleed them in the hills ten miles outside the city. We hit their supply lines trailing behind the main body first. Set everything on fire and then retreat. They'll turn back to see what has happened. So, we hit them with arrows and spears launched at their sides, then retreat again. We never try to hold ground and engage them directly. We continue to draw them inland into the mountainous regions. Then we let the land consume him as we pick them off bit by bit from higher ground."

"And the cities?" one man asked. "When do we try to take control of the cities?"

"We don't," Isaac responded. "Not yet and we certainly don't make our play for Jerusalem at this time."

There was a groan of disappointment from the officers.

"Not yet," Isaac repeated. "Any attempt to take Jerusalem now would just be for the sake of pride. We'll know when the time is right through prophecy. For now, we look at the villages and towns of Galilee. The Romans are expecting us to liberate Jerusalem first, which means they're going to keep one or two legions stationed close to there to protect it. That will divide and weaken their strength. We want to keep it that way as long as possible."

A murmur of assent rippled.

Not long after, once the military council had dispersed, Natronai sat alone in the candlelight, composing a message. It was not to his men, nor to his allies in

Judaea but instead back to Ctesiphon in Persia. He took great care with his words. Each one chosen like a general picks a battlefield.

> *To the lion of Persia, Shapur II.*
> *To the Shadow of Ahura Mazda, Shahanshah of Eranshahr, Lord of the East.*
> *It is time. My war with the Romans has begun. You once said I would be your weapon. The forge is ready, the flame is lit, and the anvil strikes. Gallus has finally sent his men to comes and crush us beneath their sandals.*
> *If you sent me men from Persia at this time, not in mass but in quiet measure, then I'm certain they would tip the balance in our favor.*
> *My men need more swords as their numbers are growing rapidly. Please send whatever you can spare.*
> *Let the Romans bleed here in Israel before they can ever reach your gates. We Jews will rise, and then you may come not as a conqueror, but as our liberator.*
> *I am the son of David. You are the son of Empire. Together, we can rewrite the map.*
> *As always, I remain*
> *Your humble servant*
> *Natronai ben Nehemiah*

He folded the parchment, placed it in a cedar tube, and then handed it to his most trusted runner, a youth from the Aramean quarter whose father once served in the Persian guard.

"Take the old road," Natronai said. "Cross at dusk. Tell no one. When you reach Edessa, look for the merchant Yazdin. He is holding our horses there. Ask him for one to complete your journey to Ctesiphon. Now go get your food and supplies and begin."

He watched the boy vanish into the darkness.

Natronai turned to Ashurbanipol who stood by his side. "I hope your King will deliver on his promises."

The general emitted his familiar grunt before answering. "Shapur will deliver as long as he is capable of doing so."

"Am I supposed to interpret what you meant by that?" The cryptic nature of Ashurbanipol's comment had escaped him.

"Something is not right," explained the Persian general. "Gallus should be heavily engaged with the Persian forces in Armenia, yet here he is able to spare five legions to send to Palestina. It should not be possible."

"Perhaps the Romans are in retreat and Gallus has pulled them back. His attack on us is to avoid exposing himself to a full second front," Natronai suggested.

"Patricius," Ashurbanipol used the term as to say you may be holding a higher rank but you should not second guess his military senses. "No, something has happened up north and we have not received word of it yet."

Natronai was now worried and wondered if he should raise the issue of Ashurbanipol's gut feeling with Isaac. He decided it was still too early.

Days passed. Meanwhile, Sepphoris had been completely transformed.

Young men trained with wooden swords in the vineyards. Women boiled bandages and hoarded barley. Teachers became captains. Priests, because of their guild training became blacksmiths.

A prophecy emerged from Isaac's lips like an ember that refused to die out. "When a lion roars in the north and the fig tree gives fruit in winter, then shall the sons of Zion rise again."

They painted it on walls. Etched it into knives. Sewed it into cloaks. It was apocalyptic. It was poetic. They believed the lion of the north to be their Patricius, the lion of Judah, or even the Emperor Shapur, the lion of the East. Either case, it was war.

One evening, Isaac approached Natronai as he sat overlooking the western road, where no army yet stirred. The rabbi's face was drawn, displaying a deep level of concern. "We must prepare them to suffer," he said.

Natronai nodded. "It won't be hard. They already have."

"But this will be worse."

"I know," Natronai agreed.

Isaac sat beside him. "Do you fear Gallus?"

"I fear the Roman's silence," Natronai explained. "The man that tastes victory, it is said, does not speak, except to give further commands. But the man that tastes defeat will vanish."

"Like Pharaoh."

Natronai didn't immediately respond. "The Romans are on the border, so they have not vanished but they definitely are not speaking."

Isaac paused. He knew immediately what Natronai was thinking. He then asked, "And if Shapur does not come?"

"Then we bleed for as long as we must. Until either God answers, or He does not."

CHAPTER XVI: THE LION STIRS

The hall of Ctesiphon was cool and dark, shaded by heavy linen with no reflection from the polished stone. The scent of cedar and burned myrrh drifted through the corridors like incense for forgotten gods.

Shapur II, King of Kings, stood motionless before the great bronze map of his empire, fixed into the floor of his audience chamber. He had not moved for quite some time.

His generals said nothing. They knew better.

The dispatch from Mahoza lay open in his hand. Natronai's words were sharp, urgent, pleading and still burned in his ears.

> 'You once said I could be your weapon. The forge is ready, the flame is lit, and the anvil strikes... Let the Romans bleed here before they reach your gates... Together, we can rewrite the map.'

Shapur's jaw was tight, but his eyes remained still. Calculating. Cold as a vulture circling above a dying lion. He knew this moment would come and he had long prepared for it.

"Speak," he said finally, without turning to his generals and advisors.

The courtiers stepped aside as Mihr-Narseh, high priest and vizier of the empire, came forward. Robed in white and gold, he bowed low. "This rebellion in Palestine," Mihr-Narseh began, "is not yet a full war. But it could easily become one."

Shapur turned at last. His beard was streaked with silver now, but his face held no weakness. Only lines drawn by campaign dust and sleepless resolve.

"Gallus has already sent forces to crush it."

"Yes, my king."

"If I send my army now, what happens?" Shapur inquired.

Mihr-Narseh hesitated. "It depends."

"On what?" Shapur was clearly irritated by the lack of response.

"On whether we wish to remain in the shadows... or show our teeth."

A second figure stepped forward, Grumbates, king of the Chionites, a fierce ally who had once ridden with Shapur through Armenia and the Zagros passes. He was younger, with wolfish eyes and scars along his cheek.

"I say we act," Grumbates growled. "Send five thousand into Syria. Quietly. Scatter them. Supplies, saboteurs, archers. Let the Jewish fire burn. Let Gallus flinch."

"And if Rome calls it war?" Shapur raised a brow.

Grumbates shrugged. "Then give them war."

A cone of silence returned over the remaining advisors. Only the rustling of torches and the distant creak of palace doors disturbed it.

Then Shapur spoke but not to anyone in particular in the room, but instead to the ghost of his father, Hormizd II, who had been murdered in a palace coup before Shapur was even born. It was said Shapur had been crowned while still in his mother's womb, the empire swearing fealty to a yet-unseen king. He had ruled ever since with iron.

"Rome speaks of order," he said softly, "but all they bring is fire. They call us tyrants, but they break the Temple and ban the blade of Abraham. They cry for peace but build walls across our borders." He turned fully, his voice rising. "And then they tried to place my brother on my throne."

The room stiffened.

"They have be interfering in Armenia, stealing bits and pieces of Mesopotamia, and now they march to crush the last sons of David."

He pointed eastward, where on the wall hung a mosaic of the sun rising over the mountains of Media. "Why should I wait for the eagle to roost at my gates, when I can snap its wings in the Galilee?"

Mihr-Narseh bowed again. "Shall I summon the border satraps?"

Shapur nodded. "Tell them this: No banners. No war declarations. No trumpets. I want ten thousand on the move within a fortnight. Riders. Scouts. Medes. Sagartian archers. And gold. Bribes work better than swords with the Syrians and Nabataeans when used first."

"And their overall goal?"

"To keep the Prince of Israel alive."

Late that night, after the court had retired, Shapur remained in his library, an ancient chamber filled with scrolls, tablets, and half-forgotten architectural projects. He pulled down a Babylonian chronicle of the House of David. He studied the line, through Solomon, Zerubbabel, his son Hasediah, through Pelatiah, down to Shefat and the beginning of the Exilarchs. He found the name: Natronai ben Nehemiah.

"Do you truly believe," he whispered to the parchment, "that you are the key?"

He turned then to a second scroll, one given to him by Jewish scholars in Susa, the text of the prophet Isaiah.

'And they shall rebuild the ancient ruins… they shall repair the ruined cities, the devastations of many generations.'

He closed his eyes. He saw not only Judea but also Armenia restored, Nisibis returned, the Euphrates unchained from Roman garrisons. If this rebellion succeeded, it would tear open a fault line in the Roman East. Shapur didn't need to conquer Rome.

He only needed to watch it bleed itself to death.

Three days later, his messengers rode out from Ctesiphon, bearing gold and sealed letters:
To the Marzban of Hatra: prepare the men.   To the commander at Singara: weapons, not flags. To Natronai ben Nehemiah: Your forge has heat. Let it now have iron.

By the time the spring sun warmed the orchards of Galilee, the first Persian volunteers had already crossed into Syrian territory. Not in uniform, not under banners, but cloaked in merchant robes and tribal colors. They brought bows, coin, camels, and news. They brought hope.

And behind them, but further east, Shapur began mustering his own greater legions, not yet to fight, but to be seen and reported by the Roman spies. It was a message specifically meant for Gallus:

'I am coming. Strike at Palestine, and you risk fire on both flanks.'

The banners of the Shahanshah rose like twin fires across the plains of Adiabene.

Spring came early to the Tigris. The air was crisp, but the earth cracked under iron sandals. When the Persian host began to move, it was not in thunder, but in shadow.

Shapur did not declare war. He did not need to. In the borderlands, action was its own declaration.   The first strikes came swift and silently. Outposts near Singara and Bezabde, isolated Roman fortlets and watchtowers taken by surprise at night. Archers crept up in the fog, slitting sentries' throats before setting the wooden gates alight with pitch. By the time the smoke reached the horizon, the lion was already inside the cage. The first major prize was the Roman fort of Vitra, a garrisoned supply base on the eastern road between Nisibis and Nineveh. Vitra sat atop a ridge, thought by the Romans to be impenetrable from the east. Its towers bristled with Syrian slingers and Armenian auxiliaries. The walls had held for two generations.

But Shapur approached not with catapults but with miners. For three days, his engineers dug beneath the foundations. On the fourth night, the Persians set fire to the wooden braces and collapsed a section of the wall. At dawn, his elite Savaran cavalry poured through the breach. What followed was not a battle. Instead, it was a massacre. Romans fled down the western slope, only to be impaled on Persian spears. When the gates fell, the city's stores of grain, coin, and war material fell with them. Vitra burned.

From its walls, Shapur sent a message to all the governors of Mesopotamia, "This is not conquest. This is reclamation. Any that swore allegiance to Rome and forgot their Persian heritage would suffer the same fate."

But Mesopotamia was only half of the Persian theater. Shapur had not forgotten Armenia where his men thus far had been engaging in small skirmishes with Roman units. Neither side had committed firmly to taking the conflict in Armenia to greter heights of an actual war. Armenia now considered itself to be Rome's eastern vassal state, the buffer kingdom now turned Roman proxy. Its king, Tigranes VII, had once sent spies into Persia. He had hosted Roman dignitaries and praised the Nicene creeds from atop Mt. Ararat.

This time there would be no forgiveness. Armenia would see war. Shapur responded with fury. A second army rode north through the Araxes valley, led by Sasanian cavalry and Chionite mercenaries, ravaging the Armenian countryside as they advanced. Fortresses were torched. Monasteries ransacked. Nobles were dragged in chains behind the columns for the purpose of being publicly executed later. Tigranes himself was captured in his summer palace near Lake Van. Shapur ordered him blinded, not killed for the sake of spectacle. The puppet prince, Arshak II was installed in his place, beholden to Persia and forbidden to swear allegiance to Rome.

The northern passes to Anatolia were now vulnerable. For the first time in decades, panic reached as far west as Antioch. Shapur focused his attention on his next target, Nisibis. The jewel of the frontier. A Roman fortress city of near-legendary strength, Nisibis guarded the upper Tigris like a dagger pressed to Persia's throat.

Shapur had laid siege to it twice before. He had vowed never to retreat a third time. But Rome had learned well from its past encounters. The walls had been reinforced under Constantine. The defenders were now veterans from Illyricum and were commanded by a steely bishop by the name of Jacob of Nisibis, who inspired resistance with prayers and curses in equal measure.

Shapur arrived with siege towers, scorpions, and massive iron-headed battering rams. For two weeks, he hammered the walls by day and lit the sky with fire by night. At one point, he diverted the Mygdonius River to flood the city from beneath, attempting to rot the foundations. But the Romans countered by digging emergency drainage tunnels and holding fast.

Persian ladders were hurled back with boiling oil. Sappers were buried alive. Jacob himself stood on the parapets, calling lightning in the name of Christ. Three times Shapur ordered general assaults. Three times he was repulsed.

Gallus knew that he neither possessed the manpower nor the generals to defeat this Persian juggernaut having stripped his legions and directing them to Syria-Palestina. The fall of Nisibis would only be a matter of time. And when that happens, he knew his days as Caesar would be over. The Persian king's armies had grown larger, his siege lines tighter, his resolve unshakable. The Sassanian banners ringed the horizon like a noose, their flame-tongued emblems rippling in the dry wind. Upon receiving the reports, Gallus could see the writing upon the wall. He was Caesar in name but scapegoat in practice. Emperor Constantius would never forgive the loss of Rome's most vital eastern stronghold.

Gallus tightened his fingers on the sun-warmed stone parapet of his palace. He turned away, his mind racing. He knew how the accounts of his managing the war would read. A Caesar who lost Nisibis would not be remembered for courage; he would be remembered as a traitor or incompetent, and Constantius II would waste no time removing the embarrassment. Gallus could already hear the chains approaching along the palace hallways.

Then he remembered the map. It lay rolled in the corner of his war room, marked not with Roman provinces but with the shifting tribal lands beyond Persia's eastern frontier. Lands of riders and raiders, where kingdoms rose and fell with the speed of a galloping horse. The Huns, the Khazars, the Turkomen, the Kidarites; names that to Rome meant chaos, but to Gallus now meant possible salvation.

He summoned his advisors that evening, the lamplight flickering over their tense faces. "We cannot break Shapur's siege from here," Gallus said, his voice low, measured. "But we can strike him where he is weakest."

One of his generals frowned. "You speak of the eastern frontier. We have no allies there."

Gallus's lips curled into the faintest ghost of a smile. "The horse-lords of the steppe don't need to be our allies. The Persians fear them as much as we do. Their loyalty is as changeable as the wind, but their greed… that is constant."

He paced the room slowly, letting the silence draw tight. "We send gold. Jewels. Promises of trade and plunder. We tell them the truth that Shapur's armies are rooted before Nisibis, leaving his eastern lands ripe for the taking. Let them smell blood in the east. If even one of these tribes rides against him, he will be forced to turn his gaze from us."

The room was still. One tribune, older and iron-haired, spoke. "If they refuse, Caesar? If they take our gold and sit idle?"

Gallus stopped pacing. His eyes caught the lamplight. They were sharp, and unblinking. "Then Nisibis falls and so will probably all of us. But if they ride, then Nisibis lives and we do too."

Within two days, the plan was in motion. Couriers, men chosen for their speed, loyalty, and knowledge of the frontier, slipped out of Antioch under cover of night. They carried chests of coins stamped with the emperor's face, bolts of silk, finely worked Roman arms, and promises written in Greek and translated into the tongues of the steppes. To the Khazars, he promised the spoils of Persian caravan routes. To the Turkomen, grazing lands and cattle taken from Sasanian estates. To the Huns, captives for slavery and ransom. To the Kidarites, Persian gold and the honor of striking at their ancient foe.

Every departure was a gamble. The roads east ran perilously close to Persian patrols, and the messengers risked death. Gallus knew that at least some of them would never reach their destinations. But all he needed was one tribe, one chieftain with more ambition than fear.

That night Gallus did not sleep. He knew his plan hinged on the throw of a die. And if the tribes stayed in their steppes, unmoved by gold or promises, then Gallus's head would adorn a pike in Constantius's court. Still, he felt something he had not felt in weeks; a possible path forward. However narrow, however treacherous, it was a path he had chosen.

By dawn, there was a dust storm rising on the Syrian horizon. Gallus watched it come, letting the grit sting his face, imagining that somehow it had originated from the pounding of hundreds of thousands of hooves against the parched earth of the eastern steppes. Somewhere beyond the reach of his sight, men on swift horses might be deciding his fate. He had placed his life, his crown, and the city of Nisibis into the hands of strangers who measured loyalty by the weight of a purse.

It was madness.

It was brilliance.

It was his only chance.

It was on the twenty-third day of the siege that a courier from the east arrived in Shapur's camp, clothes torn and bleeding. He whispered one word in the king's ear.

"Kidarites."

The camp fell silent.

The Kidarites, horse-lords from Bactria and beyond the Oxus, had invaded before, many years ago, when Shapur had been too young to remember but now, they were stronger, bolder and unified.

They had swept down across the Iranian plateau, attacking Persian outposts from Merv to Herat, plundering trade caravans, and blocking the Silk Road. Worse still, they were moving west. Toward the Persian heartland. Toward Ctesiphon.

Shapur's rage was volcanic. He had not come this far to be recalled like a thief in the night. But an empire is a fire. If you feed it too long in one place, it burns behind you. Reluctantly, he ordered the siege abandoned.

The withdrawal was brutal. Scorching. Farms were razed. Roman prisoners were impaled along the road to Vitra. Persian units destroyed supply caches so they wouldn't fall into Roman hands. Engineers sabotaged the siege equipment. Shapur left behind a border smoking but not conquered. As the last of his legions crossed the Tigris, he cast one final glance at the blackened horizon and murmured, "I am sorry my brother, Natronai."

By summer's emergence, Shapur was back in Ctesiphon, marshaling new forces for the eastern frontier. The campaign against the Kidarites would become its own terrible chapter. But in Antioch, there was relief. And for Constantius Gallus, the implications were immediate. He had weathered the storm and the eastern theater was stable once again, leaving only the south to deal with. He was free now to crush Natronai. To reclaim Palestina in Rome's name.

CHAPTER XVII: BEIT NETOFA

The skies above Lower Galilee flushed pink as the first breath of summer stirred the groves and valleys, casting warm golden rays over the land. Budding almond trees swayed along the ridges, a deceptive peace settling upon the hills. But beneath this tranquil dawn, two men, Isaac of Sepphoris and Natronai, now more commonly hailed as Patricius, prepared to strike a blow that would echo far beyond the Jezreel Valley.

Isaac stood atop a limestone outcrop, looking down upon the Roman customs post nestled in the narrow defile between the twin ridges. The Roman engineers had built it precisely, coldly efficiently: a stone fort reinforced with timber barricades and iron portcullises. From this elevated vantage, Isaac noted every patrol rotation, the timing of the gates, the length of torchlight patrols along the parapet. He had observed them for eleven nights, charting patterns, noting hesitations, listening to the cadence of soldiers' boots echoing off walls. Isaac was not a warrior. He was a planner, a patient dissector of enemy weakness.

Behind him, Natronai shifted with impatience. He paced like a caged lion, armor half-assembled, already rehearsing the attack in his head. Unlike Isaac, Natronai burned with urgency. For too long they had hit supply trains, raided food stockpiles, cut water lines. Always harassing, never confronting. This night was intended to be different. This would be the first true clash, the first time their banner would fly over Roman stone.

"You've watched long enough," Natronai muttered, his voice edged with frustration. "The men grow restless."

"I grow restless," Ashurbanipol inserted his own feelings.

"You can all learn to wait." Isaac turned, his eyes calm. "If we strike too soon, we lose the advantage. And the mystique of Rome remains intact."

Natronai growled. "I don't care for their mystique."

"Neither do I," the Persian general growled.

"I do," Isaac replied. "Because if we take it tonight, the people will see what is possible. Not just raiding. Not hiding but victory. A victory even without the Persian army coming to our aid."

The plan was delicate. Two units of slingers would position themselves in the olive terraces northeast of the fort, ready to distract and draw attention with noise and missile fire. Meanwhile, a small team of climbers would ascend the rear wall where the stones, worn by years of neglect, had begun to crumble slightly. They would infiltrate, quietly eliminate the interior guard, and open the gates from within. Timing would be everything. If the alarm was raised too soon, they would face heavy resistance.

As twilight sank into night, the rebels moved into position. Isaac walked among them in silence, laying a calming hand on trembling shoulders, murmuring final instructions. Natronai donned his helm, the lion crest catching moonlight. He clasped wrists with Ashurbanipol, their arm grieves ringing as they did so, signaling his readiness. To the rest of the men, the Patricius was not merely their commander, he was a symbol of the eternal flame of their people.

A hoot of an owl, three short bursts signaled the slingers' opening volley. Stones thudded into shielded towers, metal rang out as guards scrambled to arms. Flames from torches flickered wildly as Roman soldiers clustered to repel what they thought was just another hit-and-run raid.

It was then that Eliab, the climber, scaled the rear wall with uncanny ease. One by one, his team followed, shadows against the mortar. Knives flashed silently. Throats opened. No screams, just the shuffle of armor falling.

The next few minutes passed like hours. Then, with a creak that would be remembered for generations, the bar across the inner gate was lifted and the huge doors swung open. From the trees, Natronai let out a roar and charged, sword raised. Behind him thundered several hundred men, farmers and shepherds turned into fighters, descending with fury.

The Romans, caught in a state of shock between the slingers' barrage and the opening of their own fortress, reeled. Panic split their ranks. Resistance came, but scattered, uncoordinated and never able to mount a significant defense. Natronai struck like a thunderbolt, cleaving through the centurion who tried desperately to rally his men. Inside the walls, Isaac and Eliab secured the armory, distributing pila and short swords to those rebels that attacked with nothing more than hammers and pitchforks. Within an hour, the post was theirs.

The Roman eagle standard was torn down and thrown into the mud. In its place, Natronai raised a banner hastily stitched from linen and marked with Hebrew letters: 'HaAm Chofshi', signifying that 'The People Are Free.'

Silence followed the storm. Men stood, chests heaving, staring at the blood-slick stones beneath their feet. For a moment, no one moved. The impossible had happened. They had taken their first Roman fort. Not just looted it, but now able to hold and secure it.

It was Natronai who broke the silence, stepping to the parapet and bellowing into the darkened valley: "Beit Netofa is free! Blessed is the God of Israel."

Cheers erupted, wild, unrestrained. Tears flowed. Some collapsed, overwhelmed by the enormity of what had just occurred. They had not merely defeated soldiers; they had shattered the illusion of invincibility that Rome cloaked itself in. The eagle had fallen.

Word traveled fast, faster than the Romans could control. By week's end, messengers on foot and horseback had spread the tale across Galilee and down into the Jezreel Valley. Villages that had once looked away now sent food and volunteers. Fishermen from Magdala arrived with nets full of dried fish and bundles of arrows hidden beneath. Shepherds from the Golan came with goats and stories of Roman cruelty. The rebellion, which was once an ember, was now ablaze.

In Antioch, the news struck almost as bad as if Nisibis had fallen. The praetorian prefect of the East, Domitius Modestus, dismissed it at first as exaggeration. But when a cohort of reinforcements failed to report from their march south, fear took root. For the first time, in over two hundred years, a Roman outpost had fallen to an organized rebellion in Palestine.

Back at Beit Netofa, Isaac insisted on order. The post was fortified, patrols set, supplies inventoried. He and Natronai argued, often and loudly, about strategy. Natronai wanted to strike again, urged on by Ashurbanipol who understood the value of possessing momentum. He insisted it was time to take the next outpost at Arbel, to push the advantage.

"No," Isaac insisted. "We must consolidate. Train. Arm. Prepare for the retaliation that will come."

Natronai spat. "They are reeling! Listen to Ashurbanipol. He has experience fighting the Romans and knows exactly what is going on in their heads."

"They are regrouping," Isaac insisted. "That is what they are doing. And when they come back, they won't send a century. They'll send legions. You can't fight that with courage alone. You fight it with readiness."

"Then make us ready," Natronai urged.

In the weeks that followed, Isaac turned the Beit Netofa post into a command center for the rebel army. Engineers dug new wells. Scribes compiled lists of volunteers and supplies. Blacksmiths fashioned blades from ploughshares. He appointed a former Pharisee, Eleazar ben Yochanan, to act as quartermaster. Every night, Isaac and Natronai met beneath the olive trees to review reports, argue, compromise, and dream.

"Beit Netofa is not the end," Isaac said one evening. "It's the breach."

"No!" Natronai corrected him. "The Romans have gods of war. But we have the one and only God of the universe."

It was the summer of 351, Beit Netofa had become officially a symbol. Children sang songs of its seizure. Old men who had once cowered now lifted their heads. The Roman mystique, that aura of unquestioned supremacy and superiority had cracked.

In Constantinople itself, Constantius II heard the name "Patricius" whispered in his court, no longer with disdain, but with apprehension. The rebellion had become officially a war. Beit Netofa was its genesis.

CHAPTER XVIII: A FIRE IN LOD

  The sun hung low over the flat roofs and olive groves of Diospolis, its dying light glinting off the white stones of a city with a soul torn between heaven and earth. Once known as Lod, the city had become a stronghold of rabbinical teaching and debate, a sanctuary of words amid the bloodied land. But now the dust of war was kicking at its gates, and the name Diospolis rang with a Roman clang, echoing from marble inscriptions and the hobnail sandals of soldiers.
  Yet Diospolis was no longer just a city of scholars and scribes. Not this day because Patricius had come. He arrived not by the main road, but through a lesser-known ravine that led from the lowland orchards into the southern edge of the city. It was a simple goat path used by shepherds, seldom patrolled. Scouts had surveyed the Roman garrison quartered near the northern forum, and Isaac had bribed a local grain merchant to signal when the watch shifted, providing a window of opportunity to enter into the city. The Roman presence in the city was cautious but skeletal. It would not be a threat as long as Natronai's men did not bare their weapons. Ever since the defeat at Beit Netofa, the regional commanders avoided overcommitting forces to Jewish centers unless fully mobilized. They preferred instead to observe, to report, to prepare, exactly what the small force at Diospolis was prepared to do.
  Diospolis was now a city of scholars and scrolls, of fasts and festivals, of law and legacy. But it was also a city with sons. And those sons, seeing for their first time the man that had become legend, this face of defiance on horseback and, hearing the tale of how the garrison post was taken from Rome's grip, were both restless and eager to join the war effort.
  Patricius took full advantage of their enthusiasm. He lodged not in the city center but at an abandoned threshing floor just beyond the southeastern wall, surrounded by thickets and olive trees. From there, he could leave and reenter the city at will, during the morning hours, but always in disguise. Sometimes as a merchant, sometimes a scribe, never wearing the same clothing twice. His speeches were never announced. They simply erupted. One moment, the marketplace would be humming with vendors and the next, Patricius would be atop the speaker's stone quoting the Psalms and calling men to arms, surrounded by a collection of banners he had brought with him to the city. The lion of Judah stitched in gold upon blue told everyone immediately who they were listening to. Isaac of Sepphoris stood beside him, his face shadowed beneath his hood.
  The mood in the city was tense, crackling with the static of prophecy and rebellion. Word of the victory at Beit Netofa stretched into the narrow alleys and

public courtyards, inspiring whispers, tantalizing fears, but most of all spreading a dream that had been desperately trying to break free for centuries.

Natronai wasted no time. On the first morning after he entered the city, he made a point to address the crowd in the central square to demonstrate he had no fear of Rome. A column of young men gathered beneath the balconies of the yeshivot, their sandals slapping against the stone. They watched their Patricius climb the steps of the ancient mikveh and raise his arms victoriously.

"Brothers of Lod! Sons of the soil! I am Natronai, whom you have called Patricius. You have heard the Romans say this land is theirs for over two centuries, but I say it is yours and forever will be. These Romans tax your fathers; they patrol your cities beating you for the slightest offense; they sneer at our covenant with God. Let them tax us, let them beat us, but when it comes to making offense against the Lord, Almighty, that is when I say they have gone too far and must be punished. I, Natronai ben Nehemiah, of the Royal House of David through my father, and the House of Aaron through my mother, am the instrument of that punishment."

Isaac, standing beside him, scanned the crowd. The rabbis had come, standing cloaked in their dark robes beneath the colonnades, frowning like storm clouds. He drew Natronai's attention to them.

"Welcome teachers of God's words. It pleases me that you have come to hear what must be said," Natronai grinned. "Words which you have tried to deny as you groveled before your Roman overlords."

"Our Torah teaches restraint," shouted one, a tall scholar with a lion's beard and fiery eyes. "It teaches patience! Not revolution. You defy the yoke of Edom, and in so doing, you risk bringing destruction upon us all."

A murmur of agreement ran through the older men. But Patricius did not flinch. He stepped forward, eyes shining like molten bronze. "I do not ask you to forget Torah," he said. "I ask you to remember that even in the Tanach there is a limit to patience. Did Moses wait for Pharaoh to suddenly grow kind and cooperative? Did David flee forever from Saul, abandoning any thought of taking his crown? Did Esther wait for her husband Artaxerxes to summon her before speaking up? We are not sheep that wait to the last minute before slaughter before they realize it is too late!"

The square erupted with opposing opinions. Fists were raised. Young voices cheered. Older men shouted curses. The clash was more than political. It was generational, philosophical, existential. And in such a cauldron, Patricius thrived, his gift of oratory able to harden the will and resolve of his true followers.

Isaac looked upward and made a faint whistle, catching Natronai's attention. "Now's your moment. If you don't win them now, we'll lose them forever. You better make this good!"

Natronai was well aware that this was the critical moment. He could see the restlessness within the crowd. Some young men, eyes blazing, clutching slings and sticks as if ready to march that very night. Others older, perhaps even grayer, folding their arms, lips tight, eyes full of doubt. Natronai deeply breathed in the air thick with the combination of dust and fear. He adjusted his position on the stone platform and raised his voice so it could cut through the noise.

"Brothers. Sisters. Sons of Israel. Daughters of Zion. All I ask is that you listen to me and weigh out my words with a balanced heart. I know what you are thinking. You see Rome's shadow stretching from the Euphrates to the sea and you think, 'Who are we to stand against it?'

You think of your sons dying on some nameless road, your schools shuttered, your homes burned. You think if we keep our heads down, they will spare us. But tell me, when has Rome ever spared the proud? And we are a proud people. Proud of our history. Proud of our existence while other nations faded away. But most of all, proud of our God, who chose us from all the nations of the world to be his children."

He lets the words hang. The older men glanced down at their sandals, feeling somewhat ashamed.

"Was putting our trust in Rome a shield at Masada? Did it keep the Temple standing? Was it the belief in Rome to mend its ways that made us think there would be salvation of those carried in chains to Rome's markets and sold like cattle?" Or perhaps the thousands of our people that hung from their crosses that lined our roads for miles until the crows plucked out their eyes and their flesh rotted convinced you. Our fathers were patient and held out hope. They bent their necks, hoping the sword would pass over them. But each time the sword fell. There is no such thing as Roman mercy!"

Natronai's voice hardened, as he spat the next words. "I tell you this, false hope is the chain they tighten around your throat. And you are teaching your children how to wear it well!"

A murmur ran through the younger ones. The older crowd shifted uneasily.

"They call this city Diospolis now. City of Zeus. Not Lod. They take the name first, then they take the soul. Trust me, they will not stop at the name. They will come for your Torahs, your teachers, your bet midrash, and your sons. And when they do, they will tell you it is for the peace of the Empire. But what peace is there in the silence of slaves?"

Natronai's voice rose, deep and rough. "I have faced Rome's garrisons. I have looked their centurions in the eye. At Beit Netofa, they thought themselves gods in iron. They bled like every other man. They died like any other man. And when they died, the land beneath our feet rejoiced in remembering it was ours!"

Pacing the speaker's stone like a lion, Natronai summoned his remaining oratory skills. "Do you think we have no hope because Shapur no longer sends troops to us now? He is far to the east, bleeding against the Kidarites but we have never been stronger because we have the Lord Almighty fighting by our side, or have you forgotten! This is the hour God has set before us. If we do not believe God is leading us into battle then we are not deserving to consider ourselves to be his children. If we do not fight in the Lord's army, then we will be like the man who saw the Red Sea parted and refused to walk through! The man that lacked faith to believe in his own God!"

He stopped, pointing at the oldest man in the front. "Do you deny the power and strength of your God?"

The man shook his head. "I will march wherever the Lord leads me!"

He pointed at another, "You there. Do you not fear the Romans will close your schools? Then mark my words, the only school Rome leaves open is the one where they teach your grandchildren Latin and teach them to forget they were ever children of Israel!"

The younger men cheered. The older ones looked stung, but they were listening now.

"You speak of odds. You think Rome cannot fall. I say Rome is already rotting from within. I say an Empire that cannot crush a rag-tag army of farmers and stonemasons without calling legions from Antioch is an Empire that can be broken. And I tell you this, with the conviction of my soul, I would rather my bones bleach in the sun as a free man than live another day kneeling to a foreign god!"

The roar from the youth sounded like a pride of lions, their fists pumping in the air.

"You, men of Lod, have a choice. You can die in your bed fifty years from now, if Rome chooses to let you live that long, remembered by no one, or you can stand in the breach now, so that in fifty years your grandchildren will say, 'Here is the place where our fathers took back their freedom.'"

Natronai's voice softens for the first time, almost breaking, "If not us, who? If not now, when?" He raised his fist high. "I say, let it be now!" He threw his arms open as a cue for the crowd to shout back.

"Now!" came the reply

"To Jerusalem. To the hills. To the war that will make the world remember the name of Israel. Come with me and let us make Rome fear our names!"

As Natronai's fist rose for a second time, Isaac pushed forward, making sure to be at the very edge of the stone platform, his own arm raised. He shouted, "Lod will march!" and the young men echoed it instantly.

The chant began, ragged at first, then pounding like a war drum: "Lod will march! Lod will march!

At that moment, all the tension that had existed in the town shattered. The younger men rushed forward shouting their readiness to fight. Even the older skeptics, shamed and stirred by his words began muttering their assent, their eyes alight with a spirit they had forsaken for many years.

Over the next few days, Natronai established his quarters at an old inn on the outskirts of the town, where recruits came in droves. Blacksmiths worked day and night making swords and spears, along with arrow points. Tanners fashioned leather jerkins and assorted body armor. Isaac oversaw supplies, always wary of the enemy, keeping an eye open for any wandering Roman patrols that were advance scouting for the legions that were still encamped beyond the boundary of the province. Any squadrons that did venture too close to the town, never returned to base to report their findings.

But it was not the Romans that Isaac worried about, it was the Rabbis. He knew their entire existence relied on their maintaining favorable relations with Rome. Without the governor's approval, their schools would close, their ability to preserve and follow the traditions and customs would be curtailed and most of all their livelihoods would be lost. At that moment they would perceive Natronai as the greatest existential threat to their way of life. That would make them desperate and desperate men are always dangerous. He knew that at some point they would try to stop Natronai, even if they did appear to be supportive now.

It did not take long before Isaac's suspicion became reality. That desperation that drives good men to do evil things finally arose in the form of sabotage. One morning, a fire broke out in the stables. The horses panicked, several were lost but fortunately for Isaac and Natronai, their horses were not the ones lost that day. That same night, a young follower of the Patricius was found stabbed in the alley near the market. At his moment of death, the victim must have grabbed on to the knife with an unbreakable death grip and the murderer must have panicked and ran away from the scene, leaving the knife behind. The blade was a ceremonial slaughter knife, the kind a rabbi, known as the shochet, would use when performing the ritual slaughter of animals.

That knife was all the proof that Isaac needed to see. Accompanied by the towering form of Ashurbanipol at his side, he confronted the elders. "This cannot continue. You are playing with fire," he shouted.

The rabbis denied any wrongdoing. "We teach Torah," said one. "Not murder."

"Did I say anything about murder?" Isaac questioned those assembled. "I'm pretty certain I didn't mention it, the same way I'm certain you had a hand behind it. I only came to warn you that I would not hesitate to expose your hypocrisy if you choose to continue to confront us. You won't have to fear losing your lives at the hands of the Romans, I will ensure that you all hanged for treason before they ever come. Consider yourselves warned." With that they left.

Still, the city simmered over the next few days. Fist fights broke out between the rabbinical students and the youths of the city desiring to break free of the Roman yoke. As punishment, one of the rabbis was dragged through the streets, his beard shorn in a public display after he was heard to curse the family of the exilarch. Word was passed that every rabbi in the city would be humiliated in a similar fashion unless the Patricus was permitted to speak without opposition. Natronai was informed of their defiance and he was not pleased. He came and addressed them at midnight, standing beneath torchlight, quoting scripture and mixing it with his revolutionary fire.

"Jeremiah warned of doom, and the king placed him in prison. He cautioned for us not to fight among ourselves because we shared a common enemy. But the

King and the people would not heed his words and because of this we lost a kingdom. But the prophet also promised our return when Babylon fell. And so, we built again! Seventy years we were in exile while our kingdom lay fallow. All because we could not unite under Jeremiah's warning and stand against that common enemy. Will some of us still sit idle while Romans drink wine in our vineyards? Or will we unite and say together that two hundred and eighty years of watching our kingdom lay fallow, its fields salted by tears shed as a result of Roman occupation has been long enough! I have had enough. Will you not shed your personal vanities and finally stand with me?"

The effect was surprising, as many of the students defected from the rabbinic masters, choosing instead the firebrand over parchment. Neither Isaac nor Natronai had anticipated such a favorable response.

But Isaac still had concerns and warned Patricius, "Yes, that was an unexpected win for us, but those rabbis will not take the loss of so many students calmly. They feel threatened, especially by you, and that means they will be willing to remove us by any means from now on."

Natronai's face was expressionless. "I know what you are suggesting and I will not do it. I will not silence them by eliminating them. There is no common ground between a man standing and a man kneeling," Natronai explained. "But that does not mean silencing one's opposition through bloodshed."

"But they will not hesitate to attempt to assassinate us," Isaac protested.

"How can you be so certain?"

"You forget that I was one among them for many years and believed like them that the preservation of our schools and teaching was all important even if it meant forsaking our basic freedoms. Until I realized that a man without freedom is a fool for a teacher. To preserve the world in which they live in, they cannot afford to have us regain our freedom because then we'd restore the Temple and re-install the priesthood, and all the power they gained over the last three centuries will be lost. They must eliminate us. It is what I would do if I was still one of them."

Natronai could see his point but was still unwilling to shed his principles. "Should they try to eliminate us then we must make certain that we do not die. If we can do that, then we will win." With that, Natronai ended the discussion.

CHAPTER XIX: DEADLY INTENT

The rabbis knew they had no other choice but to try and stop the tide of students that flowed towards Patricius following his most recent speech in the town square. In the shadowed chamber beneath the old Yeshiva in Diospolis, the air was heavy with the scent of oil lamps and damp stone. Behind the concealed wooden panel that masked the entrance to an underground study hall, seven men gathered under the veil of night. These were the chief sages and elders of the city's yeshivas, the self-appointed guardians of Torah, keepers of halacha, and wielders of immense spiritual authority. At the head of the table sat Rabbi Zadok, an octogenarian whose eyes shone as sharp as his logic, his beard a silvery shroud that framed a face worn by years of fasting, intense study, and unchallenged leadership.

Outside their secret hall, Diospolis simmered just below the boiling point. As far as this cabal of sages was concerned, they were the only ones that appreciated the danger they all were facing. Only they could stop the coming insurrection and with it what they perceived as the end of Jewish civilization.

It was Rabbi Eliezer who first broke the silence. "We are men of Torah, not of the sword," he said, his voice heavy with apprehension. "To kill a Jew, especially one who is a descendant of King David, would definitely violate the Sixth Commandment. Thou shalt not murder. Since when can we condone such a heinous act?"

"Lo tirtzach, yes," replied Rabbi Zadok slowly, his eyes never leaving the flickering flame of the lamp before him. "But tell me, my brother, does that commandment restrain a man from stopping one who is in the pursuit of innocents, in order to kill them?"

The room was still as they wrestled with the intent of Zadok's words.

"That is the law of the rodef," murmured Rabbi Meir ben Nahum, adjusting his robe. "If one is pursuing another to kill, we are commanded and I emphasize, commanded, to stop him. Even if it means his death in so doing."

"Yes, but he's not pursuing any single man," countered Rabbi Hoshaiah. "He is waging a rebellion. And yes, he has caused Roman blood to spill. But who are we to judge this war as unjust? Perhaps it is God's will. I think we must refer this matter to Reb Hillel, the patriarch in Tiberias."

"Why?" Rabbi Meir countered. "Do you think because he too claims to be from the House of David that make him special and more knowledgeable than us."

"Do you question the authority of the Patriarch?" Rabbi Samuel questioned. "He is the leader of the Sanhedrin after all. His word would be final on this matter."

"No!" snapped Rabbi Zadok, slamming his palm on the wooden table. The flame quivered. "Do not take this matter to Reb Hillel and do not cloak this madness in the veil of prophecy. This Patricius is not the long awaited Messiah. He risks all by his call to arms. Every soul in this Yeshiva, every child in Lod. He lures our students with tales of glory and vengeance. He claims the mantle of the Judges but rejects the halacha! If Rome turns its gaze fully upon us, this entire city will burn. If that does not constitute his pursuit of our young men in order to kill us all, I don't know what else would."

Silence fell upon the cabal again. Rabbi Hananiah sighed, the oldest among them. "You propose that we judge him as a rodef?" he asked. "That we may kill him... lawfully? That is your intent."

"It is not murder," Zadok replied. "It is self-defense. Communal self-defense. He threatens the community of Israel."

"But how?" asked Rabbi Shimon of Lydda, his fingers nervously tapping the carved edge of the bench. "You wish to send men to stab him? Strangle him in the night? If murder is so easy for you, then tell us how it is to be done."

"Not by the means of which you speak," Zadok explained. "He is surrounded by loyalists, many of them our own former students. He is not a fool. But... he must eat."

They all looked at him now.

"We have learned," Zadok continued, "that one of our former students, Simeon bar Hezekiah, has joined his ranks. A bright boy, too bold for his own good. But a mind that can be easily bent, as I have experienced, if the right words are used. He works in the food tents. He helps prepare the rations for Patricius and Isaac."

"You would make a student into a killer?" Rabbi Eliezer asked.

Zadok leaned forward. "No. I would make a student into a savior."

Three nights later, under the cloak of darkness, Rabbi Zadok and Rabbi Shimon of Lydda slipped through a side alley to the back of a candle shop in the quarter. There, behind stacked crates of beeswax and olive oil, stood Simeon, now twenty years old, wearing the patched tunic of a rebel quartermaster. His face was placid but his eyes bright with fire and fear.

He bowed respectfully, uncertain. "Masters, you are seeking me?"

"You are still one of ours," said Rabbi Zadok, his voice quiet. "You learned the law at our feet. I still love you as if you were my own son."

"I serve the cause now," Simeon said, standing straighter. "The Patricius gives us hope. Not just words. He..."

Zadok raised his hand. "We did not come to argue. We came to ask something of you, something that no one else can do."

Simeon hesitated. "You want information?"

"No," said Rabbi Shimon, glancing out the back curtain. "We want an act. Quiet. Final."

Simeon frowned. "What are you saying? It sounds as if you want me to commit murder."

Zadok stepped close. "The Patricius is a danger to all of us. The Romans will not tolerate his victories. They will come, and when they do, Lod will be the first to suffer. Our children will pay for his glory. Unless… he is removed. You can do that. Not with a blade. With something silent. Precise."

There was a long pause. Then Simeon asked, "You are suggesting poison?"

Zadok looked towards Rabbi Simeon. "See I told you he was one of my brightest students. A clever boy who will recognize the serious threat that Patricius represents and know immediately what needs to be done."

"Yes, you are right," Shimon agreed. "He is the one that can save us all from death. He has the strength and wisdom to be the savior of the Jewish nation. He has a good heart and cares for the safety of his people."

"For an eternity our people will sing your name, recognizing our continued existence was all because of your stance against tyranny," Zadok's portrayal of Simeon as a hero suddenly captured the young man's attention.

"Would I really be saving our people?" Simeon asked.

"Of course, my son. Just like Jael saved us from Sisera raising another army against Barak by driving a tent peg through his skull as he slept. It wasn't murder but fulfilment of God's will. You see, this is the same," Rabbi Shimon explained.

Rabbi Zadok nodded. "A small dose. Enough to mimic a fever. A belly sickness. He will be gone in days. No one will suspect. No one will ever know except us that you are the hero that saved us all from extinction. But we will record it so that future generations will praise your name."

"I… I have served him food," Simeon said slowly. "They trust me. I portion the lentils and barley. I carry his bowl. That is all that I do."

"Exactly why you must be the one to do it," said Zadok. "Not for us. For your people. You do care about your people, don't you?"

Simeon's hands trembled. "I still believe in him. But… if what you say is true, if his rebellion will bring destruction to Lod… then I must believe in something higher."

"Not something," Zadok corrected him. "But someone higher. The Lord would not permit us to even suggest this if it was not the right thing to do."

The poison had already been procured from the apothecary near the Jaffa Gate, under the pretense of treating worms in livestock. Rabbi Hananiah carefully prepared the dosage himself, mixing dried oleander with crushed bitter almonds. It was enough to weaken, to sicken, and then finally kill over several days. He pressed the bottle into young Simeon's hands.

"Remember Simeon," Zadok continued to emphasize the importance of the mission. "As is written in the Masechet Sanhedrin under the ancient ruling of the rodef, 'If one pursues his fellow to kill him… then he may be stopped, even by taking his life.' You remember that ruling from when we studied it together."

"But…" Simeon could think of the words to form his objection.

"No but," Zadok cut him off. "Heaven will forgive us. God will forgive you. This is the price of peace."

Two nights later, Simeon carried a bowl of lentils laced with the deadly nightshade. He knelt before the rebel prince and presented the meal.

Suddenly, Ashurbanipol intervened. He recognized the trembling hand; the quivering lip; the eyes that refused to look up from the ground. He lunged forward, placing himself between Natronai and the boy.

"Eat not of this," he warned, as he knocked the bowl from Simeon's hands and it spilled across the ground.

The Patricius looked into Simeon's eyes and saw the betrayal. He then turned to Ashurbanipol. "How did you know."

"I have seen many of his kind in the Emperor's palace. Their body always betrays their intent."

"You would poison your brother?" Patricius questioned the young man. "For whom? For your Pharisee teachers who dine with Rome and line their pockets with Roman gold?"

Simeon remained silent.

Ashurbanipol withdrew his sword from its scabbard. "I will make the dog talk."

Patricius raised his hand to stop his bodyguard. "No need for swords when words will do."

The sword returned to its covering but the sound of disgust from Ashurbanipol's lips suggested he was not happy about it.

"Talk to me brother," Patricius spoke softly. "What could they possibly say that would make you even consider such a heinous crime. I know payment would not have been a factor since everyone that has joined my army did so with the knowledge there was no payment other than freedom promised. For you to commit murder and thereby condemn your own soul to Ghenna could only mean they confused you with their words and took advantage of your nature. Redeem yourself in my eyes and tell me the truth.

Simeon broke, sobbing, as he fell to the ground. He was able to stem the flow of tears long enough to tell Patricius of the entire plot.

Once he had obtained all of the information, Patricius brought Simeon before the men that had assembled into his camp and pardoned the young man. The gesture earned him even more loyalty and once the story spread, even more youths from Lod came to join his army as fresh recruits.

But the city of Lod was on edge as those opposed to Patricius awaited some form of retribution. There was another concern; Roman patrols were sighted in the nearby hills, watching Patricius's camp grow in size but never approached for a close look, fearing being captured. The stories regarding the size of the rebel forces reached the ears of the governor in Caesarea, and due to the lack of any other official reports reaching his office, he ordered a closer investigation of the city. It didn't matter. After spotting their initial patrols scouting the city, Natronai knew it was time to move their encampment away from Lod.

As the several cohorts of Roman soldiers marched into the city, searching house by house, their probing found nothing. Natronai never had any formal headquarters inside Lod. His army moved between date groves and ruined threshing floors, drilling without fanfare. Their armory was hidden in a cave known only to Isaac and two others.

The centurion in charge of the search mission issued a report back to the governor in Caesarea: "No open rebellion here. Just noise and the usual arguments between Jews."

Patricius had relocated his new army in the plain, five miles outside the city. Nearly five thousand strong, many of them being the youths from Lod. He ordered drills, formations, discipline, carried out under the command of Ashurbanipol, whom Patricius had promoted from bodyguard to general of the Army of Israel. Isaac stood by Natronai's side, offering strategy, and wherever possible cautioning restraint.

"The rabbis have issued a cherem, a religious ban," Isaac warned. "Let none support this man, they declared. He brings judgment upon us."

"I guess having the Romans search their homes frightened them. For the first time they saw how truly vulnerable they are. Does that mean they've given up trying to kill me?" Patricius questioned with degree of humor in his tone.

"If the opportunity arises, they will seize it," Isaac replied calmly.

"Then let's send them a declaration of our own. But let it be done publicly. I want an orator to read it at every square within the city. Let them say, 'I do not war against Torah. I war against those who have made it a fence around fear! I war against those that have made the law serve only themselves, whether they be Roman or Jew. I wage war against those that live in luxury, feasting from the hands of those that occupy our land. I take offense to those that claim to share the same birthright of my family without any evidence for such a claim. Their use of the title 'Prince of Israel' sickens me. I will fight against those that put their own words into the mouth of Almighty God and spread their lies as truth. Adonai will bring down his judgement against them, so shall it be!"

"You want to create conflict with the House of Hillel. The patriarchy hasn't said a word yet out of Tiberias. Why rattle their cage now?" Isaac questioned why Patricius would even mention those that claimed descendancy from King David. "Hillel had nothing to do with events in Lod."

"Or so you believe," Patricius cautioned. "That house has everything to do with why we are still subjugated by Rome. He is guilty, even if the crime is not apparent. Now see to it that my words get spread throughout the city."

The effect was immediate. By late afternoon, an elder rabbi, Nahum bar Yosef, approached Patricius's camp and was permitted to speak to the prince in private. They spoke for an hour beneath the shade of a pomegranate tree.

"Shall I refer to you as Prince Natronai, or this Hellenized title of Patricius I hear them calling out in the streets," the old man smiled.

"Either will do. I will leave it up to you."

"You have stirred the hearts of many," Nahum said. "But you also provoke Rome to a point that they must respond, Natronai son of Nehemiah."

"Rome was already provoked," Patricius replied. "They fear our breath, our dreams. They have done so for four hundred years since they set foot in our land. They know the Jewish spirit will not permit us to be slaves to any other nation. And thus, they remain constantly provoked."

"I want you to know that I had nothing to do with the attempt on your life. That is why they sent me to speak with you."

"I know," Patricius replied. "I have all the details and names of those involved in that decision."

"Shall they be concerned that you will exact revenge?" the elder rabbi questioned.

"They should be concerned why I haven't done so already," Patricius grinned devilishly.

"They will not try it again. They have conceded to the fact that you may very well be an instrument of God. But they still worry about the safety of Lod."

"I have raised an army to fight our battle against Rome. I do not wish to take my fight against civilians," Patricius admitted. "That is why I have spared their lives thus far but even I have a limit to my patience."

"Then let it be your army that bears the burden of this coming war," said Nahum. "Not our synagogues. Not our homes. Not our children. That is all I ask."

They struck a deal that afternoon. Patricius would leave the plains outside the city within three days, taking his army with him. In return, the rabbis would cease any open opposition. The yeshivot would remain neutral no matter which way the war turned.

Upon hearing of the agreement, Isaac was stunned. "You gave them what they wanted?"

Patricius smiled. "No. I gave them what they thought they wanted. We have five thousand men now in our army. When I arrived in Lod, we were nothing more than perhaps eight hundred. Now we are a legion. We leave Lod not as beggars, but as a force to be reckoned with. So, tell me again, who got what they wanted."

The banners rose like a crimson wave against the Galilean sky. As they marched beyond the city's regional limits, hundreds of the townspeople from Lod traveled the distance to wave goodbye to their loved ones, throwing flowers and singing hallelujah but recognizing that they may never see them again. The fire of this ancient Jewish city now called Diospolis had burned hot but now from all of the fire and brimstone that burned between them and the opposition, there rose something new: an army. But most of all, a hope.

CHAPTER XX: THE ROAD TO SAMARIA

It wound like a scar across the back of the land, carved by millennia of pilgrims and shepherds, prophets and conquerors. But for Natronai and Isaac, the journey was more than geographic, it was spiritual. And political. And perilous.

Isaac had warned him but Natronai ignored his protestations.

"The Samaritans are not like us," he said as their army of five thousand wound its way past the olive terraces of Shechem. "They hold the Torah, yes, but not the Prophets, not the Writings. They despise Jerusalem."

Natronai nodded. "And yet they share our blood."

"Blood diluted by centuries of bitterness."

"Then perhaps," Natronai said, "Rome has done us one favor. It has made brothers of bitter men."

They passed through narrow wadis, ancient vineyards, and crumbling altars half-swallowed by dust. The nearer they drew to Gerizim, the quieter and more uneasy their men became.

Even among the rebels, the name Baba Rabbah stirred a feeling of dread.

Mount Gerizim rose like a silent sentinel over the land, sacred to the Samaritans as the true site of the binding of Isaac, the resting place of divine favor. As far as they were concerned theirs was the true site of Israel's temple.

The climb to Luqban was steeper than expected.

What began as a wide, dusty trail threading through the valleys of Mount Gerizim soon narrowed into switchbacks and cliff-edged paths where the only company was the hum of insects and the dry scrape of wind over stone.

But Natronai could feel their presence, his skin itching with awareness. Eyes concealed behind the trees. Hidden, silent, ancient, fixed upon his men as they ascended the mount. There was no doubt, they were being watched.

Not a bird chirped. Not a goat brayed. Even the sun seemed to hang quieter above Mount Gerizim. The atmosphere was a mix of astonishment and fear of the unknown.

Isaac, ever perceptive, whispered under his breath as they rode, "There are men in those trees. Two on the ridge. One behind the boulder just above the bend."

"You can see them?" Natronai asked without turning. "I can't see anyone."

"I was hunted once," Isaac replied. "By Rome. The forest breathes differently when it's alone. It knows instinctively when and where something is lurking in it."

And to prove his point, his comment was followed by the unmistakable sound of a bird call, but it was sharp and out of place. They had not spotted a single bird the entire time they ascended the mountain. Several seconds passed and the call was now followed by a whistle, low and clipped.

Afterwards, a dozen men emerged as if the mountain itself had opened its stone lungs and exhaled warriors. They wore short spears strapped across their backs, curved knives at their waists, and pale linen robes tucked up for movement. Their faces were wrapped against the dust, but their eyes gleamed with suspicion.

A command rang out in a Samaritan dialect of Aramaic.

"Halt!"

The legion froze on the spot, unwilling to challenge the demand, not knowing if perhaps they were surrounded by thousands.

The Samaritan leader, a fortyish man with a jagged scar across his right cheek and a broad chest beneath his tunic, strode forward and leveled his spear toward Natronai's chest.

"Who climbs the holy mountain without summons?" the man demanded to know.

Isaac's hand moved near the folds of his robe where he kept a blade but Natronai extended an arm to block him. "No sudden gestures," he said quietly.

Natronai then turned to face the Samaritan. "You speak bravely for someone with only a dozen men, whereas I have five thousand at my back. I admire that. We come with no intention to commit any harm. I am Natronai ben Nehemiah, the Exilarch of Babylon, descendant of King David. We humbly request an audience with Baba Rabbah."

The soldier scoffed. "Every thief claims a bloodline when they're caught. That name means nothing here. Dismount. Slowly."

"And how many thieves do you catch that have their own army? I will excuse your insolence." Natronai did not hide his sarcasm.

"It matters not; you are ordered to dismount. We make the rules here," the Samaritan doubled down.

"Then I will command all my riders to dismount and my men to stay here. After all, I make the rules for them." His officers obeyed and dismounted once Natronai gave the order,

Within moments, Natronai and his party of officers were encircled. A spear butt knocked Isaac's staff from his hand, while another guard rummaged roughly through Natronai's satchel. Isaac was pushed forward, but as soon as a hand came near Natronai's back, Ashurbanipol stepped in between.

"I would not suggest you try to push me while my Persian friend around if you wish to keep both your hands. You seem to forget that it is your lives that are in my hands now should I give a single command," Natronai warned the Samaritan commander.

Neither man flinched, as they stared the other down. The tension at that moment became as thick as molasses in the midday heat.

Finally, the Samaritan captain waved his men away and commanded them to fall back in line.

Natronai stood tall, the dust streaking his brow, his patience still holding but rasping thin.

"Be aware that I am allowing you to escort the son of David like a prisoner," he said evenly. "But it is not chains that dignify a man. It is purpose. And today, I come with a purpose, so I will overlook your arrogance."

The scarred captain narrowed his gaze. "You talk too much like a Roman senator."

"Then I would have had you crucified by now, if that was true," Natronai replied.

A flicker of amusement, quickly masked, passed across the captain's face. Without further word, he motioned them to continue marching forward.

They passed under a stone archway carved into the slope, entering Luqban, a compact village fortified by its terrain and by the sheer defiance of its people. At the base of the mountain stood Luqban, the Samaritan stronghold: part village, part temple, part garrison.

Stone houses clung to the hill like barnacles on a ship's hull. Vineyards spiraled down the slopes in tight rows. At the summit, the Samaritan temple complex rose with white-washed walls and fluttering banners of the ancient letters: 'Shamarím', meaning Guardians.

Men with spears stood atop parapets. Children watched wide-eyed from behind doorways.

The air here was different. Older, to the point of being stifling. Laden with memories of poor relations between the Samaritans and their Jewish brethren.

They were led into a long courtyard shaded by a series of fig and almond trees. A simple stone platform, ringed by vines, stood at the far end. It was here that Baba Rabbah, the 62-year-old high priest and political leader of the Samaritans, had carved out a defiant kingdom-in-miniature, a sanctuary from Roman eyes and a thorn in their side.

He received Natronai not with any pomp, but with indifference. Baba Rabbah stood in the shade, leaning heavily on a carved staff in the image of Aaron's budding rod. His beard was long, white as salt, and braided into three cords. His robe bore the seven colors of the Mishmarot, the priestly divisions. His sandals were dustless, as if the ground itself deferred to him.

His eyes, however, were sharp as obsidian. His face was creased but unbowed, with wide eyes set beneath silver brows. When he saw his guests, he did not speak. Nor did he smile. He only waited.

Natronai's army waited where he had left them as their leaders were taken to the center of the open square, at which point, the captain of their escort stepped forward, tense and loud. "My lord, we intercepted these men entering our village without summons. One claims to be a prince but I say they are spies, dangerous men; possibly agents of Rome."

Baba Rabbah raised a hand. No words. Just a gesture. And the captain fell silent.

The old man stepped forward, descending from the platform with the deliberate stillness of a high priest or a man whose bones had too often been broken by grief. His staff struck the stones with soft but sovereign rhythm.

He stopped just short of Natronai, who did not lower his gaze. Baba Rabbah searched his face.

"You forgot to mention that this man you doubt to be a prince arrived with a full legion of men that he willingly left behind outside the gates of our village and in so doing placed his life entirely within our hands. I can tell you honestly, that is something only a man of noble blood would ever consider doing. You," he said turning to Natronai, without ceremony, "are the son of Babylon that the Judeans are all talking about."

The captain and his guards held their breath.

Then, with a voice that was more whisper than sound, the Samaritan elder said unexpectedly, "You have your mother's eyes."

The words hit the courtyard like a gong.

Isaac looked up sharply. Ashurbanipol shrugged his shoulders. Natronai's brow furrowed, trying to make sense of the Samaritan's comment.

"I don't know you," Natronai responded.

"No," Baba Rabbah said. "But I knew your father and mother before they ever married. Your father and I were boys together in Sura, before the edicts. My father had sent me there to study because despite our differences, there are still things we Samaritans can learn from our Judean brothers. Your father once told me that one day the line of David would return, not to rule over Shechem, but to stand beside it. I have been waiting a long time for that day."

"Then you knew I would be coming to Shechem."

The old man studied him. "And yet you come here like Jeroboam returning to Judah. An army by your side. Was that to convince me to submit to your leadership?"

"I come not to divide," Natronai said, "but to unite. Rome makes no distinction between Jew or Samaritan when it sends its soldiers to slaughter. They see only rebels."

Baba Rabbah gave a dry chuckle. "That much is true."

"I do not ask to rule over you. Only to fight side by side."

Baba Rabbah turned to the captain. "Leave us. All of you."

"But my lord…"

"I said go and stand outside the square."

The guards dispersed like shadows at sunrise, muttering but obeying.

Baba Rabbah closely examined his guests.

The son of David.

The voice of the Galilee.

The representative power of Persia.

And the last patriarch of Shechem.

They sat together under an arbor of grapes as water was poured and bread broken.

Isaac stood respectfully behind Natronai, his eyes still scanning the Samaritan guards, counting their weapons, their gait, their discipline, even if they were now somewhat at a distance.

Baba Rabbah addressed Isaac's concern. "If you must know I have three thousand men and all are on constant alert. I say this not to threaten, but to answer the question you've not yet asked."

Natronai nodded. "Then let me ask it plainly. Will you fight at our side when Gallus comes to crush us both?"

The Samaritan elder was silent.

A breeze stirred the fig leaves. A child called in the distance.

Then he leaned forward.

"I have watched your movement with interest, Prince of David. But your kings and your rabbis have cursed us for generations. They say we are heretics. Foreigners. Cut off."

"I am not my forefathers and the rabbis are certainly not my allies," Natronai answered.

"But you bear their name."

"We all bear names. But it is our deeds that matter now."

Baba Rabbah's eyes searched his.

"I have buried six sons," he said quietly. "Three to plague. Two to Rome. One to treachery. I have no more to give this world, except one thing."

"And that is?"

"Vengeance."

Baba Rabbah studied Natronai with a long, measured silence, then turned his gaze to Isaac of Sepphoris.

"And you, Rabbi, you are known to us. Your voice reaches even this mountain."

Isaac gave a modest bow. "And your courage echoes down into the valleys."

The older man allowed a hint of a smile. "Come," he said. "Walk with me."

They followed Baba Rabbah through a grove of terebinth trees, where the wind carried the scent of sweet sap and scent of mildew on old stone. They passed by a row of young boys practicing slingshot drills under the watchful eye of a one-eyed veteran. Further on, a pair of women were shaping barley loaves near an open flame, their laughter momentarily breaking the tension in the air.

"We are not what we once were," Baba Rabbah said. "But we are not broken. Not yet."

"Nor are we," Natronai replied. "Though Rome counts us finished."

The old man stopped beneath an arch carved into the hillside. Before them lay a vista of the surrounding lands; valleys green with early spring, distant hilltops dotted with grazing sheep, and far to the south, the barely visible line of the Roman road that cut across Samaria like a scar.

"Do you see that road?" Baba Rabbah asked.

"I do."

"It is our exile. Every stone of it, laid by men who think God speaks Latin."

He turned to face them.

"You come asking for alliance. But what is it you truly offer?"

Natronai stood tall, but his voice was without pride. "A fire. One that may burn us both but which could also melt the chains from our wrists."

Baba Rabbah lifted an eyebrow. "And when the flames die down, what then?"

Isaac stepped forward, thinking it best that he answer that question. "Then we rebuild from the ash. Together. Jew and Samaritan, priest and rebel. We have fought over altars and mountains for too long. Rome has benefited from our divisions."

The Samaritan leader said nothing, but he began walking again. They came upon a stone bench, worn smooth by time. Baba Rabbah sat, motioning for the others to do the same.

"Long ago, when you returned from exile, we came to you and said let us help you rebuild the Temple. No, let me clarify that. We begged you to let us help rebuild the Temple and you rejected our help and rejected my people. So instead, we built our own temple upon this mountain. But my people remember how your forefathers three hundred and fifty years later came with an army, desecrated our shrine, and burnt it to the ground" he said to Natronai. "How they declared Mount Gerizim to be cursed."

"And my people remember the blade you took to our pilgrims in Jerusalem," Natronai answered. "The blood has not dried."

They stared at each other. Two leaders of broken nations, sons of wounded houses.

Then Baba Rabbah reached out and placed a hand over Natronai's.

"You see, that is why we will never be able to fight together. Our memories run too deep. But we are not our grandfathers, which means we may not forget but we can forgive."

Natronai turned his hand over and clasped the old man's fingers. "I understand. We are not them but we are what bear the sins that come after them."

Silence held between them for a moment, deep and holy.

Isaac broke it softly. "Rome believes the God of Israel is fractured. Though we may not fight side by side, let us still show them that we fight for the same God."

Baba Rabbah's eyes shimmered with something ancient and raw. "My sons died believing that our hope lay buried in this mountain. Your people call you Messiah, but we wait for someone different. We wait for Assief, the Taheb, the one how knows where are temple vessels were buried and reveal them to us. If I am to raise their bones with honor, let it be in defiance of the empire that made me bury them. Are you the one that will reveal our temple vessels."

Natronai shook his head. "I am not your Taheb," he replied somewhat apologetically.

"Then we cannot join our armies under your leadership. We will fight but in our own way and at a time of our own choosing.

He looked once more at the Roman road.

"Three thousand men is all I have to take on an empire. Fighters. Good men, willing to sacrifice their lives for a good cause. But all of them know what is coming. We have trained in secret for years, under the guise of holy ritual. Rome does not know our readiness. So, you have my promise we will fight, just not alongside you."

Natronai nodded. "I understand, although I wish we could have stood beneath the same standard going into battle. At least I will know that while we fight in the plains below, you will be doing the same in the mountains above."

"We will do our part," Baba Rabbah assured him.

"I can bring five thousand, perhaps ten in time. Not a lot to take on the legions of Rome but our spirits are high, but it is good to know that I have allies in the hills fighting their own battles."

The old man stood slowly, gripping his staff. "Then let it be so. By the God who called our fathers, and by the memory of the covenant, we shall rise. Though we fight separately as Samaritans, and you as Jews, when the war comes to an end, the Romans will know they have suffered by the two sons of this land."

Natronai rose with him. "And may the Lord see unity some day in the future between us where once there was scorn."

They clasped forearms, not as lords, but as true warriors.

They spoke long into the afternoon, Isaac and Baba Rabbah at times sparring over scripture, and at other times discovering unexpected convergences, such as on circumcision, on purity, on the oppression of the foreign yoke.

At one point, Isaac quoted from Deuteronomy, "You are not to turn aside to the right or the left from the word I command you today."

To which Baba Rabbah responded, with a faint smile, "And yet you turned to Rome, whereas we did not."

There was truth in it. But there was also mutual respect.

In the end, Natronai rose and admitted, "If we are ever to rebuild a kingdom together, we must start not with temples but with mutual trust."

Baba Rabbah moved slower, his joints stiff with age but his spine still straight.

"Let us pray that day comes sooner rather than later."

They clasped hands in mutual respect.

That night, they made a burnt offering of peace and defiance. Samaritan priests in white robes sang ancient hymns, while Isaac read aloud passages from the Psalms. Together, Jew and Samaritan broke bread under the stars for the first time in a millennium. They recognized that they shared a common enemy as much as they shared blood but it was still not enough to unite them under a single banner. Each would fight the war on their own, and God willing, they would perhaps once again be united in victory.

CHAPTER XXI: TIBERIAS FALLS

Night had fallen like a velvet curtain over the Sea of Galilee, its waters gleaming faintly in the starlight, disturbed only by the silent oars of the rebel flotilla slicing through the black current. Tiberias lay before them, the Roman jewel on the lakeshore, arrogant and oblivious. From the hills above, torchlight flickered in signal; the city slept, its gates unguarded, its sentries drunk or dreaming. Isaac of Sepphoris crouched in the lead boat, his hand steady on the rudder, his eyes fixed on the shoreline with a cold, calculating stare.

Behind him stood Natronai, cloaked in black, his hair wind-blown, his face lit from within by the fire of destiny. He was not calm. He could never be calm on a night like this as the electricity ran through his limbs. It was not mere strategy that brought them to this, but a belief, both wild and holy that by taking the city of rabbinical scholarship that was controlled through a heavy Roman presence, that it would demonstrate to the people that God was clearly on the rebel's side and not that of their self-acclaimed sacred scholars that were subservient to the occupational force.

Isaac had drawn the map, but it was Natronai who had ignited the hearts of the thousands of rebels from Sepphoris, Magdala, and the hills of Perea, who now crept toward the sleeping city by land with knives sharpened and hearts pounding like war drums, while he approached by sea, sailing out of Tarichaea with a thousand men.

"Tonight," Natronai whispered to the men packed into the flotilla of fishing boats, "we do not take just a city. We reclaim our dignity. We reclaim our name."

The wind caught their sails. No moon to reveal their presence, only the stars, and the soft hush of waves upon this ancient inland sea. Then suddenly there was a signal: a glimmer of flame from the northern hills letting them know that the force approaching by land was in place. Isaac raised two fingers, waving his hand in a circle, causing the boats to fan out like the talons of a hunting hawk.

The plan had been born in secrecy beneath the great olive tree of Tarichaea. Isaac had charted every shift change, every sentry position, every escape route based on information of young recruits that fled from Tiberias to join their army. Natronai had preached to the people with the urgency of a prophet. Their messages spread like wildfire. Farmers abandoned their ploughs; fishermen left behind their nets, converting their boats into transport ships. Word was that the Roman garrison in Tiberias had grown complacent under the sweltering heat of the Galilean sun. It was one of the warmer and drier springs in the land that anyone could remember. Word that Antioch had already sent several legions and auxiliary forces to Palestina tended to make the garrisons throughout the province somewhat complacent and as a result, security measures had unintentionally become relaxed, especially along the docks of the city.

As soon as the first boat reached the shore, there was a pronounced hiss and a man jumped into the shallows and pulled it on to the beach silently. The same scene unfolded for all the other boats that followed. Isaac stepped ashore and pressed his palm to the ground. He had memorized every inch of the terrain. Once again he was back in the city where he had spent years under the tutelage of the Tiberian rabbis. The day he left, he swore he would return, not with a staff of wisdom but with a sword. His oath was about to become true and he looked forward to seeing if the rabbis would look so smug as the last time when he was banished.

Close to where they beached their boats, stood the old aqueduct, ancient and forgotten, but not to Isaac, who remembered spending many days sitting under the trees that sprouted beneath the aqueduct's joints where there was a steady flow of droplets of water falling to the ground. He remembered years ago, as a young student, he had discovered this dry tunnel that led beneath the western wall. He had spent nights mapping its twists and turns, learning them all to memory. He didn't know why then, but he knew that somehow his discovery would be important in the future. And now, one by one, the rebel forces under his command vanished into the opening.

Natronai refused to enter the tunnel, saying that it would not be proper for the scion of David to sneak into the city like a rat. Instead, the path he chose was through the southern gate. Such an approach was bold, direct, and seemingly impossible. He took two hundred men that he had selected as his personal force, consisting of veterans, zealots, and those identified as madmen or berserkers.

"We are the torch," he said, his voice low, trembling. "They do not see us yet, but we will blaze. For every one of our boys they've forcefully conscripted, for every taxed shekel they have stolen from us, for every Jewish girl that has been taken against her will, we will make them see us now and they will pay the price."

From out of the boat he sailed upon, his men brought the weapon that he knew the Roman garrison would not be expecting. Under the cover of darkness, his men assembled the battering ram piece by piece and then hoisted it upon their shoulders. Made from wagon parts and tied with fishing rope, it would serve its purpose. They didn't need to breach a wall, only the wooden gate.

As Natronai's small force advanced from the south, while Ashurbanipol led the army descending from the hills, Isaac with his men emerged like ghosts inside the city, blades drawn, darting between sleeping homes. Isaac had instructed his men that there would be no bloodshed of the civilians unless absolutely necessary. As far as the Romans were concerned, the goal was to humiliate the empire by not leaving a single one of them standing. The intent and goal of this encounter was to let Rome taste not only defeat, but shame as well.

According to Isaac's map, the Roman garrison was housed in the southern quarter of the city, near the amphitheater. Its commander, Decimus Varius, had sent reports of "calm" in the region for months, even though he knew the mood of the indigenous Jewish people was rapidly turning. The truth was that he couldn't care less if Rome went to war against the Jews or not, as he was simply a creature of wine and luxury, posted to Galilee as punishment and now slumbering in his mistress's bed, oblivious to the trap swiftly closing around him.

At once there were shouts coming from three different directions. The gate thundered with every blow from the makeshift ram, as it slammed against the wooden barrier. Again, and again the sound reverberated from the battering. Then came the cries.

"Bar-Am!" shouted Natronai. "Freedom! Galil Elion!"

The Romans snapped awake to the sound of thunder at the gate and screaming in the alleys as Isaac's men raced through the streets. Decimus leapt from his bed, grabbing for his sword beyond his reach as the door burst open and a young Jewish boy held a blade to his throat. "Come with us," the boy whispered. "Or die."

Decimus blinked, uncertain if he was still dreaming. The woman beside him was about to scream but an arrow whizzed by Decimus and buried itself in her chest. She never had the opportunity to make a sound. "Zunah," was the only word uttered by the archer, disgusted that one of his own people would find comfort lying in a Roman bed.

Outside, the gates shuddered under assault. Flaming arrows whistled over the walls from Ashurbanipol's men that had encircled the town. Suddenly everywhere that anyone looked, Tiberias burned.

Panic erupted in the barracks. Soldiers scrambled to dress, to grab arms, but Isaac's men were already among them, bursting through the barrack's courtyards, swords flailing and dragging those they did not kill immediately, stunned and wounded into the square.

Meanwhile, the southern gate buckled under the battering ram. With a final cry, Natronai launched himself at the door, hitting it heavily as it gave way. The rebels flooded in behind him like a human flood, overwhelming the remaining guards. There was no time to organize a defense, the best the Romans could do was fight in scattered pockets, outnumbered, demoralized, but mostly confused by the coordinated three-pronged attack.

Within the hour, the fortress was theirs, the city taken. By the hour before dawn, every Roman banner had been torn down and cast into the sea. What followed was an overwhelming silence. The remarkable silence of a stunning victory. Natronai and Isaac stood in the center of the forum, surrounded by prisoners, the garrison shackled, about to be executed. Tiberias, ancient city of Herod Antipas, city of scholars and scribes, had fallen, not to an invading army, but to its own children.

The first light of morning broke over the eastern hills. The waters of the lake shimmered like molten gold. Slowly, the people of Tiberias emerged from their homes, fearful of what they might find outside. First came the elders, then the women, clutching their children, and finally the young men and boys, blinking as if waking from a long-induced sleep. There, in the heart of the city, Natronai stood atop a fallen statue of the Emperor Constantine and raised his sword high.

"People of Tiberias, you are free!" he shouted.

And the crowd, hesitant at first, finally erupted.

Tears streamed down faces. Old women collapsed in the dust and kissed the stones. Boys climbed rooftops, waving makeshift banners. A horn blew, not the blare of a Roman trumpet, but the long, mournful cry of the *shofar*, and with it the hills answered. From the heights of Arbel, shepherds called out. From the northern road, farmers came running. A chorus rose, a medley of old hymns, battle songs, and chants not heard since the last great rebellion two centuries before. Isaac stepped forward and called the remaining Roman prisoners to the square. There were forty-three remaining.

He spoke not in hatred, but in judgment. "Your empire does not own this city. It never did but you pretended as if it was yours. Long ago, our father Abraham pleaded with God to spare the city of Sodom. 'Let me find ten righteous men and if I can do so, will you spare the city? God said he would.' I will make that same bargain and ten of you will return to Caesarea to tell your procurator that the Galilee is not his to own. If he chooses to return armed, marching beside the legions of Caesar, we will bury all of your bones beside the others. For hundreds of years, you have made sport of us, fighting in your arenas to satisfy your blood lust. Now, in order to decide which ten of you will return to Caesarea, you will entertain us in the city's arena.

His next words were intended for the people: "Let no man harm any of these Romans. Our justice is not Roman. We are bound by law to show a degree of mercy to those that have brutalized us. As such, I will let them decide their own fate. At noon let the people of the city gather at the arena and watch how Romans decide upon who will survive when they have been shamed in battle. They call it decimation, but we will be more generous and let ten survive. It is a message that says we will not forget what they have done to us but we are still willing to negotiate as equals. We will accept nothing less."

He turned to Natronai, who now looked not like a wild prophet but a prince, regal in the rising light. The wind lifted his hair. A child handed him a wreath of laurel and hyssop to place upon his head.

"Speak to them," Isaac said.

Natronai lifted his arms. "This is only the beginning. We have taken Tiberias. Next comes Scythopolis. And then Caesarea. But first we must rebuild our nation.

Protect these streets. Feed the hungry. Set up a council. Let the Romans look upon this city and see not just resistance, but order that says we are their equals. We are not barbarians. We are not fodder for their slave camps. We are Judean and the Jews will bow down to no foreign power. Over time many have occupied our lands, but one by one their empires have crumbled to dust. But we are still here, for this is our land and no other nation will ever take it from us!"

The crowd roared its approval.

The air in the arena pulsed with anticipation, thick with the pungent tang of sweat and from those that crammed themselves into the small stadium, which served mainly as a hippodrome for horse racing. Fifteen thousand townspeople pressed shoulder to shoulder, their voices rising like a storm tide. Men shouted, women jeered, and children clung to the walls, eyes wide with a mixture of bewilderment and awe.

They knew this would be no Roman spectacle of professional gladiators or wild beasts but instead an opportunity of exorcising their emotional demons created by decades of oppression and now demanding pure vengeance.

At the heart of the amphitheatre stood the forty-three Roman soldiers, stripped of armor, stripped of dignity, with bare tunics clinging to their bodies stained with dust and defeat. They stood in a crooked line, their faces drawn and hollow, sunken eyes flicking nervously toward the far end of the arena. Among them stood their commander, Decimus Varius, attempting to convince those around him that he still was their superior and for that reason he should automatically be one of the ten survivors. It didn't look like any of the other men were listening.

There, beneath the blazing noon sun, at the opposite end of the arena, a heavy wagon waited. Its bed gleamed with a deadly cargo: gladii scavenged from the fallen garrison of Tiberias. Short, stubby blades that had once cut down Jewish men, women, and children with impunity, now glittered in the light, awaiting one final taste of blood.

High above, in the seat reserved for the garrison's commander, Natronai ben Nehemiah reclined with calm authority. The crowd roared his name. "Nat-ro-nai! Nat-ro-nai! Patricius! Patricius! Messiah! Messiah!" they repeated over and over again as their new mantra.

Beside him sat Isaac of Sepphoris, face serene but eyes as sharp as a hawk's. His hands rested lightly on the arm of his chair, as though this day's bloodletting was another scripture lesson to be written in flesh.

Rising, Natronai spread his arms and the noise fell to a mild tremor. He pointed downward.

"Decimus Varius!" His voice rang across the stone, reverberating in every ear. "Once, you sat in this chair. Once, you looked down upon my people as you sent them to death. You made them slay their friends, starve in your cells, bleed in your streets.

But today…" He paused, letting the silence sharpen the edge of his words. "Today you look up. You look up at me. And you will stare death in the face as they once did."

The crowd thundered approval, stomping feet like the roll of thousands of drums.

Decimus Varius remained among his men, back straight despite the sweat pouring down his temple. His hair was matted with dust, his lips cracked. He said nothing, but his jaw clenched tight. He had killed enough to know how quickly hope drained from men in this position.

Natronai raised his hand. "You forty-three have a choice, though it is not mercy as you may have begged. Instead, I will call it justice, and should you survive the ordeal, then you will be granted the mercy you hope for. At the wagon are your blades. At my word, you may seize them. Fight, kill, survive. When ten remain alive, those ten will leave here as messengers to Caesar Gallus. Tell him what you have seen. That the children of Israel will no longer kneel. We will not bow to Rome. We will stand as free men."

He let the words hang. Then, with a downward slash of his arm, he cried, "Now!"

The trumpet blared.

The Romans broke from their staggered line.

Some sprinted desperately toward the wagon, sand kicking up in plumes beneath their bare feet. Others hesitated, caught between survival and the horror of what was demanded of them. The fastest reached the swords first, steel clanging, hands slashing at rivals even before blades were fully grasped.

The first blood spilled not from combat, but from a soldier shoved aside, skull cracking on the wagon's rim. His body crumpled as another seized a sword from his slackening hand.

Chaos exploded.

Men fought like beasts, snarling, swinging wildly, the short gladii hacking and stabbing in frantic arcs. Sand turned red within moments. A man screamed as steel pierced his belly; another gurgled as a blade slit his throat.

The crowd roared approval, chanting, pounding, baying for blood. They had prayed for such a day and as if a miracle, it had been finally granted.

Decimus fought like a lion cornered. No one provided him with any deference because of his rank. He seized a sword, cutting down one man with a clean thrust to the chest. He pivoted, parried another slash, and drove his blade deep beneath the ribs of his attacker. For a moment, the commander seemed untouchable, a veritable storm at the arena's center.

But forty-three men dwindling to ten left no room for legends. A soldier he had once commanded came at him with madness in his eyes. Decimus ducked, disarmed him, drove him back, only to feel cold steel bite into his thigh from another man behind him. He roared, staggering, blood running hot down his leg.

"Cowards!" he spat, fending off blow after blow.

But the mob did not care for his defiance. They screamed with delight as three more men fell upon him at once. He cut one down, but a sword plunged into his shoulder. Another struck his back. He stumbled, surrounded. His eyes lifted one last time, meeting Natronai's.

Natronai leaned forward, voice carrying over the carnage. "Look up, Decimus Varius. Look up, as you once made my people look up at you."

The final stroke split Decimus open. His body fell face-first into the sand, twitching once, then still.

The crowd erupted in a frenzy, cheering, shouting, some weeping with joy.

The slaughter dragged on. Men screamed, writhed, begged for mercy only to be silenced forever. Dust rose in thick clouds, mingling with the copper stench of blood. One by one, the number dwindled, thirty, then twenty, then twelve.

At last, only ten remained.

They stood in a circle, heaving for breath, each drenched in gore, some missing teeth, some limping, some barely conscious. Their blades sagged in trembling hands. They looked not like victors but spectres risen from hell.

Natronai rose, lifting his arms high. "Enough!"

The trumpet blared again, silencing the killing ground. The ten staggered together, dazed, waiting for the final verdict.

Natronai's voice thundered, "You are the last. You live, not because you deserve life, but because our God wills it so. He demands we show an increment of mercy even towards those that would harm us. You will go to Caesarea. You will kneel before your governor and tell him: Rome must withdraw. Let Israel live. Let us be your ally, but never again your slave."

The crowd roared so fiercely the heavens themselves seemed to tremble with joy.

Isaac leaned close to Natronai, murmuring, "The message is clear. Gallus will hear not only his governor's words, but the cries of our people in this day's blood."

Natronai nodded, his gaze fixed on the mangled corpse of Decimus Varius. "And Rome will know that we no longer fight for survival. We fight to be masters of our own destiny."

Above the arena, fifteen thousand voices screamed in one unbroken chant:

"Israel! Israel! Israel!"

And the ten bloodied survivors, battered and broken, were led away, not as victors, but as unwilling heralds of a nation resurrected.

When all was over and the people had exited from the arena, Natronai could see from the expression on Isaac's face that still not all was well. "What bothers you friend," Natronai inquired. "Are the people not dancing and celebrating in the streets for the first time that anyone can remember? This should not be a day worry."

"I do not worry about the people of Tiberias that are celebrating," he responded. "I'm worried about the ones I don't see doing so. Did you not notice whom we have not seen all day?"

"You are concerned about the Tiberian Council and the members of the Sanhedrin," Natronai determined what Isaac had been thinking about. "They do not matter."

"Yes, they do matter," Isaac quickly pounced upon his suggestion. "Do not underestimate their power and influence. You can interpret their absence in only one way. They are plotting against you. We have disrupted their world and that means we must be careful while we are in this city. Their loyalty is to Rome and Hillel will never accept you as his better. There's already been one attempt to poison you, I can only imagine what they will attempt to do while we're in Tiberias."

"If your so concerned, then let's go to them, rather than wait for them to come to us."

Isaac shook his head. "I don't think that is a good idea. One does not choose to stick their hand into the mouth of a rabid dog."

"I need to know if the dog bites," Natronai replied. "As long as there is this disunity in the land, we will always be easy prey for the Romans to divide us. And if they manage to divide us, then they will remain in control."

"This is foolishness," Isaac warned him. "Even if you were to gain the cooperation and support of the Tiberian Council and Reb Hillel's court, that in itself becomes contentious. There are those among our own army that will turn their backs on us and walk away if they knew you were willing to ally yourself to these men. They are the snake in the garden and God will reject us if you even dare to listen to them."

"How many men do you estimate we will now have in total after our victory here?" Natronai asked. "Twenty thousand, perhaps even twenty-five? How are we to break free of Rome unless we can't increase the army by four times that amount? Bar Kochba had a hundred thousand and still he lost. The only way we can recruit an army that large is if we can bring all the Jewish factions together under a single banner."

"And Bar Kochba lost because he was betrayed by the same people that were the predecessors of this Tiberian Sanhedrin," Isaac schooled him on the history. "And they will do the same to you if they think you are gaining the upper hand against Gallus. I have seen it in my visions. I swear to you that seeking them out will lead us to a path of destruction. As your friend, I need you to believe me on this."

Natronai thought carefully on what his colleague was saying. "All I am intending to do is talk with them," he explained calmly. "I am not saying I intend to ally with them, nor am I ready to reject them without giving them the opportunity to explain their position. Surely, talking with them with you at my side will not be taken as an offense by anyone among the troops. If I do not attempt to heal the rifts within our society, then what worth am I as a leader of our people? Let us just talk and see for ourselves what is and isn't possible."

"Talk…nothing else." Isaac was beginning to relax his position.

"Just talk," Natronai agreed.

That night, under a canopy of stars, the celebration in Tiberias began. Fires were lit in the square. Musicians brought out drums and flutes. Bread and wine flowed like rivers. Dancers spun in circles like whirling dervishes. Young soldiers in the rebel forces who had once trembled at the thought of going to war, now laughed openly. Old men who had lost sons during the Roman purges, sang with grandchildren balancing upon their knees.

Isaac and Natronai stood on a platform before the crowd. Their disagreement earlier that day had now been buried beneath the mood of the festivities. Natronai held up the scroll of Isaiah he had carried from Mahoza, the sacred scroll of Isaiah protected by his family for almost three hundred years, since the time that Titus brought down the second Temple in Jerusalem.

"This scroll," he said, "was written at the time when our people returned to this land after our exile ended in Persia. It was penned in tears and blood. But tonight, once again it illuminates our lives, not with prophecy, but with the hope of fulfilment."

A cheer thundered through the square.

"Tonight, we remember the martyrs of Yodfat, of Gamala and of Jerusalem. But we also remember that this land is not only stained with our ancestor's blood, but it is also soaked with the sweat of generations. We will build again. We rise again. Not for the sake of living in constant fear but for life, itself. The fulfilment of God's promise to be a never-ending testimony to his love, and in exchange for that, He will make us countless like the stars in heaven."

Another cheer rose from those assembled, as the firelight danced across the stone walls of Tiberias.

Somewhere, in the darkness beyond the hills, ten Roman riders fled to Caesarea, their faces pale with the shock of what they had experienced that day.

CHAPTER XXII: REALITY CHECK

The bronze doors of the Praetorium slammed shut behind the messenger from Caesarea. Within the vaulted chamber, Gallus stood stiffly by the window, gazing out toward the Orontes River, his thick hands clasped behind his back. The letter trembled in the hands of his aide-de-camp as he read aloud.

"Tiberias has fallen. The garrison has been disarmed, the standards cast into the lake. Survivors report a coordinated attack led by Isaac of Sepphoris and the man calling himself Natronai bar Nathan. They have declared Tiberias a 'free city of Judah' under a self-appointed council. Local Jews have seized arms. The entire Galilee stirs." The steward was relieved to have delivered such terrible news and still be alive.

The chamber went cold as Gallus turn and climbed the dais to his throne. Gallus, Caesar of the East, seated on the high marble throne at the rear of the room, did not speak at first. He wore a simple purple-edged tunic. No diadem. No ceremonial cloak. Only the thin circlet of a soldier-king and the shadow of a man increasingly cornered by events. His face was pale. Youthful. But tight with fury.

"And the Governor in Caesarea?" Gallus asked, his voice sharp as a blade drawn in fog.

"Flaccus has sealed the roads," the steward answered. "He requests immediate reinforcements. He writes that the Jews have not risen in such numbers since the days of Hadrian."

Gallus's mouth twisted. "Hadrian crucified eight thousand in the valley of Jezreel. And still they remember." He turned to General Maximius. "Are these the same rebels from Sepphoris? The ones your agents mentioned last month?"

Maximius nodded. "Natronai has rallied the northern towns. They do not act as brigands. They speak of law, of courts. Of councils. It is not mere rebellion, Caesar. It is governance."

"Then this is not a revolt," Gallus said bitterly. "It is treason."

He rose from the throne, striding toward the great map of the eastern provinces hung behind his seat. His finger stabbed at Galilee.

"Tiberias. A pissant fishing city. And yet here we are."

Maximius's silence was eloquent.

Gallus's voice dropped. "If they make this about ideas… not just hatred… if they speak of republics, councils, representation…" he let the words trail off. "Then others will listen."

Maximius cleared his throat. "With permission, Caesar, we could dispatch the Sixth Ferrata from Damascus. Quell this before it spreads."

Gallus turned on him. "We have already sent troops. Why are they all sitting in Caesarea and doing nothing. Sending another legion will accomplish anything. No. Do not send it yet. Blood will not stop an idea. We must kill the idea itself. We need a plan. I need a proper strategy."

Weeks later, across the sea and half the empire away, the scroll bearing the Antioch report arrived at the imperial court of Constantinople. Constantius II, Augustus of Rome, held the parchment with his gloved fingers, his face impassive as a statue of Aurelian. He read in silence.

When he looked up, his ministers and eunuchs waited in a half-circle, breathless.

"Thoughts?" he asked.

Eusebius the Chamberlain cleared his throat. "Gallus grows agitated. He fears he will be blamed for the Galilean breach. He demands clarity from Your Serenity on whether this rebellion is to be treated as local unrest or a threat to the Pax Romana."

Constantius narrowed his eyes. "And how does he suggest we respond?"

"He is... divided. His letters contradict themselves. One urges military force. Another urges negotiation."

The emperor rose, paced once across the chamber, and stopped beside the marble bust of Constantine the Great, his father. He stared into those cold stone eyes for a long time before speaking.

"Typical of Gallus. He is panicking," Constantius said. "He knows his crown rests on a column of putty. Who negotiates with rebels? What foolishness is this?"

He turned back to the ministers.

"This Natronai... this Isaac... they are not fools. They speak of councils? A Jewish senate? They pretend to want the same as other satraps within the empire. The truth is they intend to shame us before the world. They invite Persia, Armenia, even the Christians to see Rome as the new Babylon. No," his voice hardened. "No, we must act. There is no negotiation!"

A senator stepped forward.

"Then shall we revoke Gallus's mandate? Remove him?"

Constantius shook his head. "Not yet. Let him burn in his fear. Let him beg for our favor. And in the meantime..."

He turned to Eusebius. "Send word to Gallus. There is only one way this ends. Either I have this Natronai's head on a platter or Gallus offers me his."

In the rebel capital of Tiberias, transformation bloomed like a wildfire under a summer wind. The old Roman forum had been swept clean and redraped with banners of deep indigo bearing the Lion of Judah. The Temple tax, once collected by corrupt magistrates, had been suspended. A Sanhedrin of twenty-one elders handpicked by Isaac now sat in daily session beneath the portico of the eastern synagogue.

Women gathered in the square to petition for clean water. Traders set up booths. Boys carved slings for the city guard. A new order was rising. But beneath the euphoria there still ran threads of tension.

Inside a converted Roman villa, which they called the House of Counsel, Isaac met with the inner circle. His robes were worn. His eyes lined with fatigue. Yet his voice was sharp.

"We must not fall in love with our success," he said. "The Romans will come again. Of this, I am certain. The question is will we be ready?"

Hillel ben Avner, a scholar turned magistrate, objected. "We must end this now," he decried. "We must send envoys to Antioch. Offer them terms. Show we are reasonable. Not all Romans are butchers."

But the fisherman-turned-general Abraham of Magdala pounded his fist on the table. "You are a fool, Ben Avner. They will not bargain. They will slaughter. We must raise a militia. Walls. Watchtowers."

Natronai, seated silently near the hearth, finally spoke. "We must raise something more powerful than walls."

All turned to him.

"We must create a myth," he said.

Isaac raised an eyebrow. "Explain."

"Walls fall. Armies are broken. But myths? Myths live in the blood. We must give the people not just laws. Not just bread. But purpose." He stood, firelight flickering on his face. "Let the world hear that Judah has risen from the ashes of defeat. Let every province whisper of Tiberias the Free. Let Christians see we are not fanatics, and Romans that we are not slaves. We must write laws. Print proclamations. Send messengers to Alexandria, to Edessa, even to the bishop in Antioch."

"You would seek Christian support?" Isaac asked carefully.

"I would seek allies," Natronai replied. "We cannot win this alone. If Shapur cannot send us troops, then we must find another way."

"And if Gallus unleashes his legions?"

Natronai's eyes burned. "I ask the question why he has not done so already. He may be willing to negotiate."

"Even so, he does not have the final word. Emperor Constantius will not bend," Isaac warned. "He will see us as a threat and order Gallus to set the legions upon us."

"Then we make of Galilee a graveyard for tyrants."

Back in Antioch, Gallus stormed through the eastern hall of the imperial palace, a dispatch in his fist.

"They sent a letter to Alexandria!" he roared. "How dare they!"

Maximius watched grimly. "To whom?" the general finally asked.

"To the bishop. Pleading for support. These heretics call upon the Christian world, not as rebels, but as 'guardians of justice.' They speak of Moses. Of Daniel. They quote the Hebrew prophets and expect Christian help."

He tossed the scroll onto a table.

"They claim they are building a republic of God."

Maximius said nothing.

Gallus stared at him. "You think I will lose Antioch next? That the mobs will rise in this city too? My own wife's family has ties to the Jews. And Constantius is breathing down my neck demanding I eliminate them now!"

Maximius's brow rose. "You speak of Constantina?" His general was still thinking about Gallus's comment that his wife had connections with the Jews.

Gallus blinked. "I speak of treason."

He turned and began to pace.

"Constantius wants me to act first. To take the risk. To fail. So that he may cut my throat like Crispus before me."

Maximius remained calm. "Then don't fail."

Gallus stopped. "Send in the Sixth Ferrata?"

The general nodded. "But it's not just adding another legion to the ones already in Caesarea, Caesar. Flours has proven himself incapable of leading an army. You also need to send someone to lead them. Someone known to be ruthless."

"Who do you have in mind general?"

"Ursicinus. I hear there was a request to send him west but I'm certain he would take the first opportunity to remain in the east where he belongs."

Gallus exhaled. "Yes. He will crush them. But he must make it look like a tribal uprising. Don't let him martyr them. Don't make Natronai a symbol of rebellion for any of the other nations."

Maximius stepped back. "Then you must give the order."

Gallus turned to the wall, where hung the iron sword of his office. He stared at it as if t could speak to him. Then, finally spoke, "Prepare the order. Tomorrow it is signed. And may God protect us."

CHAPTER XXIII: WOLF OF ANTIOCH

The date groves outside Antioch swayed gently in the spring breeze, betraying none of the turmoil gathering like a thunderstorm within the city walls. Inside the palace complex, men paced, scribes hurried, couriers galloped, and all roads now led to one man: Constantius Gallus, Caesar of the East. His mission was clear, snuff out the fires of rebellion in Judaea and restore order to Rome's vulnerable flank. It should have been an easy task, now that Shapur was busy protecting his eastern border, but somehow this Jewish prince and his band of brigands was managing to take garrison post after garrison post with hardly any casualties.

Momentum appeared to be moving steadily in the rebels favor, yet Gallus did not move quickly. He would tell his generals that he was instead moving deliberately, like a chess master willing to sacrifice his pawns because he's already calculated checkmate occurring ten moves later. The problem was that not all his generals could see his strategy unfolding as planned, and they were actively sending messages to the emperor claiming that the campaign was a disaster.

Constantina had arrived in Antioch several months prior, the iron-willed sister of the emperor, along with a small but formidable entourage of secretaries, advisers, and guards from the palace back in Nicomedia. Gallus tended to rely solely on their advice rather than the generals who had spent their entire life marshalling the province of Syria-Palestina. He didn't care what they had to say.

While Constantina oversaw matters of the court, Gallus had cloistered himself inside the Praetorium, drawing maps and reading dispatches, as if only he had the military awareness and acumen on how to best combat the Jewish uprising. Though he was Caesar in name, he carried himself like a man who wanted to be the sole commander of the army, like Julius Caesar had been in antiquity. He trusted none of these generals that had been residing in the eastern provinces all this time, growing fat and lazy as he frequently described them offensively to his wife when they were alone. That being the case, his first action would not be to move troops into the Galilee, as the generals had been demanding, but to wait until an officer fit to command the legions into battle reached Caesarea. Maximius had provide him with the name of the most suitable candidate. The war would have to wait until General Ursicinus arrived in Antioch to take command of the troops.

Ursicinus was a veteran of the Danube, hardened in the frostbitten wars of Illyria, where discipline was law and cruelty was an alternative word for survival. It was said that he had once captured a rebel leader and crucified him upside down, letting his body rot as a warning to the next village that may have been considering rebellion. To Gallus, he was the perfect choice. This was the general he needed to extinguish any dreams of freedom the Jews might be harboring.

Ursicinus finally arrived in Antioch one morning, when the temperature was already sizzling. He was dressed in embossed leather and riding a black horse whose hooves struck the cobblestones like war drums. His face was scarred across the right temple, his nose obviously broken twice as deduced from its curvature, and his eyes were as dark as coal beneath an overhanging brow. He dismounted without any fanfare and walked straight into the Praetorium.

Gallus received him in the sunlit chamber flanked by imperial eagle standards positioned on either side of his desk. "Magister Equitum," Gallus greeted him.

Ursicinus bowed. "Caesar." He offered no other pleasantries.

"You know why I summoned you to Antioch,"

"Because of Palestina. General Maximius has already provided me with the details."

"Yes. The land is on fire. The generals I have there are fools. A Jewish prince claims divine right, and his cause spreads like the plague. We believe he has joined forces with other rebels that inhabit the land. Thus far he has gained control of small fortresses, nothing significant but the officers on my staff have been wailing like old whores swindled out of their fees, but I have not paid them much mind. I want these rebels to swell in self-confidence. It will be the cause of their undoing."

Ursicinus allowed a grim smile to cross his lips. "So, the old wounds bleed once again. Hadrian's generals were too soft hearted. They should have slain every last one of these Jews rather than leave behind enough that they could continue breeding. This is what happens when you only do half a job."

"My sentiments exactly," Galls confirmed. "I need this rebellion ended once and for all, not merely suppressed. I want these Jews erased. Wiped from memory."

Gallus paced the floor of the imperial hall in his toga half-slipped from his shoulder, while he fretted about the possible failure of his first real mission. "Why? Why do these Jews always make it so damn difficult? We changed a name on a map. A name! So what! Palaestina, Syria-Palaestina, who really cares? For Christ's sake! It's only a name! And yet they treat it like an abomination, like we pissed on their holy altar. It's parchment ink on a map, meant for the census clerks and tax collectors, not their blasted synagogues. Let them call it Judea and Galilee in their hearts. Let them mutter 'Israel' to each other in their prayers. No one's stopping them!" Gallus wheeled upon his general. "They can etch "For the freedom of Israel" on their gravestones. I don't care? The Senate doesn't care. The people of Rome certainly don't. And yet to them it's everything. A wound. An insult. An act of war. What is wrong with these people?"

"The Jews do not forget, my lord. Nor do they forgive easily," Ursicinus answered. "Everyone is aware of that."

"No, they do not. That's the damnable heart of it. They remember. Every offense, every slight, every syllable of their cursed scrolls, as if the world itself depends on them keeping score. We give them roads, aqueducts, grain. Do they thank us? No. They light fires in the hills and hide scrolls in caves like they're the last flicker of civilization." Gallus quickened his pace as he circled about the room, feeling his throat tighten with bitterness. "They hate us and yet they live among us. They reject our god, mock our churches, won't eat our food. They circumcise their children like carving out a brand; not just of faith, but defiance. Tell me, Ursicinus, what other people builds no idols, sings no hymns to their emperors, pays no homage at the games, and yet expects peace from Rome? Where is their gratitude?"

The general thought about it for the moment. "They are not like other people."

"Oh, don't flatter them. They know they're not like us and that's the problem. They cling to their separateness like armor. And worse, they relish it. They worship suffering. Martyrdom is their opium. You think this is about a name? This is about power. About whom gets to define what is holy and what is real. They do not care about borders. They care about dominion. Theirs. Always theirs. The Persians are enemies. The Germans are savages. But the Jews? They're an idea. You can't kill an idea easily. You can only burn it, crush it, bury it under rubble and even then it manages to survive." Gallus was beginning to breath heavily as he worked himself into a lather. "I envy them, sometimes. Only sometimes. That stubbornness. That unbreakable will. They pray in ruins and believe it sanctified. They lose their country and call it exile, not defeat. You could wipe them from the map, and they'd still claim ownership of heaven."

"So, what would you have me do in order to kill an idea?" the general asked.

"The eternal question, general," Gallus responded. "How do you deal with madness? It's exhausting. Other people bend. Other people break. The Greeks sulk but obey. The Syrians drink and forget. The Egyptians bow with grace. But the Jews; all the Jews know to do is resist. That is always their response. Resist forever. It's as if they enjoy having martyrdom along with their morning bread. They say we persecute them, as if a governor doing his job is an offense to heaven. We march and they claim we trample holy ground. We collect taxes and they wail as if we have made them paupers. Every law we pass they label as a desecration. Every command given is an outrage. You cannot govern them, because they say they are chosen. A people chosen? Chosen for what; misery? Isolation? They mock our laws behind their curtains. They count their Sabbaths while ignoring our courts. They speak in riddles, and whisper prophecy, and somehow always believe that we are the invaders, even after our being a presence there for four hundred years. But for them, it's war. Always war. Mark my words: they will rise again, and again, and again, and each time, the legions will answer. And each time, they will die in the thousands. And still they will cling to that name, Judea, Israel, Zion, as if those names have power. I will tolerate it no longer. The cycle must end and that end is now!"

"Then I must be permitted to act with precision and with force," the general suggested.

Gallus nodded his head, "Yes, put the fear of Rome back in their bones. Let them remember that the Pax Romana does not tolerate exceptions. If they will not bow, then we will see to it that they break."

"I will need men. Autonomy. And freedom from delay."

Gallus stepped forward, looking the general in the eye. "You have it. I'm placing the VI Ferrata under your direct command. There's already five legions sitting in Caesarea. Every general must bow their heads to you. Even Maximius. But bring me trophies. I need their leaders' heads on spikes for the Emperor to see."

Ursicinus turned to leave, but Gallus called after him. "One more thing. No crosses."

The general turned his head slightly. "No?"

"Crucifixion is a relic of my uncle's reign and it would appear you have earned a bad reputation for it. It also makes those hanging on to life look like martyrs. Death has to be clean and quick. I want the East governed with elegance, not spectacle. If you must kill, do it cleanly. Heads on spikes gives a more civilized appearance."

Ursicinus gave the barest nod. "Then we will make the earth clean with their blood." He was not particularly happy with the ban on crucifixion.

Within days, Ursicinus began reshaping the military apparatus of Antioch into a war machine. He requisitioned ships to supply coastal bases, forced local smiths to increase production of pila and gladii, and set up training drills in the Hippodrome, using captured thieves as mock rebels, so that the new recruits could gain the full taste of blood in their mouths.

The Legio VI Ferrata, already stationed in Syria, was bolstered with Gallic mercenaries and Arab auxiliaries. He reorganized them into fast-moving detachments, capable of striking deep into hill country, aware that much of the fighting would be conducted in the foothills of the Galilean mountains.

He also brought in spies. Under Ursicinus, Antioch became a nest of whisperers. Informants from Caesarea, Jerusalem, and even Sepphoris were bribed, tortured, and dispatched. Reports flowed daily into his war room. The rebels had camps in the highlands. They were training farmers as soldiers. There were rumors of Persian supplies arriving through Nabataean intermediaries. And one name kept appearing in all the scrolls: Natronai. Along with another: Isaac of Sepphoris. Ursicinus pinned both names to his map. He made no distinction between rabbi and prince. Only between target and threat.

Gallus, meanwhile, remained distant from the blood and iron of preparation. His days were filled with oratory, theater, and games intended to court the favor of the Antiochene elite. But behind the scenes, he was ever aware that his position was precarious. He could not afford failure. Constantius, his cousin, had already shown little tolerance for weakness. Gallus remembered the purge that followed the death of Constantine the Great, including the execution of his father and the exile of his brothers. He knew what happened to the emperor's pawns that failed to become kings.

Every scroll that arrived from Jerusalem or Alexandria was read by Gallus himself. He learned the names of rebel villages. He memorized the lineage of Natronai. He saw in Isaac the same charisma that had once drawn crowds to John the Baptist. He envied it. He desired it. But most of all, he feared it.

So, he gave Ursicinus permission to use all means at his own discretion to subdue the countryside. But if there was to be any slaughter of the civilian population, then it had to appear that it was unavoidable collateral damage.

Once on the march, Ursicinus moved across the countryside like a raging forest fire. He dispatched his forces in waves. The first struck the southern roads, destroying rebel caches and executing local sympathizers. The second infiltrated market towns, where young men were rounded up and interrogated. Many were maimed during the interrogation, others simply vanished. Their names were scratched onto walls in secret but never spoken aloud for fear of being added to the list of names to be rounded up next. By the third week of his forces being unleashed, entire communities had fled into the hills.

Ursicinus was pleased with his handiwork. "Fear does what swords cannot," he said to his sub-commanders. "It dissolves the will to fight. It crushes hope and it destroys dreams."

Perhaps it had that effect in his previous conquests, but he quickly realized it had quite a different effect among the Jews. From the heights of Samaria to the lowlands of Galilee, the people began to resist, not driven by an idealistic pursuit of freedom, but from the sheer terror of realizing what would come if they did nothing. They swelled the ranks of the Patricius's army, and little by little they whittled away at the Roman legions, focusing always at the weakly guarded flanks or rear and disappearing immediately into the hills after their lightning attack. The fast paced fury of his early success was now being mired down into a game of cat and mouse, the trouble being that the mice were learning very quickly how to keep the cat off balance.

As much as Ursicinus tried to control the flow of information, it was impossible to impede its flow back to Antioch completely. There, in the depths of his palace, Gallus turned once more to his scrolls and whispered to himself a promise: "If I must be remembered, let it be as the man who made Jerusalem bleed to death." He made the decision to pour all the manpower he had available into the province in order to bring the war to a close as quickly as possible. Another four thousand Arab mercenaries would provide him with all the auxiliaries he would need. War chariots were reinstated from desert retirement. Ballistae were mounted on wagons in order to lay siege to cities. The standard of Caesar fluttered above every century of men. And then, as dawn rose over the Orontes on a spring day, this iron tide of reinforcements began to roll south towards Ursicinus camp to join the battle. They carried with them simple orders that commanded the general to lay Galilee to waste.

CHAPTER XXIV: POLITICAL THUNDER

The sea shimmered silver this dawn, as the sun barely broke over the hills above Tiberias. The city nestled by the Galilean lake, ancient and defiant, now liberated from its Roman occupation, lay still in shadow, its stone streets quiet save for the gentle clopping of hooves as Natronai rode up the winding path leading to the compound of the Nasi.

Isaac of Sepphoris rode beside him, his eyes heavy with foreboding. "This will come to nothing," he said in a low voice, barely more than a whisper. "I still say this is a big mistake. Hillel is Rome's man. He has bargained away the dignity of his office to be their tax collector. He will not lift a finger for your cause. In fact, I swear he will do everything possible to bring about your demise."

"You give him too much credit, Isaac. As of our victory, we are the true power in Tiberias. He is nothing."

"Well, if he's nothing, why are we even bothering to visit. He should be coming to us on his knees." Isaac felt justified in his loathing of the man/

Natronai said nothing at that moment. The lines of his jaw were tight. He carried himself not only as the heir to the Babylonian Exilarchate, but as a prince in exile, a living banner for those who still worshipped the House of David. His eyes, were fixed upon the task ahead.

"We must try," he finally said. "Even a lion must sometimes speak with the fox."

Isaac grunted. "And what does the lion do when the fox has already set a trap? We should have brought Ashurbanipol with us. At least he would have no qualms slicing off the fox's head."

They reached the gates of the Nasi's estate, a high-walled enclave set apart from the city. The guards already knew Natronai was coming as a messenger had been dispatched the night before. They were admitted with due formality, led through an olive-shaded courtyard, past whitewashed columns and polished mosaic tiles that depicted the Temple in Jerusalem, the Menorah, the Lion of Judah. It was a house gilded in tradition but minimalized so as not to offend the Roman overlords.

Hillel the Second waited for them in a long, narrow chamber with high windows and cedar beams. The morning light spilled in like judgment, casting stripes across the marble floor. He stood as they entered, robed in deep blue, a man of poise and studied courtesy. His beard was long but trimmed. His hands were soft, unused to the sword. It was obvious that he had never done a hard day's work his entire life, born to privilege and catered to by wealth.

"Welcome, Prince Natronai," he said, bowing stiffly. "Son of the Exilarch Nehemiah. Welcome to my humble home."

"Peace upon you, Patriarch," Natronai replied with equal stiffness. "And upon the house of Hillel."

There was silence as the men took their seats across from each other at a low table. Dates, figs, bread, and wine had been laid out, untouched.

Isaac remained standing. He would not eat in this place. His eyes scanned the chamber, ever watchful.

Finally, the patriarch broke the silence. "So, tell me," said Hillel, folding his hands before him. "Why have you come?"

Natronai met his gaze. "They tell me that you are a very perceptive man. That being the case, you know very well the answer to your question."

Hillel gave a long sigh. "It is because you want a war. It matters not that it might result in the death of your countrymen without any change to the order of the world."

"I want justice," Natronai said. "It appears that some of us have forgotten what that word means in God's kingdom."

"Justice?" Hillel's brow lifted. "What justice lies in marching our young men to slaughter? In provoking the legions, the governors, the emperor himself? Do you think the land can survive another revolt? Do you think God demands we burn with zeal instead of enduring with wisdom?"

"And is this your understanding of wisdom?" Natronai shot back as he looked about at the lavish decorations of the room. "To collect taxes for our oppressors? To draft writs of clemency while our teachers are flogged in synagogues and our sacred scrolls are burned? The Church mocks us in the open, Hillel. Do you not see it or is the light reflecting off the gold ornaments blinding you?"

"I see it," Hillel said, his voice low but firm. "I see it more clearly than you will ever know. I see what happened to our people, Natronai, when they try to defy the natural order of the world. I saw what happened in Jerusalem. I see it in my dreams every night. I see and know exactly what becomes of us when we choose rebellion." He leaned forward. "You carry your name like a sword, and I do not doubt your courage. But courage is often another word for foolishness. Is the man that runs into a burning house to save another foolish or brave. Of course, if there is another way then you must conclude he is foolish. There is an alternative to war against Rome. It's called survival. Preservation. One might even say patience. Our people endure because we choose not to meet every blow with steel. We have learned how to bend. We know how to bargain. We write. We whisper. That is how we outlive empires."

Natronai's face darkened. "It is one thing to endure an occupation when you live in luxury, a completely different story if you are merely a poor laborer, scratching out a living. Have you ever taken the opportunity to ask those people what they would call it. I doubt they would say 'this is living.' Perhaps a living death would be more likely."

Before Hillel could answer, there was a shift behind a long silk curtain at the back of the room. A figure moved in the shadows.

Isaac stiffened. "It's a trap," he warned Natronai, thinking that at any moment a squadron of Romans they had missed encountering the day before would charge forward from behind the heavy drapes.

The curtain parted just enough for a face to emerge. It was a young woman, her skin olive and radiant, her eyes vast and dark as the Sea of Galilee. Her hair fell in curls to her shoulders, unbound, untamed. She watched the men like a ghost watching the living.

Hillel's face immediately grew stern. "Havilah!"

She did not retreat.

"This is not your place," he said, louder and more condemningly. "Eliezer, come get my daughter and take her back to her room!" he shouted to a servant that was obviously somewhere out of sight but overhearing the conversations in the room.

She stepped forward into the light.

"And yet I am here," she said, unafraid of her father's anger.

The room fell silent.

Natronai could not speak. His eyes were transfixed upon her as if he had seen an angel step down from heaven above. Something within him shifted. There was a long, drawn, inward breath that froze in the back of his throat.

Hillel looked from his daughter to Natronai and back again. Slowly, something cold and calculating entered his eyes. He rose to his feet and gestured with a wave of his hand that she should go away. "Leave us," he said.

Isaac saw it too and he hesitated. The thought kept repeating in his brain that this was not good. Whatever that look in Natronai's eyes meant, it was not good. Matters were complicated enough without adding whatever this might be.

Catching his breath, Natronai spoke first. "Please let her remain," he said, not taking his eyes from Havilah even though directing his comment to her father.

Eliezer, who just entered the room withdrew just as quickly. Havilah stood boldly between the two men, her chin raised.

"You shame me, daughter" Hillel said quietly.

"I had no intent to dishonor you, father," she replied.

Hillel turned to her, lowering his voice to something just above a whisper. "You know there is no place for a woman to intend meetings of importance. I forbid it. God has forbidden it."

Hillel turned slowly to Natronai. "She is willful," he said. "She does not understand that her meddling can have serious consequences."

"Exactly when did God forbid women from serious discussions," Natronai asked. "I'm not familiar with that passage in the Tanach."

"I thought as a scholar you would be familiar with the quotes from the Talmud. Yerushalmi Sotah 1:4 is quite clear on the matter. It says, 'Let the words of the Torah be burned rather than be handed over to women.' And also in Yerushalmi Sotah 3:4 which clearly identifies that 'Women are talkative and prone to idle chatter.' But most of all, Yerushalmi Berakhot 9:5 leaves no doubt by saying, 'The words of a woman are of no consequence.' These are all statements from the best minds of the Sanhedrin, based on what is written in the Tanach and suggesting that it is not a woman's place to be party to the serious discussions of men. Wouldn't you agree?"

"You would dare to suggest that…" Simon was cut off by Natronai before he could complete his sentence.

"What my close friend was about to say was that clearly your Jerusalem Talmud is inferior to the writings within the Babylonian Talmud which is still underway. If your rabbis of superior intellect, as you have suggested are the authors of these, then I would accuse them of never having read the Tanach at all. Or do they not know about Sarah, Hagar and Rebekah, whom God spoke directly with. Was not Miriam as much a leader of the Israelites as was Moses? Or do they forget that Deborah was appointed a judge over Israel. Are you suggesting that God wasted these efforts because none of these women were worthy of speaking with as their words were of no consequence?"

"You've taken my words out of context," Hillel protested. "These were general statements and not referring to specific women."

"These are demeaning statements and not worthy of someone calling himself, even if falsely, the 'Prince of Israel'. Would you not agree?"

The question caught Hillel off guard. He knew that he was being baited and no matter how he answered, his words would be used against him. He had to think quickly in order to prevent any further embarrassment. "You have insulted my family's inheritance, even though my only intent was to prevent you from being in an awkward situation. But I will forgive you. I know my daughter is quite beautiful and that would be a distraction to you, especially if we were to have a serious negotiation. Someone, like your colleague, might accuse me of using my daughter to cloud your thinking, and I do not want that to happen. Those were the serious consequences I spoke of. But I'm afraid that now that you have seen my darling, Havilah, you will be unable to focus on the matters that brought you here."

Isaac could only smile at how cleverly Hillel had shifted the conversation and turned the table. He could only hope that Natronai would not give the explanation any credibility.

"I can understand your concern, Reb Hillel. Your daughter is incredibly beautiful but I can assure you that her presence here will not distract me from my purpose for visiting you."

"Then by all means, let her stay," Hillel agreed. "Havilah, come meet the Prince of Babylon, the scion of David, who liberated our city just a few days ago."

Havilah stepped closer to Natronai. "You burn with fire," she said. "But fire alone cannot lead. You must have the support of the people. You must have the hearts of the elders. And you must not be alone."

Her hand brushed his. It was a scandalous gesture. A forbidden moment. But Natronai did not flinch.

"It would appear that you have a good understanding of the needs for a rebellion to succeed. And you have obviously deduced my reason for coming to your father's home. I may have the support of the people but I also need the hearts of the elders. No man, even one they call a messiah can win a war on his own."

"If you permit me, I will go before the people and pledge my support for rebellion."

"As much as I appreciate your support, if we are to succeed, then I need the support of your father's council. Although the daughter of the Patriarch will manage to persuade some of those that are reluctant to enjoin the battle, it will take your father's voice to deliver everyone to our cause. I hope you understand why I must decline your offer, as much as I appreciate it, but it is your father that I need to agree to stand before the people, not only in this city but all of Galilee and Judea."

"I understand. But I still believe I can be of much help to you."

"You understand nothing, daughter. It is not your place to stand before the people and I will not have you negotiating an engagement of war that you know nothing about." Hillel was unable to maintain the mask he had adopted in order cover his true feelings about his daughter's involvement.

Natronai turned to him. "If not her, then are you saying that you will support us?"

"No," Hillel said, cold and firm. "I will not. Nor will I involve myself further in your madness. Go back to your rebels. Fight your doomed war. But do not expect the House of Hillel to sanction it."

Isaac muttered, "Good. Then we are finished here. I told you this would be a waste of time. Let's go, Natronai."

Hillel rose and motioned toward the door. "Indeed you are finished here." Hillel crossed his arms. "If you are to continue this madness," he said to Natronai, "then do not expect me to walk between fire and stone. I have made my choice. Now leave at once."

Isaac's jaw dropped. Not even the Patriarch had the privilege to speak to the son of the exilarch in that manner. "This is your Exilarch that you chase from your house. Such action will be a curse upon you and your progeny."

Hillel's eyes narrowed. "They say you were once a promising rabbinical student. Now look at you. Nothing more than a madman's lapdog."

"So says the man that wears the emperors collar," Isaac fired back.

"If Rome asks, I am still a loyal son of the Empire. I will not let my people suffer on the whim of some foreign king that has illusions of grandeur. This is not a war you can win. Any fool can see that!"

"But father…" Havilah attempted to interrupt.

"But nothing!" Hillel shouted back. "We are done here and I forbid you to talk to this man again. Did you not see how he ravished you with his eyes. He is filled with the sin of lust. Now leave us!"

Natronai looked again at Havilah. "If I have insulted you, it was only because I was overwhelmed by your beauty? I pray you can forgive someone for admiring one of God's perfect creations."

"She has nothing to say," Hillel's face grew red. "She's spoiled little girl that has forgotten her position in this house and never should have spoken to you in the first place."

Havilah found herself smiling at Natronai's words. "I believe in you. I believe God will send us a messiah. Perhaps it's you."

Hillel showed her the back of his hand. "Shut up you foolish little girl."

"I will support you," Havilah shouted through the crack of the closing door.

As they descended the walkway from the house, Isaac stepped back in disbelief. "You would trust her?"

Natronai nodded. "No. I would trust the moment."

"What is that supposed to mean?" Isaac couldn't make sense of his comment.

"Don't tell me that you took one look at this woman and you're thinking you found your queen. You're not serious."

"Her defiance will serve us all. You will see," he responded.

"Her defiance will probably get us all killed. This is not the time to be thinking romantically." Isaac sensed a cloud of doom circling above his head.

Natronai continued to walk along the path without saying another word.

CHAPTER XXV: BEAUTY & THE BEAST

Natronai stood by the campfire, the flickering light catching the worn edges of a parchment map spread across a flat stone. Rebel commanders surrounded him, murmuring about troop placements and Roman garrisons, but their voices were like wind through dry reeds. He heard them and didn't hear them simultaneously. His mind was focused elsewhere.

"Natronai, are you listening to us?" Isaac shook the Patricius by the shoulder. "We need you to tell us which city garrison we should attack next."

"I'm listening," Natronai replied gruffly, but the only word registering in is mind was 'Havilah'. Her name echoed in his thoughts like a psalm. Her face, her voice, her defiance. Every time he closed his eyes, she appeared, hauntingly beautiful and luminous. His hands, meant to be plotting a rebellion, itched only to feel that glancing touch of hers once again.

Isaac stood with his arms crossed, waiting for Natronai to say more. "Well, what should we do next, Natronai?" he asked sharply.

"I need to give it more thought," he answered.

"Patricius," another rebel said tentatively.

"Hm?" Natronai blinked. "Yes. Proceed."

The commander continued, but the gleam had faded from his voice. Even he could see what Isaac already knew for certain: their leader's mind was elsewhere.

That night, Isaac pulled Natronai aside.

"You're obviously distracted," he said plainly. "You're compromising everything we've accomplished thus far."

"You don't understand," Natronai pleaded.

"Oh, I understand," Simon stated. "Ever since we visited the Patriarch's home, your mind has focused on something else. Or should I say, someone else."

"You're being ridiculous."

"No, I'm being truthful. And I'm being your friend and saying this for your own good. We're fighting a war. Thousands of lives are depending on you. You can't sacrifice everything for the sake of one woman!" Isaac was desperate to make Natronai realize he was placing them all in jeopardy.

"She's different," Natronai murmured, finally admitting the truth while smiling. "She sees me. Not just as the leader of the rebellion. Not just the bloodline. But me."

Isaac wanted to shake him furiously. "You're not some love-sick teenager. She is the daughter of your enemy. And to be precise, she's been forbidden to see you.

You're fantasizing over some imagined love story with a woman you've only seen once."

Natronai didn't answer.

Isaac sighed, and for one of the few times in his life he was at a loss for words but he knew that he had to say something before they forfeiting everything they had fought so hard to win. "Havilah," Isaac hissed the name as if it were poison. "The daughter of Hillel. Do you even grasp what you are doing? You, our Patricius, the one anointed to lead Israel against Rome, fawning over her as though she were a gift from the heavens."

Natronai's lips curved in the faintest of smiles. "Perhaps she is. You did not see her eyes, Isaac, in the way she looked at me. You didn't experience the intense feeling when she touched my hand. The Lord delivers comfort even in times of war. How do you not know that this is not part of God's intentions for me?"

Isaac slammed his palm against the table. "Comfort? Is that what you call it? Do you not recall Samson and Delilah? David and Bathsheba? Do you not see that every time a man of God allowed desire to rule his heart, he brought ruin upon himself and Israel? You think your heart burns with the fire of heaven, but you forget that fire consumes everything it comes in contact with."

Natronai's eyes snapped to him, indignant. "I am not Samson, nor am I David. My heart is my own, and the Lord knows its purity. Do you think me so weak that a woman's smile will undo what God has commanded me to do?"

Isaac leaned closer, lowering his voice, his words sharp as daggers. "It already has. Look at you. Since she appeared, you speak less of strategy, less of governance, less of the Covenant of Fire we swore to uphold. You dream instead of a woman whose father bows before Rome. If the men see her by your side, they will abandon us. Do you not understand? To them, she is the daughter of betrayal. She will undo us all."

Natronai's jaw tightened. He opened his mouth to speak but no words came. His silence was worse than defiance.

Isaac pressed on, his voice now trembling with frustration. "Do you not remember Achan, who coveted what was forbidden and brought defeat upon all Israel at Ai? Or Solomon, whose love of foreign women turned his heart from the Lord, splitting the kingdom? History is written in the ashes of men who let love blind them."

Natronai stood abruptly, his chair scraping against the stone floor. His voice thundered. "Enough! You speak as though I have abandoned the Lord Himself. But what if…what if the Lord has chosen her for me? What if, through her, reconciliation comes between the house of Hillel and the Scions of David?"

"Reconciliation?" Isaac spat. "Or ruin? You are thinking not as a leader, but as a youth chasing shadows. Love at first sight? I never thought to hear such foolishness from you. Yet here you are, willing to risk Israel's hope for the sake of one woman's face."

The air between them crackled, two brothers-in-arms suddenly turned adversarial. Isaac's breath came hard, his fists trembling on the table. He knew words would not move Natronai. Scripture, history, and reasoning but none of it pierced the armor of this madness.

And yet, he saw something in Natronai's eyes: not lust, but a hunger deeper, rawer. A longing for something more than war, for something that gave meaning to the struggle. Isaac's heart sank. He could not tear that longing from him with words alone.

He straightened slowly, voice dropping to a quiet resignation. "Then there is only one way to deal with this. Bring her here. Let her stand among us. Let the men see her not as an enemy's daughter, but as flesh and blood. Perhaps then they will not despise you for your heart."

Natronai blinked, startled. "You would do this?"

Isaac's gaze was hard, but beneath it flickered sorrow. "Not because I approve. Because if I do not, you will chase after her blindly, and we will lose both you and the war. Better she come to us than you be lured to her. At least this way I can prevent you from falling into any trap that Hillel may be setting."

For a long moment they stood in silence, the bond between them stretched taut, straining as if it might snap. They had fought side by side, sworn oaths together, built a dream of freedom brick by brick. Yet in that silence, Isaac felt the shadow of a woman, this Havilah, slip between them, threatening to sever what no Roman sword had yet accomplished.

Isaac came to the realization that there was only one solution. Let him see her. Let him speak to her and perhaps then he would come to his senses. In his heart he hoped that Natronai would see that she was not a prophetess nor a muse, just a spoiled girl, raised in privilege, tied to the man they must oppose. Perhaps then the spell would break. Though it was against his better judgment, Isaac began planning on how he could bring Havilah to their camp.

It took days of quiet bribes and whispered messages. He marked the guard patterns at Hillel's estate, questioned sympathetic servants, traced every exit and entry. Finally, on a moonless night, Isaac donned a borrowed cloak and slipped through the shadows of the Tiberian streets.

He climbed over a wall, thick with ivy, careful not to dislodge the loose stones. A dog barked once but was silenced with a tossed bone that he knew to bring through his gathering of information. He ducked into a side corridor and crept past the library windows until he reached the small garden alcove beneath Havilah's room.

He whistled, twice.

A shadow moved above. A shutter creaked open.

"Isaac?" Havilah whispered. She had received the message that he would be coming for her.

"Come down," he hissed. "He needs to see you." He then turned away and spoke in a muffled voice, only to himself. "Then perhaps he'll wake up and do what must be done."

There was a long pause. Then the flutter of linen and rope falling from her window. She had obviously prepared for this night.

She touched down beside him with surprising grace.

"He is well?" she asked.

"Too well," Isaac muttered. "Now move. We have little time."

But unknown to Isaac, another had watched all from within. Gamaliel, her brother, standing behind a thin curtain on the second floor, his arms folded and face unreadable. He did nothing. He called no guards. He made no effort to stop his sister.

"She's too clever to be kept caged," he whispered to himself. "Let her go. Let her see. Let her love him. And let her find out for herself that love is often accompanied by a broken heart."

It took several hours, following goat trails and broken paths but eventually they made it back to the rebel camp. Havilah was ushered past the sentries under Isaac's guidance and brought to Natronai's tent.

"Natronai," Isaac announced, "someone here to see you."

The air seemed to still as she entered.

He rose, disoriented.

"Havilah?"

She smiled softly. "You didn't think I'd stay away, did you? After all, you did send word to me to come to you."

He crossed the floor to her, and for a long moment, nothing existed beyond the space between them. He reached for her, but she raised a hand.

"Show me," she said.

"Show you what?"

"What you're fighting for. Not with words. Let me see it. Let me understand."

He hesitated. Her request was confusing. 'Why in the world would she want to see the overall strategy of the battles,' he asked himself. 'Could she possibly be a spy.' He quickly dismissed that possibility. His heart told him he shouldn't refuse her even though his mind was still asking a thousand questions. Finally, he nodded.

He led her to the command table, the maps, the list of sympathizers and supply lines, the strategic drawings of Roman forts. He walked her through the plan to sever Roman supply lines from Caesarea to Damascus. Showed her the names of the Bedouin tribal lords pledged to rise when the revolt crested. He found it impossible to deny telling her any of the secrets behind their missions. He wanted her to know everything.

And she listened, eyes gleaming with wonder.

"This... this is more than fire," she whispered. "This is vision."

He leaned close. "Then you believe in it?"

"I believe in you." She reached out and took his hand in hers. Natronai didn't resist.

Outside the tent, Isaac waited, pacing like a nervous uncle. Inside, the romance began to burn bright.

The moon rode high over the Galilean hills, pale and full like a watching eye. The Sea of Galilee shimmered far below, quiet and silver in the night, its surface undisturbed except for the occasional whisper of wind that stirred its glassy stillness. From the ridge above Magdala, the cluster of tents could just barely be seen. They stood as silent sentinels in the dark. The enemy forces would have to be directly upon them before they would be noticed. The location of their camp had been chosen well. Large enough to conceal twenty thousand men but hidden so deep in the forests that even the wild animals barely tread that way.

Somewhere among the towering pine trees and whispering cypresses, Havilah stood beside Natronai, cloaked in a borrowed mantle, her eyes wide with the wonder of the night, but more so of him. She was still catching her breath from the ride. No words had been exchanged for the longest time. There was nothing that their eyes had not already said. The union of the Exilarch's son fighting a war against Rome, with the daughter of Hillel II, an empire loyalist was scandalous enough. And yet, here they were. Standing side by side. Unmarried. Unchaperoned. Alone beneath God's canopy of stars.

"You could have refused to come," Natronai said softly, breaking the silence between them. "I would have understood."

Havilah turned to him, her face caught in moonlight. Her hair, unbound from the ride, curled like dark fire around her shoulders. " And you could have refused to ask me to come."

He smiled wryly, "I didn't think you'd come, though I hoped you would."

"I didn't think I would either," she admitted. "I have never defied my father to this degree before. But I haven't stopped thinking of you from the moment I first saw you."

"Nor I," he said. He looked down, then away, as if ashamed. "It's a foolish thing we're doing. Isaac thinks I have gone absolutely mad."

"And yet," she said, stepping a little closer, "we're doing it."

Their hands brushed, barely a touch. Her skin was warm. His trembled.

They stood that way for some time, saying nothing. Listening to the chirp of insects, the distant rustle of a fox in the brush, and the sighing breath of the world. Time slowed. The night stretched long.

"You know," she said at last, "my father would probably have me executed if he knew I had come to you. He'd accuse me of prostituting myself and have me stoned for the scandal I brought upon his household." Havilah then laughed, a dry, brittle sound. "Of course, he would do all that before he lifted a finger against you. But then he would attempt to ruin you. Your name, your cause. He would say it was all a Babylonian scheme, that you seduced me in order to discredit his house. And the saddest part of all is that the people, our people, would believe him."

"You believe your father's name carries that much weight," Natronai asked bitterly. "That Hillel the second. The heir of Rabban Gamliel. Of Judah the Prince himself could impose his will against the true House of David."

"Sadly, people will always believe the worst that they can imagine. They will drag their heroes through the mud with any opportunity to do so. It is far easier to tear down idols than erect them. As much as your family may be royal, you will always be viewed as the son of exile. A royal illustrious family, to content to leave their lavish lifestyle in Babylon and return to the homeland of their people."

Natronai flinched. "But I have returned."

"One out of how many generations since Zerubbabel," she questioned. "The only reason the House of Hillel has any power is because the people felt abandoned by your family. They needed a physical presence of the royal family here in Palestina, so they elevated what probably seems to you to be a low hanging branch on the family tree but it was one they could cling to, here in their own land. That is why they will believe what my father has to say, even if you think now they are committed to following you. My coming here may have been a terrible folly on your part."

Natronai frowned upon hearing her comments.

"I didn't mean it cruelly," she said quickly, touching his arm. "Only that this thing between us has always been cursed from the beginning. We're symbols to them. You stand for the future of Babylon. I for the past of Judea. But neither of us can state with any certainty when we will be gathered to a restored nation."

"Which is why I am here now," he reminded her. "If I can defeat Rome, then Israel will be restored. It is the mission that God has given me."

"Exactly the reason why neither of us can live for ourselves," she said. "To do so would be selfish. Perhaps we weren't meant to be together at this time?"

Their eyes met. Neither turned away.

"I don't want to be a symbol," she said. "I want to be Havilah. A woman. Not a banner. But you have to be someone far greater than just a man. You must be the Messiah and that would mean there is no place for me."

Natronai shook his head. "And what if I don't want to be the Messiah. Was Judah Maccabee the Messiah or just a man that won our freedom against the Greeks? I am not the madman they whisper about. Just…a man. A man who believes in his heart that we can win a war against the Romans and who loves a woman he should never have touched."

At that word, loves, a tremor passed between them.

"You said 'love.'" she murmured. "But you just met me."

"I did," he confirmed. "And I will say it again."

She searched his face. There was no smile there. No jest. Only naked truth. Painful in its sincerity.

"I think I do too," she responded.

The silence that followed was heavier than the words. He reached for her hand and this time, fully, she let him take it.

"Have you ever thought," she said softly, "what it would mean if we ran away?"

"Almost every day," he said. "But then I remember the world wouldn't let us. Not for long."

She nodded. "They would follow. They would drag us back. You to your command tent in order to fight this war. And me, if not to the stoning I mentioned, then to some betrothal bed they will have prepared as my punishment."

"To whom?" he asked curious.

"Probably some scholar. Dry as sand. With a beard that stinks of old parchment and boiled onions."

Natronai couldn't help but laugh. The sound felt wrong in this aching night, but it was genuine.

"And you?" she asked, with mock sternness. "Weren't they able to find some Babylonian princess for you to wed?"

"Oh, they tried," he said. "But I frightened her away. I told her that I speak with angels and walk with the dead."

"Do you?"

"Naturally. I walk with ghosts," he answered, his voice falling. "The ghosts of prophets. Of warriors. Of dreams I'm too afraid to fulfill."

"You're not afraid," she said. "Not really."

He looked at her, surprised. "How can you know that?"

"You rode to Palestina with a message that everyone was too afraid to hear. You claim to speak with God, and when you do speak it is with fire. My father calls you mad. But I have listened. And I know madness. You are not mad."

"Then what do you think I am?"

She stepped closer until they were breath to breath. "You are a man obsessed with trying to birth a new world. And like all midwives of change, you bleed with it."

He swallowed, staring at her. "You have a unique way of describing what others have labelled as madness. In fact, you speak much like a prophet yourself."

"Then kiss me and let us seal this prophecy with something real."

Their lips met beneath the stars of Magdala, where long ago the one the Christians called their Messiah had walked. Perhaps the stones remembered. Perhaps the breeze that stirred the trees carried echoes of another time, another love, another rejection.

When their lips finally parted, their foreheads touched. They said nothing as they sat beneath a broad branch of a cypress tree, speaking in whispers of what might never be, of dreams better left unsaid because of the risk of futures stolen and cities to be burned. Of the Temple that once was, and the Zion that might still yet come. They watched the constellations shift as the heavens rolled slowly across the sky.

In the dark silence just before the dawn, Natronai said, "If I ever do become what your father fears I will become...promise me you'll stand by me."

"My father only fears that you are truly the Messiah. That though terrifies him. Even without me, your future is determined but I promise I will remain by your side." Her smile was sincere. "Even if I must hide in your shadow. Even if the world of my father calls it a sin."

He kissed her again. This time softly, sadly. As if there was some doubt as to what the future held in store for them.

They did not sleep the remainder of that night. Neither did they speak again of forbidden love, or rebellion, or death. Two souls on a path beyond their control. A man. A woman. A proclaimed Messiah and patriarch's daughter. A Prince of nation waiting to be reborn and an heiress of a world under threat.

And when the morning came, they rose from the earth like figures from a dream, hearts heavier than when they had arrived. But bound by something stronger than chains forged of iron. It was as if they had touched eternity and now they simply waited out the final act of a tragic play.

CHAPTER XXVI: ULTIMATUMS

The sun had barely risen over Tiberias when the shouting began in the home of the patriarch. Hillel II stood in the inner courtyard of his house, his robe loose, his hair wild with fury. He was pacing back and forth like a caged lion his hands trembling, his voice ricocheting off the walls like a baying wolf.

"She is gone! Vanished! My daughter, how could she do such a thing. She has disappeared like a thief in the night! While the whole country teeters on the brink of madness, she slips out and…what? Could it be true that she is consorting with the likes of that madman holed up in the hills of Magdala?"

His son Gamaliel stood still beneath the carved archway, arms folded, following the constant circling of the courtyard by his father until the point that his eyes suffered from exhaustion. He had been up since the servant came running into his room just before dawn, breathless and pale, whispering that Havilah's bed was empty, her sandals missing, her cloak gone. Gamaliel already knew, he had seen her disappear the previous night accompanied by Isaac of Sepphoris.

"She's not a child Abbah," Gamaliel spoke up at last. "She's over twenty. She's always been independent. You should have married her off a long time ago and you wouldn't have this problem."

"She's a woman!' Hillel roared. "A woman of this house! An elder's daughter! And she is consorting with a man who claims to speak with the Almighty Himself! Do you know what they will say? That we have joined his delusions. That we endorse him! That Babylon and Jerusalem are conspiring together to topple Rome! We are doomed and it's all your fault."

"How is her behavior my fault?" Gamaliel challenged him to explain.

"You watched her leave this house with that wretch of a disgraced scholar and you said and did nothing! You didn't even tell me until this morning. What kind of son and brother are you?"

"The kind that sees opportunities even if you cannot. Let them talk," Gamaliel instructed. "It's not like you're going to watch them bring about the end of the world."

"You are speaking of the end of our lineage! That's what they can bring about, if you could see past your own personal objectives." Hillel stepped forward, stabbing a finger toward his son's chest. "If she defies me publicly, if she so much as dares to side with that man…we will be undone. All of it! The House of Hillel, disgraced. The

Mishnah we've all worked upon, tarnished. I will not allow it! You should have stopped her when you saw her leaving."

"Me? What could I have possibly done? She doesn't listen to you, so why would you even think she'd listen to me."

"You let it happen, so now it's up to you to fix this!" Hillel demanded his son pay for his mistake.

"And what would you have me do?" Gamaliel snapped at his father, eyes flashing now. "Storm the Galilean hills? March into the camp of a man half the country already believes to be the Messiah? There are rebels around him. Zealots. Men who would slit my throat as soon as they knew I was your son."

"You are her brother!" Hillel thundered. "Find her!"

"And then what?" Gamaliel was curious as to how his father thought this would all end.

"Just bring her home. By any means necessary."

Gamaliel clenched his jaw. His knuckles whitened as he recognized the impossibility of the task. "And if she refuses?" he asked pointedly.

"Then let her know that she will be cut off from this family." Hillel's voice turned to ice. "We will sit shiva for her. As if she were dead."

The words sank in like iron into water. A long silence followed. The weight of it pressed into the walls. Even the birds in the almond trees outside seemed to hush upon hearing Hillel's remark.

"You know, I think you're looking at this all wrong," Gamaliel tried to explain. "Natronai represents a threat to you because you can't control him. But she can."

"What are you trying to say? That I dangle your sister in front of him like a whore and in return he has to do me favors? Is that what you're suggesting?"

"That's not what I'm saying," he rebutted his father's suggestion. "If you'd listen, you would understand that through her you have leverage over him. By manipulating Havilah to do things for you, she will in turn manipulate him, as long as she thinks what she is doing will not bring him into harm's way and is for the good of the people. Pretend that what you may be offering to her will be to their mutual benefit and I am certain she will get this Patricius to agree."

"You really believe so?" Hillel had his doubt but he was well aware of the persuasive power women had over men.

"It is a fact father. Given the right circumstances and the proper motivation, she can be the perfect enticement to lead to his downfall."

"You would have me do such a thing to your own sister?" Hillel sounded both shocked and ashamed by the suggestion. "I cannot," he insisted. "It is one thing to cast her out of the family, but completely another to make her a pawn to simply remove an opponent's king from the board. She would never forgive me."

"Whose forgiveness are you seeking father? Hers, or as you were saying, Rome's in order that our family survives. I just ask that you think about it. This could be an opportunity. Most important now is to make Rome see you as an ally."

"No, I cannot. Just go and bring her back to me," Hillel waved away any further discussion with a swat of his hands.

Eventually, Gamaliel bowed his head. "I'll find her but think seriously about what I have said, father."

By late afternoon, word had traveled quietly through alleys and whispering halls. A silver coin here, a favor owed there. Gamaliel sat alone at a fountain near the spice market, the hood of his cloak low over his brow.

When the hands came, they came silently, gripping his arms, pulling him to his feet. A black cloth was draped over his face. He struggled, but not much. Any effort to break loose would have been useless. After all, this was what he wanted, although he had hoped he would be able to see where the rebel encampment was located when they took him to see his sister. That was impossible now.

He was placed on the back of a donkey and led through narrow streets, then into the hills. The scent of thyme and dust filled his nostrils. He heard murmured voices, footsteps over dry leaves. The ride seemed to last forever, twisting and turning designed in a way to confuse him should he be trying to memorize their route. At last, the cloth was yanked away.

He stood at the edge of a small encampment. Tents were nestled between rock outcroppings. There were men posted on ridges, watching him closely. They wore no uniforms, but their eyes were sharp and he could tell immediately that they had no respect for his family by the way they sneered at his presence.

And then came Havilah. She stepped from behind one of the tents, hair wind-tossed, cheeks flushed with color, eyes wide with alarm. "Gamaliel," she breathed excitedly, "Why did you come here?"

"Isn't it obvious sister?" he replied coldly. "You disappear in the middle of the night to do who knows what, and yet you ask such a question. Father and I were concerned about you. But clearly that was not a concern of yours. So, this is where you've run to. To the middle of nowhere. To do what? Join the rebel cause!"

She stepped toward her brother, but his body was stiff, unmoving. The warmth of the childhood was long gone.

"You shouldn't be here," she said.

"No. You shouldn't be here. I have come to take you back where you do belong."

They faced each other like two soldiers on opposite sides of a battlefield.

"You don't understand," she attempted to explain. "He's not what you think."

"How can you even guess to know what I am thinking right now? What kind of woman throws herself at a man? A man she has only met and knows nothing about. A man through his reckless disregard for the safety of our people will probably get us all killed. What is there for me to understand?"

"I know it sounds ridiculous but I love him. I knew it from the moment I saw him. He represents the hope of our nation. You and father should be supporting him, not trying to rally the people against him," she pleaded. "But you won't try to understand."

"Oh, I understand," Gamaliel spat. "You've been taken in by the mystic visions and the sound of his rebel poetry. I understand completely. You've thrown away your name. Your heritage. Father wishes to disown you for the dishonor you have brought upon our family."

Her eyes flickered, her lips parted. "He said that?"

"He will mourn you as one of the dead if you don't come home. He already lit the candle." Gamaliel's voice cracked. "Do you want to die in exile, Havilah? Do you want to be a stranger to your own blood? Come back now and perhaps I can convince father to forgive your sins."

"I want to be more than a name on some family scroll that simply says daughter of the Patriarch," she said, her voice trembling. "I want my life to make a difference. I want to choose my own destiny. For once in my life, I want something that wasn't written for me before I was born and to be dealt with as chattel to be married off to some old man that can line the family's pockets."

Gamaliel turned away, trying to collect himself as he felt the anger rising in his body. The pain was in his shoulders, in his hands, in his silence. What was he to do with this woman that felt entitled to have her own mind? Such defiance in the family was unheard of.

It was then that Natronai emerged. He moved with calm dignity, eyes scanning the tension between the pair of siblings. His presence was like the arrival of a storm that had already broken. He had been listening to their conversation.

"You must go," he said quietly to her.

Havilah looked at him, shocked. "No. You promised…"

"I promised to love you," he said. "I didn't promise to destroy your family in doing so."

"I don't care about that." Her eyes teared as she suddenly felt his rejection.

"You must." His voice had weight and finality. "Because I do. And because if you don't go back, they'll brand you forever. They'll close every door to you and the people will focus on your disrespect more than your faith and support of the rebellion. But if you return now, we might still have a path to resolve this matter peaceably with your father. A slow one granted, and most definitely a narrow one, but more importantly a real one."

Tears glistened in her eyes. "You're sending me away."

"I'm providing us with a possible future," he argued. "I will find a way to convince your father that our being together was meant to be."

"I fear he will never agree," she confessed to the flaw in his plan.

"To take you now, against his wishes, will be seen as an affront to our laws, our traditions and to God. We must be patient and believe that God will rectify this situation when he hears our prayers."

She shook her head, lips trembling. "It's not fair."

"No. It's not. But you know in your heart it is the right thing to do."

Natronai stepped forward, took her hand and pressed it to his chest. "I love you, Havilah bat Hillel. I would cross an inferno and the deepest sea to be with you. But not if the price is the destruction of everything you are. Go back. Be the daughter. Be the sister. And believe in me that I will find a way."

She looked at him, as if trying to memorize his face. She touched his cheek with trembling fingers. Then she leaned in and kissed him, long and sorrowful, tasting salt and dust and dreams.

When they parted, her voice was nearly gone. "Don't forget me."

"Never." His words rang true.

Another cloth was brought and Gamaliel's face was covered once again. Her head too in a light veil. Gamaliel had not bothered to say another word. Mounted on the backs of donkeys, together, they left.

As they rode in silence toward Tiberias, Havilah looked back through the veil, and thought she saw a figure standing and watching her where the trees thinned. The ache in her chest was sharper than any wound. The sky above her was still the same, nothing had changed, still eternal, except her own future, which now felt suddenly so far away.

She was going home but as of now, it felt like exile.

Back in Tiberias, Hillel was working in his study late into the night still unaware of his daughter's imminent return to his house. He dipped his quill in ink and began to write furiously.

"To the noble officer Marcus Severinus,
My greetings in peace.
In return for clemency toward my people,
and assurance that the synagogues of Galilee remain untouched
in the coming months, I offer the following intelligence..."

His script was fluid, measured. As if he had written this very letter a dozen times in his mind already. He paused, then continued.

"...regarding a meeting of rebel leaders to take place,
I have heard that they conduct their camp
north of Magdala under the leadership of one Natronai ben Nehemiah.
But as yet, I do not know their precise location.
I am working on a way in order to obtain that information.
Included are names of some of his allies he has here in Tiberias,
And what I believe are their scheduled movements from what I have been told..."

He pressed the wax seal. In his heart, a whisper of guilt stirred. But it was quickly extinguished by conviction. "I serve a greater cause," he murmured. "Not zealotry. The survival of my people."

CHAPTER XXVII: CAESAREA

The palace of Caesarea loomed silent, its colonnades white in the late afternoon glare, its halls suffused with the smell of sea-salt and wine. Guards at the entrance stiffened when they saw Ursicinus stride up the marble steps, his cloak swirling like a crimson storm. His face was black with rage, his jaw clenched so tight that even seasoned centurions flinched at his approach.

Inside, Flaccus sat at ease. Cushions cradled his thin frame, and in his hand was not a sword but a scroll containing some ancient Greek philosophy he pretended to understand. His face lit briefly with relief when Ursicinus entered, only to sour when he saw the general's hand already on the pommel of his sword.

"You," Ursicinus said, his voice low but sharp enough to cut glass. "You sit here like a eunuch while the province burns. Asochis has just fallen, in case you haven't received the news as yet. This Patricius, whoever he is, marches next against Simonias. And what do you do? Nothing. Not a spear raised. Not a cohort dispatched. The five legions in the city rust with age. You just lie there on your sedan, suffusing your mouth with grapes."

Flaccus lifted a hand in protest, voice trembling but controlled. "Violence breeds violence, Ursicinus. Do you not read the words of our Lord, Jesus Christ? These uprisings are nothing more than sparks. If left alone, they will smolder out. I have governed through patience, not the whip. Trust me, it is the only way."

The general slammed a fist down on the table, shattering a clay cup. "Patience? Cowardice is more like it! You disgrace the purple stripe you wear. You let rebels raise banners over Roman towns, and you talk of smoldering sparks? The province is aflame! As Legate, aren't you supposed to be the law? I see no laws being enforced, so what exactly is your position?"

Flaccus stood, attempting dignity, but his knees betrayed him with a slight tremor. "I am governor by decree of the Senate. You have no right to challenge me. I am…"

He got no further. Ursicinus crossed the space between them in three strides and struck him across the face with an armored backhand. Blood splattered across the cushions. The governor stumbled, clutching at his cheek.

"By right of Rome's survival, I claim this province!" Ursicinus roared. He grabbed Flaccus by the throat, dragging him from the couch like a rag doll, slamming him against a marble column. "You speak of decrees while rebels spit on our standards. You are unfit, Flaccus. You are either a coward or a traitor. Which is it?"

Flaccus gagged, clawing at the iron grip. "I… I am neither…"

The general slammed him again, cracking his head against stone. "Then you are merely useless!"

The guards stirred but froze when Ursicinus's glare fell on them. None dared move. He lifted Flaccus and hurled him across the floor. Then came the boots. Once, twice, again and again directly into ribs, into stomach, until the governor curled like a dying insect, whimpering in fetal position.

"You will yield the treasury," Ursicinus spat. "Every aureus, every denarius of silver, every measure of grain will be handed over to me. My legions will be outfitted at once. You have wasted enough time and brought enough shame upon the Empire."

Flaccus coughed blood, his teeth stained pink with it. "If you strip the treasury, you will ruin us all. The province cannot survive an endless war."

"The province cannot survive you," Ursicinus snapped, lifting him by the hair. "Give me one good reason not to crush your skull against this floor."

"Because I know this land," he sputtered. "I know these people. My connections here are invaluable and without them you will soon realize that this land will take everything from you unless you learn how to play its game. It will swallow you whole. I can help you master it."

"You?" Ursicinus laughed. "I think you've done enough damage to this province by now. The only thing I want to do with you now is put you in the slave hold of a galley and make you row your way back to Constantinople."

"You wouldn't dare do that," he protested, knowing full well there wasn't anything that would please Ursicinus more than doing so.

"You have no idea what I'm willing to do," Ursicinus growled. His leg kicked out once again and Flaccus recoiled in tremendous pain.

Perhaps it was the pain, perhaps it was fear, but something loosened Flaccus's tongue completely. His eyes rolled with desperation, and he croaked, "There… there is another way. Rome has a hold… a leash… on the Jews. Their Patriarch—Hillel. He is ours. Owned."

Ursicinus froze, breath heavy, his knuckles white. "Speak now while I've still left you breathing!"

Flaccus coughed again, spitting a clot onto the tiles. "The Patriarchate is bound to Rome. Hillel bends because we feed him, we clothe him, we let him sit in pomp while his people call him holy. He will do what Rome commands. Through him we control the Law itself, their hearts, their identities, anything we want them to do. Use him, and you can turn this rebellion to ash without lifting a sword. You can get the Jews to destroy themselves. In so doing you'll save thousands of Roman lives."

For the first time since entering, Ursicinus did not strike. He stared down at the broken governor, chest heaving, weighing the revelation.

"So," he said at last, voice grim, "the key is not sword nor spear, but this Patriarch. You say he is a friend of yours and that Rome holds his leash, and through him, all Judea. Are you willing to wage your life on this?"

Flaccus sagged in his arms, half-conscious, whispering, "Yes… yes. But if you don't handle him properly, then instead you will break the leash forever. That's why you need me to do it."

Ursicinus released him, letting him crumple to the floor like discarded parchment. He turned to the guards, who still stood frozen. "Secure the treasury. Post a cohort at every vault. The wealth of this province belongs to Rome's legions now. As for this man," he pointed to Flaccus, "Get him some help so that he's speaking again."

The soldiers snapped to attention and hurried off, eager to escape the suffocating fury of their commander. Through the colonnade, Ursicinus could already hear the echo of iron boots as his men poured toward the treasury halls.

He glanced back once at Flaccus, who lay groaning, a wreck of blood and silk. "You will live," he said coldly, "but only because you have given me a need to let you do so. Do not mistake mercy for weakness."

With that, Ursicinus swept across the chamber, the hem of his cloak streaked with the governor's blood. He climbed the steps to the outer balcony and gazed east, where the hills of Judea shimmered in the dying light. Somewhere out there, the rebels gathered strength, believing Rome to be fractured and impotent. He would show them that belief would be a serious mistake on their part.

He turned to his aide, a hard-faced tribune who had followed silently behind, saying not a word all this time. "Give the governor two days to arrange for this patriarch to come to me here in Caesarea. And if he doesn't, then send riders to Tiberias," Ursicinus instructed. "And let this Patriarch know that I personally have summoned him to Caesarea at once. Tell him Rome requires his presence. He will come willingly, or I will drag him here in chains."

The tribune bowed, signaling his readiness. "And if I should find that the governor is not taking care of the matter himself, what should I do with him?"

"Nothing," Ursicinus was quite blunt. "If that should be the case, it will be my pleasure to take care of the matter personally." Ursicinus stood tall, hands clasped behind his back. "The glory of Rome will be restored. Let the rebels cheer their fleeting victories," he murmured. "By the time this so-called Patriarch bends to my every whim, Palestina will remember who owns her soul."

The sea breeze carried the faint smell of blood from within the palace. Behind him, Flaccus's groans echoed across the marble hall.

"I think I've changed my mind," Ursicinus commented to the tribune. "I somehow doubt that the governor will be in any state to communicate sufficiently in the next couple of days. I think it best that you go immediately to Tiberias and summon this Hillel, yourself."

"I will do so immediately, excellency, but didn't the governor say something about the patriarch only responding to his requests?"

"I believe the governor may have overestimated his influence," the general replied as he looked back on the skeleton of a man still scrawled across the floor. "If there's one thing I know about traitors, it's that they march to a different set of principles from anyone else. And their first and foremost principle is self-preservation. Threaten the life of this patriarch and his family and I guarantee he will dance to our tune."

"In that case, I presume we no longer need the assistance of the governor," the tribune suggested.

"That's correct," Ursicinus agreed. "Put him on the next boat sailing to Constantinople with a message to the Emperor, 'Here lies the man who let this war get out of control.'"

"As you command, excellency."

CHAPTER XXVIII: SAMPSON & DELILAH

The moon hung low over Caesarea Maritima, looking like a dull silver coin smudged by clouds. The night air was heavy with salt and feeling damp, the sea endlessly murmuring to the shore as if reciting an old, half-forgotten sonnet. A Roman galley, shadow-black, swayed in the protected harbor like a beast at rest. Torches flickered under archways of the imperial compound, but most of the city slept, oblivious to the gathering of vipers in its heart.

Beneath the granite columns of the provincial praetorium, two figures stood cloaked in the gloom of a shuttered audience chamber. One tall and broad-shouldered, girded in armor that glinted faintly in the low lamplight. It was Flavius Ursicinus, General of the Eastern Legions. The other, shorter, wrapped in a dark mantle that concealed his form and obscured his face was Judah Hillel ben Gamaliel, known simply as Hillel II, Patriarch of the Jews of Palestina.

"Your cloak, Rabbi," Ursicinus said, his Latin thickened with the roughness of his short time on the Danube frontier, "you may remove it now." He gestured toward the chamber's oil brazier. "You will find no daggers in this room if you are concerned. Neither have I brought any scribes or secretaries with me. I assure you that we are all alone."

"And I," said Hillel, unclasping the cloak with slow, measured grace, "have brought no Torah." It was a joke but it took a while for its meaning to dawn on Ursicinus.

Finally, the general laughed. "A good one, Rabbi, as if you could convert me."

The two men regarded each other more carefully. Ursicinus, with his cruel, weather-hardened face carved by years of campaigning in Syria, Armenia, and Mesopotamia. Hillel, brown skinned and owl-eyed, lips pursed in the eternal pose of careful calculation. He did not look like a traitor, Ursicinus thought, but then, traitors rarely do.

"I assume," Ursicinus began, pouring two cups of dark wine, "that I did not summon you here so that you could deliver a sermon, nor to beg for your city's forgiveness in its siding with the rebel cause."

Hillel was caught off guard by Ursicinus's indication that he would not consider absolving Tiberias of taking part in the insurrection.

"I...I..." the rabbi stuttered. "You summoned me, excellency."

"Yes, I did. I just wanted to ensure you weren't going to bore me with a list of prior demands. I already know what you wrote to the prelate, Marcus Severinus. He passed your letter on to me. He informed me that you are a collaborator that I can trust."

Hillel did not answer at first. He accepted the cup without thanks, held it, but did not drink. His eyes wandered to the map laid out on the marble table behind Ursicinus, red ink tracing the roads of Galilee, black lines marking recent skirmishes. The names of rebels were written prominently in the margins. He saw the name Patricius scribbled beside the hill country of Tiberias. Most of the names were the ones he had provided to Marcus Severinus.

"My people," Hillel said at last, "are a stiff-necked nation. Always have been. We argue with each other more than we ever do with the Romans. We are theologians at heart, not warriors."

Ursicinus grunted. "But a collaborator is much more than someone having a difference of opinion, would you not agree?"

Hillel fell silent.

"Don't get me wrong. I have no issue with you willing to sacrifice some of your people in order to pursue peace with Rome. Considering how much damage your countrymen have already inflicted on the Roman garrisons, I find myself disagreeing with you. There are those among you that are definitely warriors. And you breed them by the thousands. Rebels, I mean. Like lice in a soldier's tunic. That's why I can appreciate someone like yourself that is an independent thinker."

Hillel's face twitched, just slightly. "Every people dreams of freedom, General. Even cattle revolt when the yoke rubs too raw. But dreams are not realities. They are convenient fictions, useful to inspire…but dangerous when mistaken for destiny."

Ursicinus crossed his arms. "Then why did I need to summon you if you have already seen through the illusion? Go and stop your people from continuing this mistake yourself and we can end this war on more agreeable terms. If you rely on me to stop it, then it will not end so well for your people. That I can assure you."

"If only it was that simple," Hillel sighed. "But as long as they think they have found their Messiah they will follow him, even if he were to go against the Gates of Hell."

"So, if you can't get the people to follow you, then I am just wasting my time summoning you here. I already know what I have to do. I thought you would have realized that your presence here meant I was going to provide you with an opportunity to save your people. Now you are telling me you can do nothing. If you cannot provide solutions then I don't need you to advise me." It was clear that Ursicinus was about to lose his temper.

Hillel stepped closer to the general. "I did come with a possible plan that I believe will interest you. I have come to offer you something your legions have not been able to take. Something that will end this farce of a revolt without burning half of Judea to ash in the process."

The general's brow arched. "Go on. You've gained my interest."

Hillel leaned in slightly, as if sharing a confession. "You hunt Natronai, whom you know as Patricius. He calls himself a warrior of the people, a Messiah, and that is dangerous. At his right hand, is the sage of Sepphoris, the one named Isaac."

"I know of their names," Ursicinus said, dryly. "I know the blood they've spilled. I know the towns they've stirred to madness. I know they move with secrecy and spirit, like shadows. So, what has any of this to do with you? You haven't told me anything I didn't already know. Don't waste my time, rabbi on worthless prattle."

"I can give them to you," Hillel spurted out the words that Ursicinus only dreamed of hearing.

A silence fell between them, the kind that stretches into the bones.

Ursicinus narrowed his eyes. "You? I have my scouts out searching for them night and day and not one of them can tell me where his men are camped. What makes you think you can find their encampment?

Hillel turned from him, taking a few steps toward the brazier. The fire glinted in his eyes like reflected sin. "I did not say I could deliver his army by locating their camp, I said I could deliver the two leaders into your hands."

The general wanted to laugh but he could see that the rabbi was being serious. "You think you can deliver the both of them. How?"

"Through my daughter, Havilah. She is…how should I say this…the beloved of Natronai. He is drawn to her like a fly to honey."

Ursicinus looked surprised. "Beloved?" the Roman said, with a grin drawn from a half sneer, half intrigue. "So, this supposed miraculous holy man has earthly appetites for the flesh? Is that what you are saying?"

"He is no holy man," Hillel replied, coldly. "He is a zealot. A charlatan. A child playing prophet. But like all men, he has a vulnerability. His flesh has been pierced, not by your spears, but by my daughter's eyes. He would do anything to see her again. Anything to protect her. She is his weakness and the way we can draw him out to be captured."

"And does your daughter return this affection?"

Hillel gave a faint shrug. "Perhaps. She is young. Impressionable. But she will do as she is told."

Ursicinus chuckled. 'I've met no such daughters in my life willing to listen to their fathers when it comes to matters of love. Yours must be the exception. But tell me why a father would betray his own daughter? You must realize that she will never forgive you for such a betrayal."

"It is a risk," Hillel admitted, "but my son has convinced me that my duty is to my people and not to the flesh of my flesh. Though I admit there is no pride in it, my son is correct. He says that God would not have permitted such a binding of hearts if it wasn't for the purpose of delivering our enemies into our hands by their own weakness. I believe he is right."

"You will risk your daughter's love for a higher ideal. Is that what you are saying to me?"

"Yes," Hillel acknowledged he was aware of the sacrifice. "If I can make her believe I have had a change of heart, then I can have Natronai summoned through her. Lured away from the protection of his forces. And with him, his companion, Isaac.

The lion and the flame, delivered into your hands without a fight, both at the same time."

"There is always a fight," the general corrected him. "Whether it be two men or two hundred, none of them ever surrender peacefully. Your daughter may even be harmed in such a scuffle. Are you willing to sacrifice your own daughter?"

Hillel didn't hesitate. "Would you not for the sake of peace?"

The Roman said nothing for a moment. Then, with brutal calm replied, "I have sacrificed sons in the name of war. I am not so certain I would have done so willingly in the pursuit of peace."

"I ask nothing in return for her safety," Hillel continued, "though I do pray that she can be spared by your men. But if she falls in the process, that is the price of peace and it would be by God's will. But I do have terms, and they are terms for my people, which are my major concern."

"Of course you do," Ursicinus acknowledged with a devilish smile on his lips. "How could I even imagine you would come here without your list of terms?" he said sarcastically.

"There will be no vengeance against the people. No fire and slaughter. You may sell Natronai's soldiers into slavery if you wish. Strip them naked and brand them with Caesar's seal, as it is what they deserve for taking arms against the empire, but the common people must be left unharmed. Their towns must be spared. They are as much a victim of this rebellion as any other innocent."

"And that is all?"

"The major learning centers of Tiberias, Sepphoris, and Jaffa must be left untouched. The Sanhedrin must be allowed to continue to function. And the Patriarchate must remain under my family."

"I have heard that this Patricius has set up his own Sanhedrin. Which one do you want me to spare?"

"There is only one Sanhedrin and that is the one under my leadership," Hillel retorted.

"Of course. So I presume you wish to continue collecting Rome's taxes, Is that correct?" The general was beginning to see Hillel's true motivation more clearly.

"Precisely. After all, my family is the only one the Emperor can truly trust with such duties."

Ursicinus laughed, brandishing a harsh bark of mirth. "You cloak your ambition in sanctity, Rabbi. You almost had me fooled and believing that you would sacrifice your own daughter for the sake of protecting the people but now I see you more clearly. But do not worry, I admire that. I have always admired snakes with silk tongues."

"I do not do this for ambition," Hillel lied, attempting to make himself sound more convincing. "I do this because if history has taught me one thing, it is that when you resist Rome, Rome buries you and erases you from history. But when you serve Rome, Rome always rewards you and sometimes, in doing so, she forgets to kill you."

The general refilled his cup. "Tell me, Rabbi Hillel. How exactly will you trap them? Isaac and Natronai are cautious. Cleverer than most in my experience. They have eluded my scouts and informants for months and I'm not even close to identifying their location. Even if your daughter summons him, how do you guarantee that he will come and furthermore bring the Sepphorian with him?"

Hillel's lips curled into the faintest smile. "I have not worked out all the details yet but I plan on giving them what they both desire most of all."

Ursicinus raised a brow. "Then why should I believe you if you don't even have a plan as yet?"

"Because for the sake of marriage, even the smartest of men will walk into an obvious trap." Hillel walked slowly towards the map on the table and tapped a finger on Tiberias. "Are you familiar with the story of Samson and Delilah, General?"

The Roman frowned. "Samson…some Hebrew folk tale? I'm a general, not a schoolteacher."

"Then let me tell it," Hillel said, quietly. "There was once a man, mighty and gifted, chosen by God. He had the strength of lions and the courage of kings. But he kept falling in love with Philistine women who indirectly served his enemies. Even though they loved him, they would still unwittingly betray him. In the case of Delilah, night after night, she coaxed him, caressed him, made love to him until he told her the secret of his great strength. She cut his hair while he slept to see if it was true. And when he awoke, his enemies were upon him. Blind and broken, he was dragged in chains to the city of Gaza, where he finally met his end."

"Sounds familiar," Ursicinus said. "We have tales like that too. Rome always wins in the end."

"And so, it shall here," Hillel said. "With my daughter unwittingly serving as his Delilah."

Ursicinus chuckled again. "And you, of course, must be the Philistine priest in this story."

"No," said Hillel, somewhat offended by the comment. "I am merely the servant of God, doing that which must be done."

"Yes, of course. If you say so," Ursicinus grinned.

The silence that followed was as thick as oil. The Roman paced once around the table, then extended his hand. "You'll have your terms. If you deliver them alive or even dead, I will honor your requests. The learning centers will be allowed to teach. The Sanhedrin will continue. Your family will remain the patriarchy. But fail me…and I will salt your cities until not even the faintest memory remains."

Hillel took the hand. It was like gripping an iron statue but at the same time slippery.

Ursicinus released his grip. "And one more thing."

"Yes?" Hillel was afraid to ask.

"I am curious. If your daughter does die in this…this betrayal of her love, will you still mourn her?"

Hillel said nothing. Only lowered his eyes. He knew the question was mocking him.

"No," Ursicinus said, answering his own question. "You won't. That is why I think I can trust you."

That night, Hillel left his chambers and walked barefoot through the corridor, towards the locked room where Havilah slept since her return with her brother. He turned the key and quietly opened the door. Inside the bed chamber, Havilah slept on the cot, her dark hair spilling like ink across the blanket. A single oil lamp flickered beside her. She looked peaceful and for a moment her father was having second thoughts regarding his arrangement with the general. He watched her for a long time, motionless.

Then, slowly, he sat beside her and whispered, "You are beautiful, my daughter. And beauty is the ultimate weapon."

She stirred faintly but did not wake.

"You will deliver our people. And you will destroy him. That is the will of God."

CHAPTER XXIX: TEMPLE REMNANTS

The spring of 352 dawned late over Judea, its winds laced with the scent of wild hyssop and dry earth. The almond trees bloomed early that year, a tender white against the battered hills. Under crystal blue skies, Patricius marched, no longer as the marauder he had once been, but as the avenger of a shattered people, a redeemer crowned not with gold, but with dust and the bitter prayers of the dispossessed.

His men came in silence before dawn, boots muffled as they tread upon the dust of centuries. The walls of Jerusalem loomed ahead. They were thick, ancient, now manned by a contingent of complacent Roman auxiliaries and half-trained Christian militiamen who assumed that no rebel force would dare challenge the might of Rome's claim to the sacred city.

This day they were wrong.

Natronai had encircled the city during the night, his men hidden in the numerous olive groves that surrounded the city and behind broken aqueducts that no longer carried water. When the first horn sounded, it was not a shofar but the horn of war. The sound was low, guttural, and primal.

Then came the fire.

Arrows ignited in pitch sailed over the walls in arcs, falling like stars upon the Roman barracks and watchtowers. One tower burst into flame as a shrieking sentry plunged to his death below, his robes smouldering. Roman soldiers scrambled in confusion, some barely roused from their beds, dragging on armor and seizing weapons as the enemy breached the Lion Gate.

Natronai led the assault himself.

He crashed through the entrance with his elite guard, his men armed with curved Judean blades and North African spears looted from their previous campaigns. The first Roman he encountered died without a sound, his throat sliced clean to the spine. A second tried to block his path with a pilum but Natronai smashed his shield aside and split the man's face down to the teeth.

Blood soaked the sandstone streets as Isaac's infantry poured through the northern breach. They met the Roman cohort near the Cardo, a narrow thoroughfare of flagstones and broken colonnades. There, the fight turned savage.

Isaac's men fought in tight formation, slamming shields into Roman lines, then jabbing low with daggers and short swords. The Romans tried to hold their ground, but their numbers were too few. Their commander, a grey-haired tribune named

Marcus Livius, rallied a unit of twenty and charged from the Church of the Holy Sepulchre with surprising fury. One of his men drove a spear straight through the chest of a Galilean rebel, pinning him against a wall like a swatted fly.

But before Livius could repel the rebel force, Natronai had arrived to support Isaac's men. He hurled a broken roof tile into the tribune's face, blinding him in one eye, then surged forward and ran him through the belly. Livius screamed, coughing blood, and died grasping the hilt of the sword still buried in his gut. The rest of the Romans broke and fled but most did not make it far. Cut down in the alleys or skewered as they tried to scale the inner wall until they suffered total defeat.

Isaac kicked over a Roman standard, blood-spattered and frayed. "They were more prepared than I expected," he muttered.

"They had time to pray," Natronai growled, pulling a javelin from a corpse's throat. "Let's make sure their god hears them."

Bodies were left to litter the streets by midday. What remained of the Roman garrison fell back to the Antonia Fortress, making a last stand atop the ruins of their once-proud tower. Flaming carts were pushed up the slope as Galilean archers rained death from rooftops. Trapped, with no opportunity to escape, a barrel of pitch was rolled into the fortress gate and set ablaze, turning the old stronghold into a blazing kiln.

By the time Natronai entered the compound, the air reeked of burnt flesh and scorched hair. He stepped over a Roman soldier whose legs had been severed and saw the man still muttering prayers. He ended the suffering with a clean thrust, murmuring the Shema under his breath.

The path to the Temple mount was now clear and Natronai led his men on to the immense platform that had been forbidden to Jews to walk upon for two hundred years. Natronai and Isaac stepped together onto the Temple mount platform, the tramp of their sandals echoing against the massive retaining walls that had once borne the glory of both Solomon's and Herod's Temples. The air was thin and dry, touched with the dust of centuries, but beneath it lay something heavier, an ache of memory, a pulse that none of them had ever felt but all somehow recognized. For the first time in generations, Jews walked once more upon the place where their fathers had worshipped, where the Holy Presence was said to have rested between the wings of the cherubim.

The soldiers, hardened men who had faced swords and fire, now stood awestruck. Some wept openly, their calloused hands brushing across the ancient paving stones as if touching the hem of eternity itself. Isaac looked to Natronai and whispered, "It is ours again." His voice trembled, half in joy, half in disbelief.

But at the heart of the mount, where the Foundation Stone lay hidden, rose an intrusion that struck them like a dagger. A small stone church, plain but resolute, stood upon the very site of the Holy of Holies. Its wooden cross cast a long shadow across the platform. Around it clustered priests and pilgrims, garbed in Christian robes, their chants filling the air with foreign hymns. They did not cower at the sight of armed men. Instead, their faces twisted with contempt, their eyes hard with defiance, as if daring the Jews to assert ownership over what was rightfully theirs.

Natronai's jaw tightened. His hand hovered at the hilt of his sword, though it was not fear but fury that gripped him. "This…" he spat, "this insult stands upon the navel of the world. Our fathers bled for this place and look what has been raised in mockery of them." He turned to his men, his voice rising with the steel of command. "Tear it down. Burn it. Let no hand or tongue stay you. This blasphemy will not remain."

With a roar, the soldiers surged forward. The priests cried out, some cursing, others clutching their relics, but none dared stand in the way of men whose hearts burned with centuries of longing. Beams cracked, stones tumbled, and smoke soon curled into the sky as fire consumed the wooden cross and rafters. The scent of incense was replaced by the acrid stench of ash.

Yet even as the flames climbed, Natronai felt no triumph. He stood apart, gazing not at the ruin but at the scar it revealed—the bare, violated stone that should have been the dwelling of the Divine. His elation of reclaiming the mount warred with a deep, hollow grief. Joy and despair mingled until he could scarcely breathe.

Isaac laid a hand on his shoulder. "Shall we rededicate it now, Patricius? A lamb can be brought, an altar raised."

Natronai shook his head, his eyes fixed upon the blackened rubble. "Not today. Not amidst the stench of their desecration. This mountain deserves purity, not haste. We will come again when the people are ready, when the city itself has been made clean. Then we will sacrifice."

The soldiers fell silent, watching their leader. Around them, the last timbers of the church collapsed into glowing embers, sparks drifting upward into the darkening sky. They stood upon holy ground, long defiled, now reclaimed, and waiting. For the first time in generations, the Temple mount belonged to them once more.

When the rest of the city of Jerusalem finally fell, it fell hard. The banner of Rome was torn down and trampled in the dust. Above the city, on the highest slope of the Mount of Olives, Natronai stood, his men arrayed behind him, as he beheld the Holy City, imagining it in its former glory. Over and over the men shouted the title of Patricius, making it clear that Natronai was now the master of Jerusalem.

Despite the accolades, their Patricius was not pleased. The vision before him was not the Jerusalem of old, praised in legends for its beauty. This Jerusalem was an abomination of what once was, laying quietly under the soft haze of the late afternoon sun, which revealed all her blemishes. Her walls glowed a pale gold as the rays reflected of disintegrating plaster. From the Mount of Olives, the city still looked somewhat majestic, sprawling across the ridges and valleys like a crown cast from stone, but as Natronai and Isaac descended into the heart of her streets, the illusion quickly dissolved.

They walked side by side, neither in armor nor in haste, their sandals scuffing ancient flagstones worn smooth by centuries. The Patricius had removed his sword in respect for the city, though the men protecting them still held their weapons. For now, the battle was over, and Natronai believed the city was too sacred to enter with his blood covered sword.

"Look at her," Natronai murmured, gesturing at the winding alleyways ahead. "She's dressed in another man's skin, like rags on a vagrant!" What remained was something deeper, leaving an ache in the bones of the earth itself.

They passed beneath an arch inscribed in Greek, which read, dedicated to Kyrios Iesous Christos, Lord Jesus Christ. The arch bore the seal of Constantine, etched over the remnants of older carvings, Hebrew letters now barely visible beneath the chisel marks of erasure.

Isaac glanced sideways. "It is the new order. Erase anything that shows the land's Jewish past."

"They have done a good job of it," Natronai commented. "It will take years to restore everything that they have defaced and defiled."

They entered the forum square, a once a bustling marketplace of Jewish traders, scholars, and craftsmen but now it stood eerily quiet, dominated by a massive basilica built in imperial Roman style but adorned with foreign symbols. A crowd of Christian pilgrims, mostly pale-skinned and wide-eyed, huddled around a man who held up a darkened piece of wood.

"That's the nail," he declared. "One of the very ones that pierced the Messiah's hand!"

They gasped in reverence, some weeping, others falling to their knees. Another monk pulled back a silk cloth to reveal what he claimed was the true garment of Christ. An old woman clutched a splinter of wood to her chest, muttering prayers in Latin.

Ashurbanipol surrounded by his officers was already by the stall watching when the two of them approached.

"Were you thinking of buying?" Natronai teased his Zoroastrian general.

"I do not understand all of this," Ashurbanipol replied, sounding confused.

"A city of relics," Natronai said coldly. "They have turned faith into a scavenger hunt. Is this what their religion is all about?"

"More like a city of fools," Ashurbanipol was far more blunt in his assessment.

Isaac's face was unreadable. "It is their way. They search for proof where none was given."

"I am surprised," Natronai admitted. "We have just taken the city, eliminated their Roman protectors, and they're not even paying us any attention. They don't have the slightest fear of us."

Ashurbanipol shook his head, staring at the pilgrims scrambling through the streets, sketching crosses into the dust, asking directions to Golgotha as if it were a shrine with a ticket booth.

"They build churches on every rock they believe he may have touched, every place he might have walked. They break open graves hoping to find his shadow. They search for the Ark but ignore the covenant. Is this what they have coveted so greedily that the Empire has fought war after war with us in order to hold on to their control of this land? I don't understand it."

"It is their justification," Isaac explained. "Take away their faith that somehow this land must be special to their god and there would be nothing to fight over, other than dust and sand. So, they fill their heads with the mystic divine in order to justify their reasons for taking the land from us."

"They think these rusted nails and splinters of wood are worth losing their lives over?" Ashurbanipol still could not fathom why the Romans would cling so strenuously to a land that has offered them nothing but corpses to fill their cemeteries.

"It is their way of believing that God has made them a promise as well," Isaac explained. "Whereas we are tied to the land through the covenant that God made with Abraham, the Christians want to believe they have a similar tie through these relics."

Natronai shook his head. "It is hard to believe that we had to fight to take a city where the only thing of value to our enemy is a street of hawkers selling counterfeit trinkets and religious tokens. Well, let us see what else there is to see."

They moved on, toward the old Jewish quarter. The heart of the city had been carved out and repaved in stone not native to Judea. Marble statues of Roman saints lined the sides of what had once been the Path of the Priests, that the Kohenim had taken on their way to the Temple. In place of study halls and Torah scrolls, there were small chapels filled with incense and golden icons of Mary weeping.

The air was thick with the scent of burning frankincense and the monotonous chant of Latin hymns. Young monks debated fiercely over which cave Mary Magdalene had cried in, while priests posted outside the Holy Sepulchre stared blankly at pilgrims, bored yet protective of the site as if it were the emperor's own tomb.

A blind beggar nearby murmured the Shema under his breath. Natronai paused and knelt beside the man.

"You are of the children of Israel?" he asked softly.

The old man tilted his head, curious as he deciphered Natronai's Hebrew dialect. "I am what's left of them. Only a few thousand now. The Romans don't like us living in our own city, so many have left. But you are not from here."

"No, I am from Babylon," Natronai replied.

"Oh," the blind man reacted. "There is word that a great leader is coming from Babylon to rescue us. They call him the Patricius. Have you heard of him?"

"Yes, in fact Patricius and his army has just taken control of the city this very day."

The old man cracked a toothless smile. "What would he possibly want with this city of dry old bones? There is nothing here for us. Not too bright if he wasted his men to take possession of this pile of trash. Nothing here worth dying for."

The words stung Natronai in his heart. Isaac looked away.

"I think he did it in order to revive a dream," Natronai offered his reasoning. "As long as Jerusalem lives, so too does the soul of the Jewish people. Some things he believes are worth dying for."

"Well, if you see him," the old man continued, "tell him that old Samuel thinks him a fool for wasting his time and his men's lives here. Jerusalem is the place where we old Jews come to die and be buried, nothing more."

"I promise to pass on your words to him," Natronai clasped the beggar on the shoulder as he stood up and prepared to leave.

As they rose again, Natronai let his eyes drift across the broad avenue. He could see it now. The Jewish city had not merely been conquered; it had been overwritten. Not destroyed but repurposed, like a sacred scroll scraped clean and inked over with foreign myths to conceal its original identity. And all of it, all this frenzy and fervour and fire, had emerged from the death of a single Jewish man.

He turned to Isaac. "How can this be? How could the crucifixion of one Jewish teacher, one heretic, upend the empires of the earth?"

Isaac walked in silence for a few paces before answering. "Because they choose to make of him much more than a man."

Natronai stopped walking. "That still doesn't tell me the 'why'. Even we," he said slowly, "had prophets. Men of miracles. Even Elijah, who called down fire from heaven, did not turn the world upside down. But this Jeshua, they crucified him like a common criminal and yet here we are… churches built in his name and Rome bending the knee to a Jew they never knew."

He gazed up at the massive dome of the Church of the Resurrection, standing where the tomb of a Davidic king should have been.

"This is madness," he whispered. "Not faith. Utter madness."

They walked on in silence, descending further into the remains of the Jewish quarter, a cramped cluster of narrow alleys and soot-stained walls. Hebrew letters marked doorposts, often scratched hastily above crosses. Fear hung in the air like damp smoke. The few thousand Jews who remained peered out from behind shuttered windows. Their eyes did not light up at the sight of their Patricius but only flickered with dull recognition. They had seen liberators before. But more than that, they had seen what followed.

A mother tugged her child inside as they passed. A young man, wearing a Roman tunic adorned in Jewish fringes, simply turned away.

"They don't believe it will last," Isaac muttered.

"Perhaps they're right," Natronai replied. "Unless we find a way to end this war quickly and begin to rebuild the city, then there is no place for them here. Not anymore."

The sun began to dip below the ridge. The shadow of the western wall stretched long and thin across the street like a wound. They returned to the steps of the Temple Mount. The smell of charred wood still lingered from the dismantled church. Nothing remained intact.

Natronai looked back at the city behind him. Jerusalem, the once beautiful bride of God, now dressed in unfamiliar garb, chanting songs to a man she once crucified. He sat on the step and whispered aloud, "She doesn't know who she is anymore."

Isaac didn't answer. There was no answer.

Only silence.

And the echo of old prayers lost in new tongues.

For the next few days, Natronai had sealed himself away from his closest advisors and officers. He needed time to think, time to question why he had come to Jerusalem at all. Their camp in Jerusalem had become quiet; eerily so. Bells occasionally rang from towers that bore not any Hebrew call to prayer, nor the echoing of a shofar, but the solemn peal of churches dedicated to foreign saints. Crosses gleamed atop domes where once the synagogues had been housed. Greek inscriptions, not Hebrew, lined the lintels of great stone halls. The Roman Church, with Constantine's blessing, had reshaped the city in its image. Jewish life had been boxed into a miserable quarter along the eastern wall, its inhabitants cowed, hollow-eyed, and wary. They emerged only after it was apparent the Roman soldiers had either been killed or driven out, staring at Patricius and his men with something between awe and disbelief. Still unable to trust that they had been liberated and for the first time in their lives, they were free.

It was time. Natronai knew he could not leave the Temple Mount desecrated. Isaac walked beside him in silence, the weight of history pressing on both men. The Temple Mount, *Har HaBayit* and the *Bayit Hamikdosh* had become an obscenity. They climbed it in a state of mourning. The small church that once sat atop the ruins, was now nothing but charred ashes blowing in the wind. The Roman-built homes whose courtyards had sprawled irreverently across the ancient foundations beside the church were now nothing more than patches of black tar staining the massive stones.

Natronai reflected on the fact that children had been playing in the very courts where Levites had once sung psalms. And olive trees now grew wild between the broken paving stones. There was no trace of the Ark, no menorah, no altar. Only weeds. And defiled stones.

Natronai said nothing. He simply walked until he reached the old Foundation Stone, barely visible beneath the soil and ash of centuries. He knelt, hands trembling. He touched the rock as if it might still pulse with memory. He had dreamed of it since childhood. The very name, *Yerushalayim*, burned in his chest like an eternal flame. But this day, when he climbed the Mount, he found no gold, no choirs, no fire from heaven. Natronai stopped. His knees clashing against the ground. "No," he whispered. "No…"

Isaac knelt beside him.

"There used to be courts here," Natronai said, gesturing wildly. "The altar, the inner sanctum…right here! And now…this?" While still on his knees, he wept. Not just for the ruins, but for what had become of his people. Not conquered but essentially erased by Rome. Tears fell, not as a soldier's grief, but as a son's grief for a mother exiled, for a people degraded, for a God who seemed so distant from this place. His sobs broke through the silence of the Mount, and even his guards turned away, unwilling to look upon their commander so undone.

"We must clean away the sins of the past," their Patricius stopped crying and gave an order. "I want the soil scraped, the Mount washed in water and sprinkled with hyssop, according to the rites of old. It is time to take back what is rightfully ours."

It took three days. As instructed, the Mount was washed with water and scrubbed clean with hyssop. Priests, the descendants of a forgotten caste, were summoned from the Jewish quarter, their hands trembling as they recited ancient litanies. And then, with the sun setting in a burnished flame over the Judean hills, Natronai stepped forward once more, this time in linen robes hastily stitched by women from the Jewish quarter. They incorporated remnants of priestly patterns buried in memory. He stood before a crude stone altar rebuilt from the old Temple's foundations. Isaac stood nearby, arms crossed.

"You shouldn't do this," Isaac muttered. "Let one of the Kohenim from the Jewish Quarter complete the rites. Remember, the Hasmoneans did both, acted as both priest and king and look what happened. They cursed our line with their arrogance."

"I am no king," Natronai said softly. "Only a servant. My father is a scion of David. My mother is a daughter of Aaron. Unlike the Hasmoneans, I am both."

The lamb was brought forth, trembling in the arms of a Levite.

Natronai laid his hands upon it. "Blessed are You, Lord our God, King of the Universe," he recited, voice wavering, "who brings justice upon the earth, and remembers the covenant of Abraham, Isaac, and Jacob."

He drew the blade. The animal cried only once and then fell silent.

The blood was caught in a basin, then sprinkled on the stones. The fat was burned. The altar accepted the offering. Smoke rose high into the sky, dark against the burning red of dusk.

A hush fell upon everyone that witnessed the ceremony. And for a moment, one would swear, the holy mount held its breath. Some say the wind stilled. Others said they heard music on the breeze. But Natronai simply stood there, unmoving, as the fire consumed the offering. Then he turned away, robes stained with ash and blood.

Isaac looked on with mixed awe and dread. "We've taken the city," he said. "But can we actually restore her soul?"

Natronai, acting as Kohen Gadol, didn't answer. His hands were soaked with blood. His eyes with tears.

The celebration following the rededication of the Temple Mount was a poor excuse for a celebration. In the old hall of the Sanhedrin, which had been converted into a church library, Natronai sat with Isaac and his generals. The wine was untouched. The mood was solemn. Night had fallen over Jerusalem, and a chill settled into the stones of the city. Lanterns swayed gently in the breeze, their flickering light casting long shadows on the crumbling columns. The smell of roasting meat mingled with the lingering scent of burned incense, an odd marriage of both victory and sorrow.

"There is nothing for us here," Natronai said finally. "The city is lost to its past. It has become something else. God will deal with it, in His time. I was mistaken to think we could use it as our capital."

"You could rebuild, Patricius" one of his men offered.

"No," Natronai replied. "The glory of Jerusalem was not in her stones, but in her covenant. And that has been torn. We've taken the city, but her heart has already been broken ."

Later that night his generals and advisors spoke in hushed voices, hunched over maps and tally scrolls, debating supply lines, garrison strengths, and Roman retaliation.
But Patricius heard none of it. Instead, he stared at the flames. Not with the sharp gaze of a general plotting his next move, but with the hollow stare of a man who had just seen the ghost of something he'd spent his life searching for and realized it could not be touched.

"Tell me," he finally said suddenly, his voice cutting through the murmurs. "What did we actually achieve here?"

The generals fell silent.

Isaac frowned. "Jerusalem, my lord. We've taken her. The city is ours. That alone is a miracle."

"No," Patricius replied, shaking his head slowly. "It's not ours. Not really. Not in the way that matters. Others have come and changed her into something else."

"We can change her back," one of the generals offered a solution.

"We walked her streets. We saw her stones. Her faces. Her crosses." He let out a long breath. "Jerusalem is not asleep, waiting to be woken. She's dead. Her soul... necrotic. Eaten from the inside."

No one challenged his opinion. Even Isaac remained still.

"She has become a reliquary," Natronai continued bitterly, "a shrine for a god who never ruled her, for myths birthed in Roman tongues. The covenant has been paved over. The Law has been silenced. The Temple desecrated by tourists who weep over a hill and call it holy because a dead man once bled there." His hand gripped the hilt of his sword, then loosened. "They chant his name in the city of David. They sing to the cross while the blood of prophets cries out from the stones. I saw churches where study halls once stood. Saints where sages once taught. The city has changed hands but in the process her heart has been broken."

Isaac leaned forward. "The desecration can be undone. The Law can be restored."

"No," Patricius said, with a terrible stillness. "Not this time. Perhaps some time in the future but not now."

He looked around at the men who had followed him through fire and blood, who had watched him slaughter Romans at Beit Netofa, liberate Tiberias, and now stand upon Zion's ruins. He had always spoken with clarity, with conviction. But now... now he was no longer certain.

"Do you understand what this means?" he whispered. "If Jerusalem, the jewel of Israel, the city of the Great King, if she cannot be restored... then what are we fighting for? If the soul of this land has already been claimed by another god, how can we speak of freedom or covenant or redemption?" He ran a hand through his hair, fingers trembling. "I thought we were raising the bones of Israel. But what if all we're doing is animating a corpse?"

The words hit like stones.

Ashurbanipol exhaled sharply. "So, what then? We surrender?"

"No," Patricius replied. "Never surrender. I will fight to my very last breath against the scourge that is Rome. But..." His voice trailed off. He stood slowly, stepping away from the fire, gazing into the night toward the Temple Mount, its dark silhouette crowned now with emptiness. "I thought victory would taste like honey," he murmured. "Like wine poured on the altar. Like psalms returned to the wind."

He turned back to them, eyes raw with disillusion. "But it tastes like ash."

Isaac rose at last, placing a hand on Natronai's shoulder. "Then we don't fight to restore what was," he said softly. "We fight to prepare what will be. Your dream was to restore the ancient land of Israel. I say that dream has long since passed. We fight now to create a new Israel. The Israel promised by Isaiah, Micah and Zechariah. This is the age that they prophesized. The age of a new Israel and a new Jerusalem. First, we restore the land to the people and then later we build a new city to dedicate to God. We look not to the past but to the future!"

It was the first time that night that the men began to cheer, not for what once was, but for what will be.

Natronai didn't answer right away. His gaze lingered on the broken skyline. His soul felt untethered, drifting somewhere between the ruins of a dream and the harsh dawn of a new truth. "Yes, we will build a new Jerusalem in the same way that Zerubbabel, Ezra and Nehemiah did. Not relying on the bones of the past but on the soul of the future."

The Jewish army left the city of Jerusalem the next morning. Before he departed, Natronai wrote a message and had it posted on the walls of the Praetorium, the former Roman stronghold, knowing that once they had left, the Romans would return.

To Gallus, Caesar of Antioch:
You hold a city you do not know, and rule a people you do not understand.
You have crowned the ashes of Zion with your own image, but God sees.
And one day, what you have defiled will be made holy again.
This city does not belong to you. Nor to me. It belongs to the God who named it.
Remember that.
Natronai ben Nehemiah, Patricius of Zion.

And then, with his banner furled and his army solemn, he rode north to Galilee, leaving behind only the echo of shofar blasts, the blood of a lamb on the altar, and a city still aching for redemption. Behind him, Jerusalem stood silent. Cleansed but empty. Claimed but hollow.

A city waiting, once more, for the glory of God.

CHAPTER XXX: THE MIRROR CRACKS

The march northward had been hard and shrouded in disillusion. Dust clung to the soldiers' cloaks, and the sound of iron-shod sandals beating the earth echoed with the rhythm of a cause believed righteous. But the desolation of Jerusalem said otherwise. That their cause might be unreachable within a single lifetime. From the hills above, the city of Simonias came into view. Small and modest, walled against an outside world, its stonework reflected the late afternoon sun with a deceptive warmth. To many of Natronai's men, it looked like a prize awaiting their embrace, another city to swell their numbers, to give bread and refuge to the soldiers of Israel's rebirth. A reason to forget their experience in Jerusalem, the Holy City.

But as they descended into the valley, the silence from Simonias felt wrong. No banners were unfurled. No delegations of elders came forth bearing bread and salt. The gates remained shut, the towers watchful. A few curious heads appeared along the walls, then vanished quickly, replaced by Roman-crested helmets. The message was clear enough; Simonias would not receive them as brothers.

Natronai slowed his horse. Behind him, the column stretched long: farmers turned soldiers, zealots still drunk on sour dreams of Jerusalem's restoration, hardened military men like Ashurbanipol. They, too, saw the city's refusal, and murmurs spread like a pestilence.

"This is not what they promised," one of the younger men muttered. "Are they not Jews behind those walls?"

"Aye, Jews," another spat, "but Roman Jews. God save us from such."

The words stung Natronai more than he let show. To see Jews standing beneath Roman standards, especially here, far from Caesarea and the coastal centers of imperial power, was to feel betrayal in the marrow of his bones. He had imagined that his coming would stir something long buried in their hearts. Yet the city's shutters closed tight, and the silence of its streets told him his presence was not the herald of liberation, but the approach of a threat.

Ashurbanipol rode up beside him. The Persian was a great block of a man, scarred and sun-worn, with eyes narrowed into permanent suspicion. His voice was steady, low, made for command. "They know we are here, and they hide. That is all the proof you need, my lord. They are no friends of yours. They are enemies and should be treated as such."

Natronai's gaze lingered on the walls. "They are Jews, Ashurbanipol. Sons of Abraham. Would you have me raise sword against my own people?"

The general gave a shrug, as though the thought meant little. "A people divided against itself cannot stand. Today they are Jews, yes, but tomorrow they will be Romans in heart. Better to cut away rot before it spreads."

Natronai said nothing, but inside him a heaviness settled. He thought of Jerusalem, a week earlier, when he had mounted the Temple platform. The sting of finding a church upon the Holy of Holies had nearly unmanned him, yet he had told himself that God had chosen him, that the city would rally in time. But here, in Simonias, it seemed even the Jewish heartland was not waiting for his coming.

The column pitched camp outside the walls. Smoke rose as fires were lit, tents pitched in orderly rows. The sound of hammers striking stakes rang out against the stone cliffs. From the battlements of Simonias, the inhabitants peered down, not with awe, not with reverence, but with suspicion, even disdain.

As twilight deepened, the city gave no answer. No emissary sought parley. Only the dim glow of lamps behind shuttered windows betrayed that life continued within.

Natronai sat alone near his tent as the stars emerged. The men were restless. Some boasted loudly that the city would fall by morning if their Messiah willed it. Others whispered fears, wondering if this was a sign of things to come? What if the revolt was not heaven-blessed after all?

Natronai, hearing both voices, found his thoughts circling like wolves around a fire. Simonias was small, but it was symbolic. The ancient city of Shimron. To pass it by was to admit that not all of Israel was with him. To take it by force was to draw first blood against his own brethren. Either way, his mission would bear a scar.

When Isaac approached, the rabbi's steps were silent on the grass, his beard catching silver in the starlight. He knelt beside Natronai without speaking, and together they looked at the city on the hill.

Then Isaac murmured: "They have shut their gates to you, as Jerusalem shut its gates to the prophets of old. Do not forget what was written: those who deny the Lord's anointed will share in the fate of the wicked."

Natronai flinched, for Isaac's words struck where Ashurbanipol's had only scraped. He had hoped for welcome, for affirmation. Instead, Simonias had given him the bitter taste of division. And with that, the night deepened, heavy with choices to come.

The following morning, a gray mist rolled down from the hills, cloaking the camp in damp silence. The soldiers woke uneasily, their fires guttering. The walls of Simonias loomed above like a reproach, their towers indistinct behind the veil of fog. Natronai summoned his closest advisors to the command tent. The air inside was heavy with lamp smoke, wool cloaks dripping from the morning dew.

Ashurbanipol stood near the center, his armor stripped save for a heavy belt and sword. He had the air of a man who had already decided the matter. Isaac, by contrast, sat cross-legged on a mat, his hands folded over his staff, his eyes burning with the certainty of scripture. Several captains ringed the tent, men who had fought in the initial clashes against Roman patrols, their loyalty tested but not yet unbreakable.

Natronai remained standing, arms behind his back, his face pale with sleeplessness.

Ashurbanipol began without ceremony.

"My lord, there is no profit in hesitation. The city is small. Its walls are stone, yes, but not high, not Roman-built. A siege would be brief. If we storm Simonias now, we will claim provisions, weapons, and a stronghold from which to strike northward. If we linger, their silence will fester. The men are already whispering. They expected triumph, not this… waiting."

One of the captains, a weather-beaten man from the Galilee, nodded grimly. "The people do not open their gates because they do not fear us. That cannot stand. If we pass them by, others will follow their example."

Isaac lifted his staff, the gesture small yet commanding. His voice was calm, but every syllable struck like stone. "The Torah is clear. When Israel turns away from the Lord, judgment comes. Have you forgotten what Moses commanded concerning the towns that lead Israel astray? You shall put the inhabitants to the sword, and their cattle, and their spoil, and you shall burn the city with fire. Such is the justice of heaven against those who betray the covenant."

The tent fell silent at his words. Even the captains, hardened men, shifted uneasily. Natronai looked at Isaac, pain etched in his brow.

"Rabbi… my friend…these are Jews. They pray in the synagogues, they read the Law. Would you have me burn them as idolaters?"

"They pray in synagogues, yes," Isaac said coldly, "but under Roman protection. Do you not see? They place their trust not in the God of Israel but in the legions of Caesar. And by shutting their gates, they have denied God's chosen one. The Messiah has come, and they have spat in his face."

Ashurbanipol interjected, his rough voice cutting like a blade. "Messiah or not, rebellion cannot afford softness. You think the Romans will stay their hands because you spared one city? No, they will march with fire and crucifix. Mercy to traitors will only weaken you. A leader who will not strike when the moment demands it, is no leader at all."

Natronai closed his eyes briefly. Their words pressed upon him like weights, each heavy, each deadly. He imagined the streets of Simonias running red with blood, children clinging to mothers, elders cut down by men who only yesterday sang psalms with them. Yet he also saw the other vision, a Simonias untouched, its people emboldened to mock his claim, word spreading that Natronai the Messiah was too weak to compel allegiance even from his brethren.

The captains murmured among themselves, watching their lord wrestle. One finally spoke:

"We have marched with you, Natronai, because you promised Israel restored. But restoration cannot come if every village refuses us. Simonias is the test. Show us you have the strength to command."

Isaac's eyes gleamed. "Even now the Lord is watching. Will you prove faithful, or will you falter before kinship of flesh and blood? Did not Abraham lift the knife over Isaac when God required it? Obedience to heaven is above all things."

Natronai stiffened at the words, for Isaac had named the very paradox tormenting him. Was not his own name tied to that ancient sacrifice? Was he not himself now the patriarch, asked to raise the knife against his sons for the sake of a promise greater than blood?

Ashurbanipol leaned forward, his scarred hand slamming against the table. "Decide, lord! Every moment we delay, the city grows bolder. Their courage rests on your hesitation. Crush them, and you will crush doubt in your ranks. Spare them, and you will plant doubt that will grow like weed through your army."

Natronai looked at them both, the foreign general and the rabbi of his army. Two voices, one of steel, one of scripture, yet each demanding the same outcome: destruction. The council chamber seemed suddenly small, its walls closing in like a tomb.

He spoke at last, voice quiet, almost broken. "You ask me to slaughter Jews. To raise fire against a city that has known the covenant since the days of Ezra. You tell me God demands it, or Rome demands it. But what of the God who commanded us to love our neighbor, to preserve life? What of the promise that Messiah would gather Israel, not destroy it?"

Isaac's face hardened, his disappointment clear. "The Messiah is also to judge. Do not mistake softness for righteousness. To spare them is to deny your calling."

Ashurbanipol growled. "Spare them, and you prove yourself unfit for kingship. Kings are not made by mercy, but by victory."

The air in the tent thickened, the silence drawn like a bowstring ready to snap. Natronai's hands trembled as he gripped the table, torn between the two absolutes laid before him.

At last he dismissed them with a weary wave. "I will decide before daybreak. Leave me."

They departed reluctantly, Isaac glaring with prophetic fire, Ashurbanipol muttering curses in his Farsi tongue. The captains filed out, whispering doubts. Natronai remained alone in the lamplight, the maps before him blurring, the city of Simonias waiting outside like a verdict yet to be spoken.

Night fell heavy over the camp, a darkness deeper than the mist of morning. Fires burned low, their embers glowing red against the damp ground. The soldiers had quieted after their evening meal, but their silence was not the silence of rest. It was the silence of men waiting for a verdict, listening for rumors, glancing toward their leader's tent.

Within, Natronai sat alone. A single oil lamp flickered, its flame wavering with the drafts that crept through the seams of the canvas. Maps lay unrolled before him, but their lines blurred together. He had tried to study them. Routes northward,

Roman garrisons, supply trails, but every path seemed to converge on Simonias, as though the entire revolt hinged upon this one small city.

He pressed his hands against his face, fingers digging into his brow. Since Jerusalem, the weight upon him had only grown heavier. Standing upon the Temple platform, beholding the church where once the Ark had rested, he had felt both chosen and betrayed. Chosen by God, for who else could reclaim such ground? Betrayed, for the people had not risen as one to follow him. And now, Simonias deepened the wound with another refusal, another denial.

The tent flap rustled. A young scribe, no older than twenty, ducked inside, bearing a cup of water. His hands trembled as he set it down.

"My lord," he whispered, "the men ask what tomorrow brings."

Natronai looked at him, and for a moment saw not the boy but his own reflection as a youth: eager, believing that destiny was a fire that could not be quenched. He could not answer. The boy bowed and withdrew, leaving Natronai once more with his silence.

He lay back upon the bedding and closed his eyes. Sleep did not come easily, but when it did, it brought visions that were half-dream, half-accusation.

He walked through the streets of Simonias. They were empty at first, their stones gleaming with an unnatural brightness. Then the cries began, children's wails, women's shrieks, the clash of steel. He looked down, and his hands were red with blood. His sword dripped upon the stones. All around him, Jews lay fallen, their faces twisted not with hatred but with betrayal. They reached out to him, lips forming words he could not hear, but their eyes spoke clearly enough: The Messiah has become a butcher.

He turned, and in the distance saw the Temple Mount. But it was no longer crowned with a church, nor with the lost sanctuary. It burned. Flames consumed it, black smoke rising into the heavens. And in the smoke, a voice thundered, not with words, but the weight of judgment itself.

Natronai awoke with a start, his chest heaving. Sweat drenched his cloak. He pressed a hand against the ground, steadying himself, but the image lingered; the Temple in flames, his own sword dripping with the blood of brethren.

He rose and stepped outside. The camp was hushed, only the distant murmur of sentries exchanging watchwords. Beyond, Simonias lay cloaked in shadow, its walls faint outlines against the starlit sky. He wondered what the people inside were doing. Did they huddle in fear of him? Did they whisper prayers for deliverance? Or did they sit in quiet confidence, trusting that Rome would save them from their own kin?

He walked aimlessly until he found himself near the edge of camp, where the fields sloped upward toward the city. There he sank to his knees, pressing his forehead into the damp earth.

"O Lord of Hosts," he murmured, his voice hoarse, "why have You set this trial before me? I asked to be Your servant, not a slayer of my own people. I asked to gather Israel, not to scatter her again. Have I mistaken the sign? Am I deceived by my own heart?"

No answer came. Only the rustling of wind in the grass, the distant cry of a night bird.

He thought then of his father, a stern man who had taught him the Law. He remembered being told that the Messiah would bring peace, that the lion would lie with the lamb. And he wondered: was this peace? To storm Simonias? To silence its refusal with fire and sword? Could such a beginning lead to the kingdom foretold?

And yet another voice gnawed within him. The voice of Isaac, reciting scripture of judgment. The voice of Ashurbanipol, promising strength through fear. The voices of his captains, demanding proof of leadership. To spare Simonias might mean losing them. To destroy Simonias might mean losing himself.

He sat in that torment until the stars wheeled overhead. By dawn, his face was hollow, his eyes red-rimmed from weeping unseen. But his resolve had hardened, though not as his counselors had hoped.

He would not destroy Simonias. Better to risk his crown than to drench his mission in the blood of his own people.

Yet even as he formed the decision, he felt the fissure within himself widen. For he knew Ashurbanipol would call him weak, Isaac would call him faithless, and his soldiers would whisper that their Messiah's sword was blunted by sentiment.

The crack had begun. He could hear it already, like the splitting of stone beneath hidden strain. Perhaps it was the sound of the morning light breaking, pale and cold. The mist had lifted, leaving the valley washed in sharp clarity. Simonias stood quietly on its hill, its gates still barred, its walls unmoving, as if the city itself waited to hear what judgment would fall.

Natronai summoned the leaders once more. They gathered in the open air this time, before the assembled soldiers. Ashurbanipol stood like a coiled beast, his jaw set hard. Isaac's expression was one of stern expectation, already certain that heaven would demand fire. The captains lingered, eyes darting between their general and their messiah. The rank and file pressed close, murmuring, their breaths clouding in the morning chill.

Natronai stepped forward, cloak heavy upon his shoulders, face drawn by the sleepless night. His voice carried, though it trembled.

"Men of Israel," he began, "you have followed me through hardship, believing the Lord has chosen this hour for the rebirth of our people. I have called upon you not for plunder, nor for vengeance, but for restoration, so that the covenant might shine again."

He paused, scanning their faces. Some glowed with fervor, others already shadowed by doubt.

"Now we stand before Simonias. It is a city of our brothers, our own flesh and blood. Some of you even have relatives and friends behind those walls. Yes, their gates are closed. Yes, they have not yet seen the truth of our cause. But shall we answer their blindness with the sword? Shall the kingdom of God begin with the slaughter of Jews by Jews?"

A ripple ran through the crowd. Some bowed their heads, moved. Others shifted angrily, fists tightening on spear-shafts.

Natronai's voice rose, steady now, as if conviction had finally found him. "No. I will not raise my hand against them. Simonias shall be spared. Let the world see that the Messiah does not conquer by destroying his own, but by summoning them to repentance. We march forward, leaving their gates intact. If they will not follow today, perhaps they will follow tomorrow. Their blood shall not stain the foundation of Israel restored. I need you to remember that I have marched with you through hunger and thirst, through fire and sword. You have followed me not because I am stronger than you, but because we all share the same wound, the wound of exile within our own land, the wound of humiliation, the wound of seeing the house of Israel trampled underfoot.

Now we stand before Simonias. A city of our own people. Flesh of our flesh. Blood of our blood. Some here cry, 'Raise the sword, take it by force, bend them to our cause.' But I tell you this: a sword lifted against a brother cuts twice. Once into his flesh, and once into our own soul.

If we destroy Simonias, what will we have won? A pile of ashes where once stood a city of our kin. A victory that reeks of Cain's jealousy more than David's courage. We would be no better than those Romans who set fire to Jerusalem and laughed as her children burned.

I will not be Rome. And I will not make you Rome.

Do you think our enemies will not cheer if Jew slaughters Jew? Do you not see their trap? They hope to watch us devour each other, until nothing remains but ruins and slaves.

No. Our battle is not with Simonias. Our battle is with the empire that crushed our fathers and denies our sons a future. Our brothers in that city are afraid, yes, but we must never assume that fear is treachery. They are not our enemies. They are lost sheep who need a shepherd, not wolves who deserve the spear.

I swear to you, by the God of Abraham, Isaac, and Jacob, we will not waste one drop of Jewish blood on this day. Let the Romans come, they will find us united, not divided. Let them strike us and we will stand shield to shield, not blade to blade.

When our children speak of us, let them not say, 'the Patricius raised his hand against his brethren.' Let them say, 'In the day of decision, Israel remembered she was one people, one heart, one covenant.'

So lay aside the anger that clouds your vision. Stand with me, not as men thirsty for slaughter, but as guardians of Israel's soul. For only a united people can be a free people.

So, I ask you, will you follow me still?"

For a moment, silence held. The words hung in the air like a verdict delivered. Then Ashurbanipol spat upon the ground, his voice a growl. "You show weakness before friend and foe alike. Do you think Rome will tremble because you spared one city? No, I guarantee that they will laugh. And these people, safe behind their walls, will whisper that the Messiah was afraid. Fear spreads faster than faith, my lord."

A murmur of assent rose from some captains. Others remained uncertain.

Isaac lifted his staff, his voice ringing out, "You defy the command of heaven. Did not the Lord Himself order the cities of apostasy to be destroyed? You claim to bring restoration, yet you set aside His judgment. Beware Natronai because the Lord will not be mocked. To spare them is to betray your calling."

The words of his closest advisor stung sharper than Ashurbanipol's rebuke. Some soldiers nodded with the condemnation, others shook their heads, confused.

Natronai stood firm, though his hands trembled at his sides. "I am answerable to God alone. And I believe He does not call me to slaughter His people, but to gather them. I will let you judge if it is God's bidding that I am performing or not. For I have not spoken all. Last night, as I lay upon the ground, wearied of counsel and torn by anguish, I cried out to the God of our fathers: 'Lord, show me the path! Am I to lead Israel into glory, or into ruin?'

And sleep overcame me. But it was no common sleep. I beheld a mountain blazing with fire, yet not consumed. From its summit there poured a river, bright as molten gold, that divided into two streams. One stream flowed into fields, and the fields brought forth grain and fruit in abundance. The other stream turned to blood, and everywhere it touched, the ground withered and the people fell dead.

Then a voice, both terrible and sweet, like thunder wrapped in song, spoke to me, saying:

'Son of Israel, the sword of your hand is mine to command.
Do not turn it against your brother, lest the river of blood flow and the harvest be lost.
For I am not served by the death of my children, but by their unity.
Spare Simonias, and I will be with you in the day of battle.
Strike Simonias, and you will walk alone, and your name will be cursed among the generations.'

I fell upon my face in dread, and when I awoke, the earth beneath me was wet with tears. Brothers, I swear by the Holy One of Israel, I did not invent this. I saw it. I heard it. And I trembled. Would you call me liar? Then you call God Himself liar. Would you defy me? Then you defy the One who led us out of Egypt, who split the sea, who gave us His covenant on Sinai.

I would sooner cut out my own tongue than pretend the words of God. And yet I speak them to you now for the sake of your lives and for Israel's future. Simonias must be spared, not by my will, but by His command. This is the Lord's decree."

For a long moment after Natronai finished, there was only silence. The men stood as though the air had thickened around them, their spears and shields forgotten at their sides. Some shifted uneasily, glancing at one another, waiting for someone to laugh, to call it a ruse. But no one did.

The rawness in Natronai's voice, the trembling in his hands, the tear-streaked face of their commander, none of it looked like artifice. It looked like a man who had been scorched by something greater than himself.

A grizzled veteran broke first. He dropped to one knee, pressing his forehead against the hilt of his sword. "If the Lord has spoken thus, then who am I to resist?" he muttered, loud enough for all to hear. Others followed, first a handful, then dozens, until the sound of knees striking earth became like a drumroll across the camp.

Some wept openly. Some stared wide-eyed at the sky, half-expecting to see fire and cloud descend as in the days of Sinai. The army, restless a moment before, now bent beneath the weight of fear and awe.

Even Isaac, ever defiant, stood frozen. His lips parted, but no words came. He looked into Natronai's eyes searching for deceit but found none. Ashurbanipol, whose hand had been resting on his sword, slowly released it. His shoulders sank, and he gave a low growl, not of victory, but of surrender. "If this is truly from your God," he said, "then we cannot stand against it. Not I, not Isaac, not all the legions of men."

The murmur of assent swelled, rippling through the ranks: "Not against God. Not against God."

Natronai lowered his hands, his voice gentler now, almost paternal: "Then let us rise as one people, not divided. The Lord has spoken, and we will obey. Simonias will be spared."

A cheer rose, not the bloodthirsty roar of men rushing to battle, but the steadier, deeper cry of soldiers bound by conviction. In that moment, Natronai's words ceased to be his own. They had become a covenant, etched upon the hearts of his army. Isaac and Ashurbanipol did not cheer, but neither did they oppose. And that silence was victory enough.

With that, he turned, signaling the standard-bearer. The banner of Israel lifted, and the column began to form. Slowly, reluctantly, the army moved, feet dragging, voices muttering. Some looked back at Simonias still longing for conquest, others with relief at the blood not shed, but more than anything they all felt as if they were walking under the shadow of God.

From the walls of the city, figures watched silently. No cheer, no gratitude, only watchful eyes as the rebel host pulled away.

And as the army filed out of the valley, Natronai felt the first true crack in his mission widen. Not upon the stones of Simonias, but within the hearts of his own men. The march from Simonias was quieter than any Natronai had ever experienced. The usual songs of zeal were absent. Even the clatter of weapons seemed muted, as though the men bore a weight heavier than their arms. They trudged forward, eyes averted, whispers passing among them like a sickness.

By midday the army halted near a stream to water the animals. Natronai withdrew beneath an olive grove with Ashurbanipol and Isaac, his two pillars of counsel, though this morning they had felt more like adversaries.

Ashurbanipol wasted no time. His words were sharp, meant to wound. "You have retained your army, Natronai but I do not know for how long. They marched here believing you would lead them to glory. Instead, you turned them away from an easy victory. They wanted bread, weapons, a city to claim but instead you gave them pious words. I do not claim to understand you Jews but I do know men, and in the end, even the words of God will not be enough."

Natronai kept his gaze steady. "I gave them something that fed their souls today. Once you know us Jews better, you will understand how the words of the Almighty can be enough. The day will come when Rome feels our sword, but it was not meant to be today."

Ashurbanipol sneered. "Rome does not care. They will speak only that a city defied you, and you walked away. They will not mention the words of your God. Only that the Jews had grown weak. That is all they will see."

Natronai opened his mouth to reply, but Isaac interjected, his staff tapping against the earth. "No, Ashurbanipol. You speak as a soldier. I speak as a servant of the Law." He turned to Natronai. "You have restored hope that God is still marching with us. After Jerusalem, I know that many a man had come to doubt it. You chose mercy and that is God's way. His word shall always prevail. That's assuming they were God's words." He turned his head to watch Natronai's reaction to his final comment. Natronai's expression never changed as if it was etched in stone. He didn't even flinch, convincing Isaac that the vision must have come form God.

The decision at Simonias had spared blood, but it made Natronai aware of something far more dangerous: doubt. Even in his own heart that doubt had taken root and was spreading rapidly. There certainly was no doubt in God but now he had doubt in himself, in his mission, and whether he truly bore the mantle of Messiah.

CHAPTER XXXI: CHANGE OF HEART

The house of Hillel II, Nasi of Tiberias, was not often unsettled. It was a household of measured steps, whispered courtesies, and the hum of scholarship echoing through its marble halls. But these recent days the air was tense, heavy as storm clouds refusing to break. Servants moved in silence, glancing uneasily at the closed door of the young mistress's chamber. For three days she had refused to leave it. For three days she had touched neither bread nor water.

Hillel himself, though a master of appearances, felt the eyes of his household servants upon him. The daughter of the patriarch was wasting away, and whispers had already begun of how a parent could mistreat his daughter in this manner. They said she was pining for the rebel Natronai, the man who dared claim himself Messiah, who drew swords against Rome and the Sanhedrin. Certainly, a man of his stature could not tolerate such an affair but how could he justify permitting his own daughter to pine away without interceding. A scandal of this sort could not be hidden but Hillel was not a man who would willingly lose control of the narrative.

That morning, he gathered the household. Servants, tutors, even the cook and the steward were called into the atrium. He stood among them in a robe of deep blue, his beard combed with meticulous care, his features arranged in a mask of sorrow and paternal grief.

"My daughter," he declared, his voice heavy with anguish, "is the very light of my house. Her joy has been my joy; her sorrow my sorrow. I would give up all, my standing, my wealth, even my very life if it meant she might once again smile at me. Shall a father not sacrifice for his child?"

The servants bowed their heads, some silently reciting prayers. A few wept at the sight of their master so undone. Hillel clasped his hands dramatically to his breast.

"Yes, I have resisted her heart's desire. I feared what the world would say if I permitted her to see this rebel. I feared the ruin of our name. But what is a name if the child of my loins withers away? What is honor if she lies pale and lifeless? Today I resolve: let her be with whom she loves, even if it be this Patricius, the man I will always oppose. I would rather see her happy and alive than righteous and dead."

A murmur ran through the hall. The steward, loyal and gray-haired, whispered, "The master is merciful. Truly a father among fathers."

Hillel raised a hand as though brushing away the praise, but inwardly he savored it. Every eye was upon him. Every tongue would carry this tale into the streets. Hillel the loving father. Hillel the man willing to humble himself for the sake of his daughter. It was the greatest role he had ever played, and his audience believed every word of it.

With a grave nod, he dismissed them and made his way to her door. The corridor was silent. Only the faint creak of wood announced his steps. He paused before the chamber, resting his hand against the carved cedar door. For a long while he said nothing, listening. Within, the silence was absolute. At last he spoke, his tone gentle, mournful, rehearsed.

"My child... my dearest one. Will you not open for me? Must a father beg at his daughter's door?"

No answer. Only the stillness of despair.

Hillel pressed on. "I know why you grieve. You believe me cruel, a jailer keeping you from the man you love. But hear me now! Know that I have relented. No longer will I stand in your way. If Natronai is the one your heart has chosen, then so be it. I will bless your union. Only come forth, only live, and do not wither yourself to death in silence."

A faint sound erupted, muffled sobs from within. Hillel leaned closer, letting his voice soften to a whisper.

"Do you think I care for the world's gossip? Let them whisper. Let them scorn. They cannot know what a father feels when his child suffers. Come back to me, my daughter. Open the door. Let me hold you."

Minutes dragged like hours. At last, a bolt scraped. The door opened a finger's width, then a hand pulled it wider.

She stood there, pale as ivory, her eyes red-rimmed from tears, her hair tangled. Her cheeks were sunken, lips cracked from thirst, yet in her gaze burned the fragile hope of one who wants desperately to believe.

"Truly, father?" she whispered. "You would allow it?"

Hillel drew her into his arms, pressing her head against his chest, his eyes glistening with feigned tears. "Truly, child. Your happiness is my only prayer. I swear it before heaven."

She clung to him, her body trembling, a broken sob tearing from her throat. She believed. She believed because she wanted to, because despair had left her nothing else to hold.

And Hillel, master of masks, tightened his embrace, hiding the cold calculation behind his eyes. For this was not mercy, but strategy. He had bought her trust once more, and through it, time. Time enough to use her devotion as a weapon against the rebel himself.

"You will let us marry?" She still found it difficult to believe.

Her father nodded solemnly. "Yes, child. I would rather have you alive and joyous among rebels than dead to me in my house."

She burst into tears, clutching him tightly, her frame racked with sobs. He held her, stroked her hair, and murmured soft words.

Within, a coldness coiled in his chest. He waited until her breathing slowed and her sobs softened. Then he drew back slightly and smiled.

"But such a union must be made lawful, holy, and public," he said. "Not a secret tryst in the hills. A proper betrothal. With a big wedding. I will permit your union no other way."

Havilah nodded eagerly. "Anything. Yes. It is what we would want as well."

"And it must be witnessed," Hillel added. "By the community at large. For the sake of all. To protect your honor. And of course, for the peace that will be forged between our two sides, no matter if it may not last. If we make such a great gesture, this bridge between Babylon and Tiberias. perhaps there will be a way to win this war."

She kissed his hand.

"I shall write to him today," Hillel said. "We shall choose a date within a week. I believe two sabbaths from now will be sufficient. Don't you think so?"

She threw her arms around him again. "You don't know what this means to me. You don't know how happy you have made me."

"I do," he whispered.

And in that whisper, he buried the invisible knife.

That night, in a private chamber of the home's basement, Hillel lit a single oil lamp and sent out two letters by a trusted couriers. The first letter was to Natronai.

To Natronai, Scion of David, Son of Israel, leader of men,

Though you and I have stood on opposite sides of thought and action, I cannot deny the bond my daughter Havilah has set her heart upon. A father's love obliges him to safeguard his child's happiness, even when it leads him down paths he would not freely tread.

Therefore, I will not hinder her wish. The marriage between you and Havilah shall be solemnized in Tiberias on the second Sabbath henceforth. The arrangements will be made discreetly, and the ceremony conducted according to our customs.

Take no mistake, this I do not for politics, nor for cause, but for the sake of my daughter. I pray you will treat her with the same devotion she has shown you, and that her joy will not be short-lived.

I trust you will understand the spirit in which I write.

—Hillel ben Judah

The second letter was sealed after writing only four lines:

To Ursicinus, Commander of the Galilean Legion:

The rebel will be in Tiberias at the hour of the third watch, eight nights hence. He comes unarmed. The wedding will be public, the gathering large. Strike swiftly. Spare none in his entourage but do not harm the citizens of Tiberias that will be in attendance.

—H.

He handed both off with no evidence of any emotion.

The courier never made it past Natronai's outer sentries. Stationed on the road to Magdala. That much was clear from the stains of dust on his cloak, the bruising on his cheek, and the way the guards shoved him forward as if he were no more than a criminal. Once they removed the blindfold, the courier realized he was standing before the Rabbi of Sepphoris. Isaac stood there in the half-light of dawn, arms folded, waiting for an explanation as to why the courier would think he could not only find where the rebels were camped but why they would even let him live if he did. The rebels were encamped in a shallow valley between Sepphoris and Magdala, as the morning fog clung to the ground like an omen. Ravens circled the ridge tops as though feasting on foreknowledge of blood.

"Caught him skulking on the lower path," one guard said. "Said he bore a message for the Patricius himself."

Isaac narrowed his eyes. He had lived long enough in the game of rebellion to know that every message was a weapon. Slowly, he stepped forward, palm outstretched. The courier hesitated, then handed over the rolled parchment. Its seal was intact, pressed with a signet bearing the image of a fly that Isaac recognized instantly. Hillel ben Judah. The Nasi. As far as Isaac was concerned, his sworn enemy.

Isaac turned the parchment over in his hand, weighing it as though it might bite him. He already knew what it contained. He could feel it. The bait. The snare. The final stone meant to crush Natronai, not elevate him. His mouth went dry.

The courier tried to speak, but Isaac raised a finger to silence him. "Take him to the rear. Give him bread and water, nothing more. I will decide what to do with him later."

The guards obeyed. Isaac was left alone with the scroll. He cracked the seal, unrolled it, and began to read.

The words were precise, measured, dripping with reluctance yet duty-bound. Hillel claimed that he had, against his will, agreed to give his daughter Havilah in marriage to Natronai. The ceremony would take place in Tiberias on the second Sabbath hence. He wrote that it was for her sake alone, not from joy, not from approval. The tone was cold, reluctant, almost bitter. But beneath the bitterness lay a truth: he was granting Natronai the very thing he desired most in all the world.

Isaac felt his stomach twist. He knew at once it was a trap. Hillel had never yielded anything without an angle. This was not an olive branch; it was a noose disguised as a wreath. But Natronai would not see it that way. Natronai would see only Havilah.

For several long breaths, Isaac did not move. He closed his eyes, trying to master the panic that threatened to overwhelm him. Then he turned toward the inner camp. The letter crinkled in his fist.

Natronai's pavilion stood at the center of the camp, striped cloths of black and crimson swaying in the morning breeze. He was already awake. Isaac could hear the muffled sounds of steel being polished, the low murmur of aides reciting numbers of supplies, weapons and recruits. Natronai was a man who rarely slept when the scent of Rome hung near.

Isaac entered without ceremony. The guards at the entrance bowed their heads but did not dare question him. Inside, Natronai sat at a broad table covered with maps. His dark hair fell loose around his shoulders, and his eyes, those burning eyes, were fixed upon a line of Roman fortifications sketched in charcoal. He looked up as Isaac approached, and a rare smile flickered across his face. Not for Isaac, but for the scroll Isaac carried.

"You've news," Natronai said, rising to his feet. "I see it in your hand. From Tiberias?"

Isaac swallowed. "From Hillel himself."

That was all it took. Natronai's expression shifted from calculation to hunger, like a man who had been starved and at last smelled bread baking. He reached out. Isaac hesitated a fraction of a moment too long.

"What is it?" Natronai asked, sharp now. "Give it to me."

Isaac obeyed, handing him the letter. Natronai unrolled the parchment, and read. As the words unfolded, a light came into his face, bright and terrible, as if the sun itself had touched him. He read it once, twice, three times, then pressed the parchment to his chest.

"She has won," he whispered. "Havilah has prevailed. Even her father bends before her love."

Isaac's heart clenched. "It is not love, Natronai. It is poison. Hillel writes with the tongue of a serpent."

Natronai glanced at him, eyes narrowing. "You would call it poison because you have never felt what I feel."

Isaac stepped forward, voice urgent. "I know Hillel better than you. He has never once yielded a thing without snare or consequence. This letter is not a gift. It is bait. He wants you to walk willingly into his cage."

Natronai laughed, though the sound held more defiance than mirth. "Cage? You speak of cages while offering me the keys to heaven? I will not turn away from her."

Isaac's voice broke. "Then you are walking into death."

For the next hour, Isaac threw every weapon he had, not steel, but words sharpened on the whetstone of experience. He spoke of Hillel's reputation, of his dealings with Rome, of his long history of manipulation. He reminded Natronai that the Nasi had denounced the revolt, had branded them heretics, had sought Roman favor over Jewish freedom. "Do you think such a man would bless this union honestly? No, he invites you so that he may end you."

Natronai's replies were calm, almost tender, yet unyielding. "You mistake bitterness for honesty. His words are cold, yes, but that is because he yields not to me, but to his daughter. Havilah has bent his will. Do you not see? She loves me. She waits for me. She has persuaded him, against his heart, to grant what he would not grant otherwise."

Isaac shook his head, desperation rising. "Even if that were true, the city of Tiberias is no sanctuary. It crawls with Roman supporters. You set foot there, and you set foot into the jaws of the lion. He has chosen the time and place. He will not let you leave alive."

Natronai's eyes flashed. "I have faced lions before. I did not flinch."

Isaac slammed his hand against the table, scattering the maps. "This is not battle! This is assassination. There will be no honor, no clash of arms. only betrayal, only ropes and blades in alleys. You cannot fight what you are unwilling to see."

But Natronai only smiled faintly, folding the letter again. "You fear too much, old friend. Love is a fortress stronger than Rome. She will not let me fall. No father would ever place his only daughter in danger on the day of her wedding. It's unimaginable to think otherwise."

By midday, Isaac felt as though he were drowning. No matter what he said, Natronai turned it aside, as if Isaac's words were arrows bouncing off armor. Yet it was not armor of steel, it was armor of obsession. Havilah's name was the shield, her imagined love the sword. Natronai's heart was already in Tiberias, kneeling before her. How could Isaac drag him back?

He left the tent, staggered into the sunlight, and pressed his palms to his eyes. Around him the camp bustled. Men sharpening weapons, loading carts, and tending fires. They all looked to Natronai as their savior, their leader. None of them were aware of how close he stood to ruin.

Isaac walked among them like a ghost. Every face he saw seemed to accuse him: Why can you not save him? Why can you not pull him back from the edge? He thought of every word he had spoken, every warning, and felt them crumble into dust. Hillel's trap was too perfect. It exploited not Natronai's weakness for power or glory, but his one unguarded spot: his love for Havilah.

That night, Isaac could not sleep. He lay awake on his cot, staring at the canvas above, hearing in his mind the echo of Natronai's voice: Love is a fortress stronger than Rome. He wanted to scream. A fortress could be stormed. A fortress could fall.

The next morning, Isaac tried again. He entered the pavilion while Natronai was breaking bread with his captains. In front of them all, Isaac spoke boldly.

"Patricius, I must warn you again. This marriage is not a blessing. It is a dagger aimed at your heart."

The captains shifted uncomfortably. Natronai raised a brow. "You persist."

"I persist because I see the snare tightening," Isaac said, his voice loud enough for all to hear. "If you go to Tiberias, you will not return."

One of the captains muttered, "Perhaps the rabbi is jealous of the match." Laughter rippled.

Isaac ignored it. He locked eyes with Natronai. "If you will not believe my words, then test them. Send spies ahead. Search the city. See if I speak lies."

Natronai considered it. For a moment, Isaac's heart leapt. But then Natronai shook his head slowly. "To send spies is to admit doubt. I will not insult Havilah's honor with suspicion."

Isaac's hands curled into fists. "This is not about honor, it is about your survival!"

"I have already discussed my marriage plans with the captains here. They all agree that this is a great opportunity to unite the Houses of the Exilarch with that of the Patriarch. The people will see it as a divine blessing that once again we are a united nation. When word is sent out, even a town like Simonias will join our cause. What you see as disaster is a golden opportunity that has been handed to us by God."

"Yes, she is beautiful; yes she comes from a noble family," Isaac agreed, "But the only opportunity I see here is for our capture. Why not hold the wedding n Sepphoris where we at least know we will be surrounded by those loyal to our cause."

"Because the House of Hillel rules in Tiberias. It is where their family has influence. It only makes sense that the wedding takes place there."

Tiberias and Havilah will bring about our end," Isaac was adamant.

Natronai leaned forward, voice low and dangerous. "Enough. I will not hear another word against her. She is the light by which I see. You may doubt, but I will not. If you cannot accept this, then perhaps you no longer belong at my side."

Those words struck Isaac harder than any blade. He staggered back, throat tight. To be cast away now was unthinkable. Yet he had no choice but to bow his head. "As you command," he whispered.

That evening, Isaac tried one last time. He found Natronai alone, seated by a low fire outside his tent, the letter unfolded in his lap. The Patricius stared at it as though the ink itself whispered promises.

Isaac sat beside him, his voice stripped of anger now, bare with sorrow. "Natronai, I have stood with you through every battle, every hardship. I have seen you bleed and triumph. But this… this is the one battle you cannot win, because it is not fought with swords. It is fought with shadows. And shadows always consume the light."

Natronai's eyes softened, but his words remained the same. "You do not understand. When I was a boy, I dreamed of Jerusalem restored. When I became a man, I dreamed of Rome undone. But when I met Havilah, I dreamed of nothing else. She is the dream that swallows all others. Even if it is a trap, even if it leads to my end, I would go to her. For a single glimpse, a single touch, I would risk everything."

Isaac felt tears burn his eyes. "Then you are lost."

"Not lost," Natronai said gently. "Found."

"Then let me start stationing men within the city. Simply to provide security. I will see that they remain concealed and none will be the wiser for their presence."

Natronai nodded. "If it make you feel better then do so."

"I would like to move the army into positions on all the major roads leading into Tiberias as well," Isaac suggested.

"We have already taken Tiberias. Our presence there will only remind the people of the horror of when the city fell to us," Natronai warned his companion. "Even now they still talk about the show we put on with the death of Decimus Varius and accuse us of being more barbaric than even the Romans were to them. I cannot afford to stir such sentiment at my own wedding. Keep the army far enough away that the people are not threatened."

"You are inferring that I keep them up in the hills but that would mean they are hours away from Tiberias if an alarm is sounded." Isaac was not happy with that order.

"I have already sent back message to Reb Hillel that I will be there. That being the case, the only sounds heard at a distance will be the blaring of the wedding trumpets."

For the remaining days of that week, Isaac searched for proof. He sent trusted scouts to shadow the roads near Tiberias, bribed informants, questioned travelers. Yet all reports were inconclusive. Some said the Romans were gathering quietly. Others swore the city was calm. The only one story they all shared was that they could see that the city of Tiberias was preparing for some huge event on the Sabbath and the word was that it was going to be a wedding. Nothing he could bring to Natronai as undeniable proof. Nothing to shake him from his course.

Each evening Isaac returned empty-handed, and each evening Natronai grew more excited about his approaching wedding. The Patricius planned his procession to Tiberias, spoke of wedding garments, even laughed, which was a rare sound since his return from Jerusalem. The men of the camp began to whisper of peace, of alliance with the Nasi. But no matter how they spoke of a brand new alliance, Isaac sensed they were marching not to a wedding, but into a slaughter.

The days slipped like sand through his fingers. Each hour brought him closer to the second Sabbath. Each hour the trap tightened. Isaac felt the weight of destiny pressing down, crushing his ribs, suffocating him. He had always been the voice of caution, the shield of wisdom beside Natronai's sword of fire. But now, his voice had turned to dust. His shield was splintered. And Natronai walked forward, smiling, into the abyss.

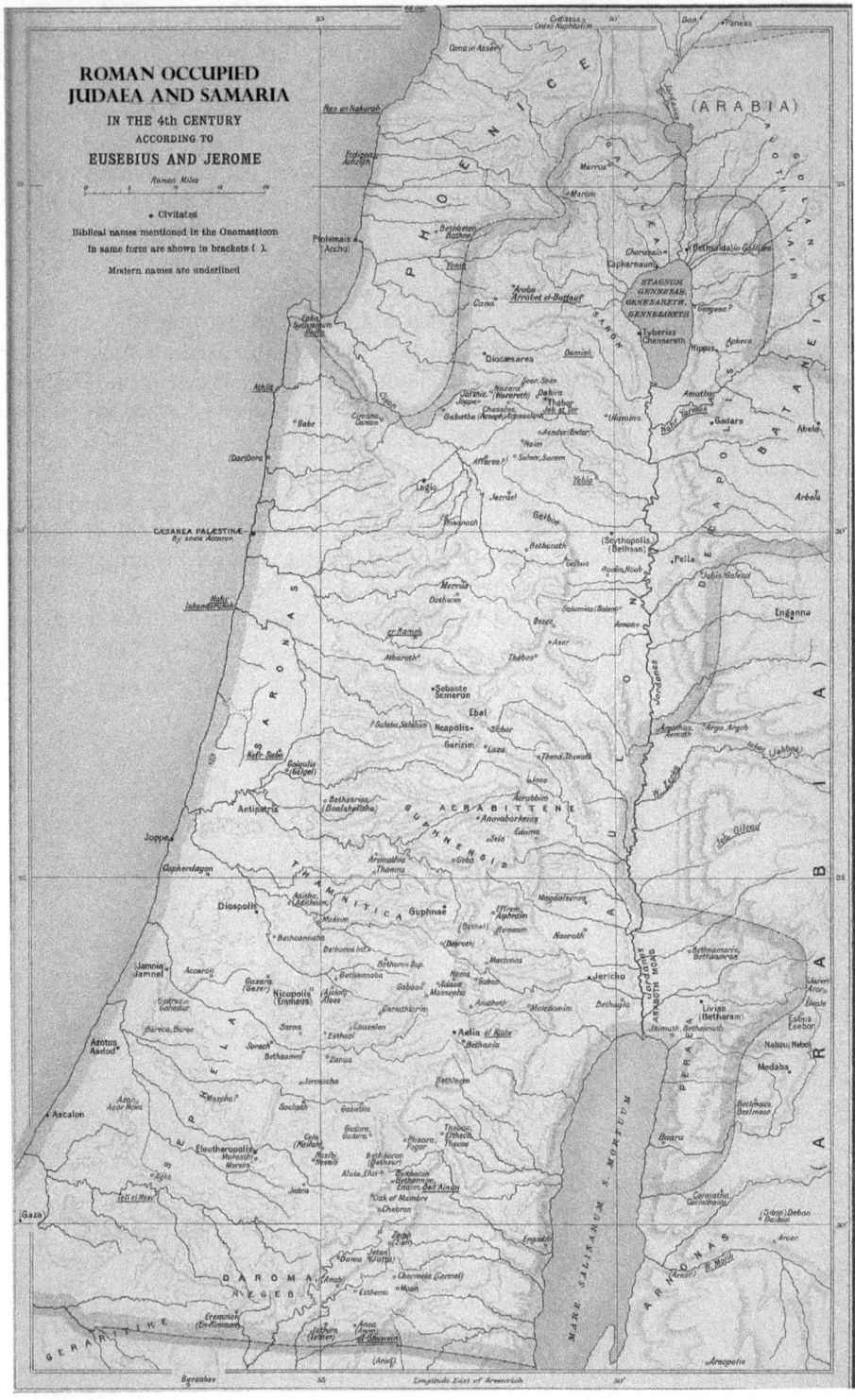

CHAPTER XXXII: THE BINDING

The approach to the wedding Sabbath was not all peace and quiet. Word of the first public executions came from Emmaus. A teacher named Eleazar, caught with a copy of the Covenant of Fire, was burned alive with the scroll tied to his chest.

But his last words were recorded by children who escaped and repeated them: "This fire is not Rome's. It is the fire of Sinai. You may consume my flesh, but the flame will leap into your children."

The next morning, thirty more joined the ranks of the Redeemed, pledging themselves to the rebel army. In response, Natronai and Isaac added a new section to the Covenant: the Oath of the Martyrs.

> "Should I fall, let no man mourn for me as the pagans mourn.
> Let him sing the Song of Ascenders, and lift high my blade.
> Let my bones be buried in the soil of the rebellion,
> And my name be etched not in stone, but in the breath of the living."

Entire villages began taking the Oath. Boys not yet of age swore it. Grandmothers with withered hands whispered it as they prepared flatbread over fire.

Isaac watched in wonder. "What is happening?"

Natronai whispered: "They are becoming one people. The people who crossed the sea. The people who heard the voice on the mountain. They have heard Hillel's pledge to marry his daughter to me and now they are convinced this is God's holy rebellion. This is the sign we have been waiting for since Jerusalem."

It was the night before the wedding; Isaac awoke from a dream. He stumbled to where Natronai was sleeping beneath the stars at a small cove outside Tiberias.

"I saw the people marching," he said. "Not with rage, but with song. A hundred thousand singing the Songs of the Ascenders. They carried the scroll on their shoulders like the Ark."

Natronai's voice was hoarse with fatigue. "Then you see, this wedding is all part of God's plan."

"But they weren't dressed like us," Isaac interrupted. They had clothing that I have never seen before. I don't know, but I don't think it was us."

"Of course it was us," Natronai calmed his concern. "When we enter into the time of God's prophecy, He will adorn us with heavenly clothes. That's why you couldn't recognize it."

Isaac was still uneasy about his dream. They walked together down to the lake. In the distance, boats were burning lanterns as they did their night fishing. Natronai looked across the water.

"It will come with blood," he said. "But also glory. The kind that echoes from Jericho to Zion. We must be patient. This is the Lord's timeline."

Isaac nodded.

"And all of it," he commented, "began with ink and fire."

"Such is the will of the Almighty," Natronai confirmed.

They walked back to their tents but Natronai knew he would not sleep, being too excited about the morrow's events. He was confident that everything would go well. Isaac's men that he had concealed within the city were reporting back that all was quiet. Since their taking of Tiberias, the city gates were now manned by Jewish sentinels bearing a red cord woven through their cloaks that signified they were part of the rebellion. Roman graffiti had been scraped from the walls. Baskets of flowers lined the street of the synagogue, interlaced with ribbons, all in preparation for the wedding.

At the synagogue, where once sat elders loyal to Hillel, a new seat had been carved from olivewood and placed before the ark. It was flanked by torches and covered in embroidered linen, designed with the crest and symbols of the Exilarchate. The seat alone was a symbol of the city's welcoming for the new deliverer of Zion.

By morning tens of thousands gathered around Tiberias. Farmers, scribes, women with infants, shepherds from the heights of Gilead. They brought bread and wine, olive oil and honey, and goats for sacrifice. For most, this wedding would be the biggest event of their lifetime. The city was awake, and more than awake, it was alive, pulsing with an energy that made the very stones of the streets seem to hum with a concealed energy.

The entire week whispers had carried the news from village to village, town to town: Natronai, son of the Exilarch, the leader of the Galilean revolt, was to wed Havilah, the daughter of Hillel II, the Nasi of the Sanhedrin. To the people, it was not simply a marriage, it was the weaving together of two ancient lines, the house of priestly scholars and the house of warrior princes. In their hearts, it felt like the rebirth of the kingdom was at hand, the restoration of pride long dulled by Roman chains. An end to the servitude and humiliation.

Now, as the morning air filled with the smell of baking breads, spiced lamb, and honeyed cakes, a steady stream of people poured into Tiberias. Families arrived in long processions, children skipping barefoot beside carts laden with figs and pomegranates, their laughter mixing with the bleating of goats and the clatter of merchants setting up stalls. The narrow lanes overflowed with garlands of flowers consisting of carnations, oleander, and wild poppies strung in chains and draped from balconies. Everywhere one looked, a barrage of color and sound reigned.

Musicians had come from as far as Sepphoris and Beth Shean, their lyres and flutes lifting melodies that danced in the streets. Drums echoed like heartbeats, urging the people into circles of traditional dance. Old men, their beards white as snow, clasped hands with children and whirled around in steps they had not danced since youth. Women clapped, their voices rising in ululation, their bright scarves flashing like flames in the morning sun.

"Blessed be the Lord!" cried one voice, and the crowd answered with shouts of "Hallelujah!" The words rolled like thunder through the city, not as a rote prayer but as an anthem of joy. For once, there was no fear of Roman soldiers at the gates. Rumors placed them far to the south, embroiled in their endless wars against Natronai's forces in Judea. Here, in Tiberias, the people let themselves believe in peace, even if only for this one day.

Along the lake shore, rows of food-sellers called out to the throngs. Skewers of roasting meat turned over coals, the fat sizzling as it dripped. Baskets overflowed with olives and dates. Wine flowed freely, poured into clay cups that passed from hand to hand. Children smeared honey on their fingers and licked them clean, giggling as they darted between dancers. The whole city had become a festival, as if heaven itself had opened its gates and spilled its bounty upon them.

At the heart of the city, near the great synagogue, banners of blue and white fluttered in the breeze, sewn with the Star of David and symbols of the tribes. They proclaimed to all that this was not merely a wedding, but a covenant. The names of Natronai and Havilah were on every tongue, spoken with reverence and expectation. For some, it was as though David and Micah had risen from the pages of scripture to walk among them once more.

And everywhere, joy reigned supreme. Men who had known only hardship now lifted cups and sang. Women who had buried sons in the war now let themselves smile and sway to music. The young, those who had never known what it was to live in a kingdom of their own. glimpsed for the first time what their ancestors had spoken of: freedom, dignity, and a future worth dreaming of.

As the sun climbed higher, its rays glinting off the waters of Galilee, the city of Tiberias became a tapestry of light and laughter, of hope and devotion. This was not merely a wedding day. It was a coronation in the hearts of the people, a celebration to be remembered for generations.

But while Tiberias sang, the south screamed. With six legions under his command, Ursicinus had ordered three of them south to rape, pillage and burn. In the plains around Lydda and Emmaus, Roman patrols had descended like wolves. Villages were set to the torch, their men cut down with pitiless efficiency, their women and children herded together, slaughtered as warnings, their cries carried on the smoke. Merchants on the roads were stripped of wares, their caravans reduced to ashes. Olive groves and vineyards, the product from centuries of labor, were hacked to stumps and left to burn.

These were not random acts of cruelty by a general without a strategy. He was a soldier of cunning, if not of mercy. He knew the Jews of Galilee would be watching the south nervously. So much so that they'd be distracted from events in their own surroundings. So, he allowed the news of such raids to trickle northward, not too fast, not too close. Rumors that claimed the Roman legions were tied up in Judea, that their reach could not stretch to the Galilee in time to disrupt Natronai's marriage. A calculated illusion, considering the ability to distinguish between the involvement of three legions as compared to six would take a military strategist to tell the difference. He let the people believe the threat to their own province lay days away, when in truth, his dagger was already poised at their throats.

For even now, as the sun gilded Tiberias and the streets filled with laughter, an entire Roman legion marched in disciplined silence along the valley roads. Their armor glinted in the morning light, shields locked in endless rows, spears bristling like a forest of death. Standard-bearers carried the eagle high, its wings spread wide as if to mock the songs of freedom rising in the north. Every mile brought them closer to the unsuspecting city.

And on the eastern shore of the Sea of Galilee, at Hippus, a flotilla of Roman galleys had already pushed off. Their oars dipped in unison, the waters foaming in their wake. Soldiers packed the decks, their helmets shining like a sheet of bronze, their eyes fixed westward. By mid-afternoon they would be in Tiberias harbor, and the joyous cries of children would be drowned beneath the clash of steel and the wails of the dying.

In Tiberias, no one could see it. The people danced, drank, and lifted their hands to heaven in thanksgiving. They praised the Lord for the day He had given them, blind to the shadow gathering beyond the hills and waters. The city had never known such joy, nor would it ever know such peril again.

CHAPTER XXXIII: FAMILY TIES

In the days that followed Hillel's announcement of the wedding, Tiberias hummed with strange preparations. Hillel's servants were dispatched to source fabrics and wine. Invitations were discreetly prepared. Havilah began to eat again, to bathe, to sing softly under her breath. The color returned to her cheeks.

She believed.

So did the scholars. Many were stunned. Some murmured against it. Others claimed it was a political masterstroke. uniting the Babylonian mystic with the house of the Mishnaic sages.

Only Gamaliel said nothing. He watched his father closely, noting the curve of his words, the coldness behind his smiles. He remembered how swiftly his father had shifted from fury to peace. He saw the gleam in his father's eyes when others weren't looking.

One night, he approached him in the study.

"You would risk her life for this."

Hillel looked up. "I would risk much more."

Gamaliel's face twisted. "I told you to find a way to trap the rebellion's leadership, not get my sister murdered. She will be killed. Do you think Ursicinus will distinguish between rebels and brides when he attacks the city?"

"She is a sacrifice," Hillel said calmly. "Did not Gideon sacrifice his own daughter in order to guarantee victory. Such things are meant to show our loyalty to the Lord. It's a lesson we must all bear. A painful one, I admit, but one for the preservation of Israel. Would you prefer she bear his child? That she become the mother of a false dynasty?"

Gamaliel turned away in disgust. "I thought you would prepare a pre-marital feast instead for the men of the city and invite him to attend. And during that event you would have the Roman's surprise us and no one would know that you deliberately betrayed him. But this! This is too much! To have them both march to the bimah and prepare to exchange vows, while you open the gates to the Romans, that is something that not even God will forgive you for. You have no soul."

"I do what I must do. I have a nation to protect. I have a legacy that I must see survives," Hillel replied. "And I intend to save it so that you will have something left to reign over when this is all done."

"What makes you so certain I won't tell my sister about what you have planned?"

"Will you also tell her that this was all your idea. That you urged me to find a way to deliver Natronai over to the Romans," his father taunted him. "Yes, go and tell her but tell her everything. I would not have considered any of this if it was not for you. Go ahead and let her know everything."

Gamaliel hesitated. He knew that he could not confess the truth to Havilah. It would destroy their bond forever and merely result in the canceling the wedding and her running off into Natronai's arms regardless of an official marriage or not. And it was true; the thought of her bearing offspring to the son of the Exilarch curled in his stomach. He would prefer her dead than have such an even occur.

Meanwhile, Havilah spent hours preparing her garments. She wept with joy as she held the veil her deceased mother had worn. She whispered to the stars each night, thanking God.

Natronai wrote her daily. And in each letter, he told her of his hopes: that this union might finally bring peace to their people, that they might heal the wounds between exile and home.

The night before the wedding, Hillel stood alone at the window of his study, watching the lights of the city flicker. He had told no one the truth save his son and the Roman commander. Not even the council. He would disclose the truth to them just prior to the wedding so that no one revealed the truth too early.

He had calculated every angle. The soldiers would descend just prior to twilight. They would slaughter the zealots in attendance first. Natronai next. The bride, if caught in the chaos, would be mourned as a tragic casualty of misguided love. Her name would be preserved. Her memory honored. And Hillel would emerge with both power and pity. His eyes closed.

And for a brief moment, he let himself feel it, the weight of what he had done. The echo of her sobs in his arms. The warmth of her voice saying, 'You don't know what this means to me.' He wondered if this was the same feeling that Akiva experienced just before he betrayed Bar Kochba. If it was, then if Akiva, the sage he worshipped with all his heart could survive with such guilt, then so could he. He let the moment of feeling any remorse pass, and he turned away from the window.

He blew out the candle as the sun dipped low, casting molten gold across the city's eastern walls. He could see the guests begin to arrive from the Galilean villages and cities. Some came by donkey, others in litters.

Somewhere, out there beyond the walls he knew that Natronai with his escort had arrived, quietly, avoiding main roads. Isaac would ensure that they kept a low profile. He knew his charade would never deceive the Rabbi of Sepphoris but like Samson, the heart would outweigh common sense and there'd be nothing that Isaac could do to stop it. It was why he was so certain is plot would succeed when he finally detailed it to Ursicinus. Love will make fools of even the wisest man.

On the sabbath day of the wedding, Natronai wore robes of deep crimson and gold. His hair was bound in cords. No sword hung from his hip because he refused to bring a weapon under the wedding canopy. All he brought was a small pendant, a shard of flint taken from Beit Netofa, where his rebellion had begun.

Isaac walked beside him, silent and wary. As they approached the gates, he said, "One word from you, and we vanish. No one would blame you."

"No," Natronai said. "We go forward."

"I don't like it," Isaac protested. "There are too many people crammed into the city. Once we're inside, we will be barely able to move. It is the perfect scenario for an ambush. We should have never agreed to hold the wedding in Hillel's own city."

The gates opened and they passed through.

The wind over Tiberias carried the scent of cedar and roses, mingled with the distant heat of the lower valley. The old Roman amphitheater, last used by Natronai to force the Roman garrison to fight among themselves, had been transformed into a gathering place for the unusual assembly of pitched tents for all the visitors from outside the city. Banners of white and gold fluttered in the breeze. Flowers were strewn upon the stone pathways. Hillel had spared no expense in making the wedding feel both holy and grand.

Once inside the city gates, Isaac's nerves began to panic. In all his life he had never seen such press of humanity. He became skittish upon hearing the beat of drums from the synagogue courtyard, and the sound of laughter mingled with the braying of donkeys and the squabbling of merchants. He felt as if he was drowning in a swollen hive, packed so full that every alley stank of sweat, wine, and dust.

As a corridor opened upon recognition of the arrival of the groom, the people began to cheer wildly for Natronai, their Messiah Patricius, their savior, the man who had defied Rome and promised freedom. Natronai smiled broadly, waving as though he were already a crowned king. His face shone, not from exertion, but from joy. Beside him, Isaac kept his jaw tight, his eyes narrowing as he scanned every balcony, every rooftop, every shadow.

Something gnawed at his chest. Not hunger, not thirst, but that cold sensation that had saved his life countless times before: the instinct that a battlefield was about to swallow him. At first, he could not name it. But as they pressed deeper into the city, as the throngs swelled, as the air grew hotter with the crush of bodies, the truth assembled itself in his mind.

Five thousand men lay concealed just outside the city walls, under his orders, seasoned fighters who would die for Natronai. But inside these walls? Inside this suffocating anthill, they would be useless. A sword cannot cut through a crowd without dulling itself to nothing.

During the week, he had infiltrated a thousand more into the city, chosen men, veterans who could blend into the crowds and rise when summoned. They had been spying and reporting any activity out of the ordinary but thus far had reported all was calm and usual. Yet what good would they be now? In this press of flesh, they could not even lift their blades without striking down women and children, or each other. They were squeezed like seeds in a pomegranate.

And then came the third realization, the one that made Isaac's gut twist until bile rose to his throat. Twenty thousand more of their brothers waited in the hills above Magdala under Ashurbanipol's command, a formidable force, but too far. Far too far. Even at a forced march, it would take them hours to descend upon Tiberias. By then, the city could be in flames or drowning in Roman bloodshed.

Piece by piece, the puzzle came together. The overcrowding. The timing. The fact that their enemies would likely know of the wedding with all the publicity it had garnered. What better lure could Rome devise than this? A city swollen beyond capacity, defenses crippled by the very crowds that celebrated, and their own forces divided by distance.

A perfect trap if someone was to open the gates.

Isaac's hand clenched so tightly his knuckles whitened. He turned to Natronai. "Patricius," he said low, his voice nearly lost to the roar of the crowd. "This is folly. Look around you. The city is too full. If the Romans are near, if they strike, our men inside these walls are useless. Our fighters will be pressed too tight to be of any aid. And Ashurbanipol's legions? They are hills away, blind and deaf to what happens here."

Natronai, still smiling at a group of children who ran alongside, barely glanced at him. "You worry too much, Isaac. Today is not a day for irrational shadows. Today the people rejoice, and so must we."

Isaac's temper flared, though he bit it back. "You think I see shadows? No, Patricius, I see reality. This is how Rome wages war. Not with fair declarations, but with surprise, with cunning. They would wait for the day you are most distracted, most vulnerable. And here we are, trapped in a city that could become a slaughterhouse."

Natronai laughed, light and dismissive. "Slaughterhouse? Look at them!" He gestured to the sea of faces. "Do you not hear their voices? These are our people, Isaac. They would not permit harm to come to us. Five thousand men beyond the gates, a thousand within, twenty thousand more in the hills. Even Rome, with all her might, would hesitate to challenge that."

"They would not hesitate," Isaac growled. "They would seize this chance with both hands. And if they do, our numbers mean nothing. They have chosen the field, Natronai, not us. This is not strength, it is weakness. What use is your Persian escort of twenty men if we cannot find a way to exit the city if attacked?"

But Natronai had already turned away, basking in the adoration of the masses, his eyes shining as though the world had already bent itself to his will. Isaac saw in that gaze not strategy, not calculation, but love, love for the woman he was about to wed, love for the triumph he believed destiny had granted him. It blinded him more surely than any bandage.

"Trust me," Isaac urged, his voice low and urgent. "If I am wrong, I will beg forgiveness. But if I am right, and we linger in this city, we are lost."

Natronai finally looked at him then, and for a fleeting moment Isaac thought he saw doubt. But it was gone in an instant, washed away by a radiant smile.

"You are my shield, Isaac," Natronai said warmly. "If danger comes, you will find a way to deal with it. That is why you are at my side. Today, I am not a general. I am a groom. Let me have this day and leave the shadows to you."

The words struck Isaac like a blade to the ribs. He wanted to seize Natronai by the shoulders, to shake him until the illusion shattered. But he could not. He knew the man's heart was set, and no argument could wrest him from it. So, he bit down his fury, his dread, his bitter certainty.

And as their procession moved deeper into the choked city, Isaac felt as though the walls themselves closed around them, narrowing, tightening, preparing to snap shut like the jaws of a wolf.

Throughout the day, the signs multiplied. Every rooftop, every colonnade seemed to bristle with figures, some cheering, some merely watching. And who could tell, in such a crowd, which were innocents and which were Roman spies?

The marketplace was impassable. Twice their entourage nearly stumbled over fallen children, trampled by the press. Men jostled against each other as they attempted to touch Natronai's robes, tempers flaring, voices raised. A single spark could ignite the entire city into panic.

Isaac muttered to himself as they continued on. He began to play the game in his mind of 'what would the Romans do' if he was their general. It was then that he came to the realization if the Romans came from the lake with ships, they would be inside the harbor and then the city before anyone could even raise a signal. That force would have one mission: to open the gates to any forces stationed outside the city. If they were to strike from the hills at legion strength, they would cut the roads and sever the city from the five thousand he had stationed outside Tiberias. And if they were to infiltrate through the southern gate, then he would never even see them until the first torches were thrown.

One by one the scenarios unrolled in his mind, and each one ended in disaster. He searched Natronai's face for even a flicker of concern but found none.

Natronai was consumed by thoughts of Havilah, by the ceremony to come, by the promise of binding his destiny not only to a people but to a woman. His heart was already pledged, and his mind followed it blindly.

Isaac realized then, with a hollow chill, that this was how great causes perished. Not by the strength of the enemy, but by the weakness of their own leaders. One man's desire could undo the work of thousands. One man's blindness could squander the sacrifices of armies.

And yet, Isaac remained silent. He had spoken his warnings, and they had been dismissed. He would not plead again. Instead, he gripped the hilt of his sword, feeling its familiar weight, the only reassurance left to him.

CHAPTER XXXIV: RED WEDDING

In the center of the city, where the synagogue stood proudly, the rabbinic elite gathered in elegant white. Scribes with trimmed beards, elders with prayer shawls, scrolls, and solemn faces. Not all knew the full truth. Some came thinking this was a gesture of unification. Others, less naive, sensed something sinister in Hillel's sudden generosity. And then there were those that Hillel had just explained his intentions that morning to and they were merely going along with the charade, staying silent and pretending to be enjoying the frivolity of the occasion.

During the morning, Havilah sat in a courtyard garden surrounded by maidens and candles, cloaked in a robe of ivory silk. Her veil hung nearby, resting on a bronze stand. The veil shimmered like starlight, embroidered with doves and pomegranates. Her eyes were wet, but not from sorrow.

"Do you think it's real?" she asked softly.

Her closest friend, Elisheva, tilted her head. "What is?"

"This peace. My father's change. Do you think he truly meant it?"

Elisheva hesitated. "I think… he loves you. That much is true."

Havilah bit her lip, then smiled. "He does. And perhaps this is God's hand, not his."

She looked up at the sun filtering through fig leaves. "When I see Natronai this afternoon, I will know. He will look at me, and the world will make sense again."

Hillel stood at the center of the synagogue's courtyard, arms behind his back. He wore full rabbinic dress with tallit, crimson hemmed robe, and his family seal: the fly. When he saw Natronai approach, he smiled.

It was perfect. The crowds were thick. The seating arranged. The guards that had been Natronai's escort were absent from view, but present. Always present but Hillel paid them no attention. They were too few to foil his plan.

"Welcome, son," Hillel said.

"Father," Natronai said, trying the word for the first time.

They embraced. It was hollow, but none could tell.

"I am honored," Hillel said. "To think, this union might bring about not just peace between men but between heaven and earth."

Natronai smiled, uncertain. Where was the trap that Isaac spoke of? He scanned the courtyard but saw nothing. Only children gathering flowers, elders clapping hands, guests filing in.

Isaac stared at Hillel with cold silence. The two men had nothing to say to the other.

It was time as the fourth hour after noon dawned. Natronai grew nervous and then he saw her.

Havilah stepped forward, radiant, trembling. Her gown shimmered with threads of silver. Her veil concealed her face, but her eyes brimmed with tears of happiness. She prepared to march down the aisle. And at that moment, everything else disappeared.

"Are you happy?" he asked her, voice trembling as she waited by the entrance to the paved courtyard.

She nodded. "I can hardly breathe."

"Then it is real," he whispered. "And nothing else matters."

The stone-paved square at the heart of the synagogue was lit by a hundred oil lamps, their golden glow shimmering off the columns of the old building. A raised bimah stood at the center, draped with linen and adorned with olive branches. Guests filled the benches in orderly rows. Children clutched palm fronds. A cantor softly hummed a wedding hymn. The ceremony began as Natronai entered the synagogue and headed towards the bimah accompanied by Isaac. Havilah remained in the corridor awaiting the proper time to enter.

But in the hills beyond Sepphoris, the horn was about to blow. Isaac's game of pretending what he would do if he was the Roman general was not far from the truth. At the far southern side of the city, in the rocky hills and forests beyond the sight of the revellers, ten Roman cohorts directly under the command of Ursicinus lay in wait. He had split his remaining two legions so that one would completely surround the city of Tiberias after everyone had settled into the city, while the other would go further north, searching for the main encampment of Natronai's army. He had left the operation of the flotilla to his auxillaries. Those with him had their orders: wait until the sun began to set, then strike fast and without warning. By then the flotilla sailing across the lake would have taken the harbor and stormed the gates. As soon as they entered, all exits were to be sealed. There would be no survivors among the rebels or anyone else that got in their way.

Natronai stood beneath the canopy, flanked by two witnesses. His heart beat fast, but not from fear. It was the anticipation of joy, of something sacred. He could feel it drawing near. He looked out toward the long aisle framed with the burning lamps. There, behind the crowd, the bride was preparing to step forward, escorted by her father.

Havilah was breathtaking. A halo of candlelight kissed the folds of her gown. Her eyes locked with his, a mix of nerves and adoration.

But Natronai could tell something was wrong. He watched as Havilah looked behind her. She paused and then began to look frantic. Her father, whose role it was to come forward and take her arm was not there.

The guests around her began whispering. Some of the benches that had been full earlier now stood half-empty. The crowd, once thick and expectant, had thinned alarmingly. At least half were gone. Disappearing without anyone even noticing with all the commotion.

Natronai's pulse skipped.

He looked to his right. Isaac stood motionless, staring toward the synagogue's massive doors. Isaac wanted to say, "I told you so," but it was even too late for that.

A gust of wind swept across the square, rustling the white canopy. The oil lamps flickered. Natronai turned slowly in place. He scanned the balconies, the shadows behind the draperies but saw nothing

A priest from Tiberias, near the front row rose and quietly exited. A few women followed. Then, as if on cue, another handful of guests stood and slipped away.

The silence in the synagogue grew heavier.

Isaac stepped up beside Natronai. "Where is Hillel?" he whispered. "Where is that snake?"

Natronai's throat tightened.

Havilah stood frozen midway down the aisle, her hands clasped nervously. She looked toward the doors, back toward the canopy. Her lips moved: Where is he?

Isaac's hand slowly dropped to his belt. "They're gone," he muttered. "All the Tiberians are gone. Look! All that's left are foreigners to the city. They have all vanished. We have fallen into a trap"

Natronai's eyes shot toward the open doors and then they heard it.

A single blast of a war horn.

It echoed through the canyoned streets of Tiberias, chilling the marrow of every soul still in the square.

Then came the sound of boots. Boots marching in unison.

From the southern gate poured men in glinting segmented armor, rows upon rows of Roman legionaries, bearing the scarlet banners of the VI Ferrata Legion. At their head rode Ursicinus himself, face hidden behind a plumed helmet, sword drawn.

Panic broke.

At the synagogue, guests screamed and fled in all directions. Tables overturned. Lamps spilled fire across linen coverings. The cantor's voice dissolved into a cry of alarm. Havilah stood paralyzed, her hands to her mouth.

Natronai's voice rang out. "GET HER OUT!" It was the only priority he gave to his guards.

Isaac moved like lightning. He grabbed Havilah by the arm and pulled her into a side passage just as the first Roman bolts whistled through the air inside the synagogue corridor. One struck a bystander in the throat. The man crumpled instantly.

Natronai leapt from the bimah and drew a dagger he had hidden in his sleeve. He may not have carried a sword but he had not been foolish enough to be entirely defenseless. "TO ME!" he cried to the scattered remnants of his guard.

But there were too few.

The trap had worked.

The streets were sealed. Legionaries flooded in from all sides. The false wedding had drawn them into a cage, and the door was now swinging shut.

Natronai ducked behind an overturned table as arrows rained down. He could hear Isaac's voice shouting somewhere in the chaos. The clash of steel, the wailing of women. Another horn blast signaled the second wave.

Natronai turned to run but found himself blocked by a Roman auxiliary.

The soldier lunged. Natronai sidestepped, slashed upward, cutting the man across the jaw. Blood sprayed. He grabbed the fallen soldier's gladius and pushed forward, deeper into the maze of smoke and fire.

He had one thought only: Save her.

Elsewhere in the city, Hillel moved with chilling efficiency. Hidden behind the ancient synagogue, a private passage led to a stable where horses had been kept ready. Gamaliel and the other members of the Tiberian delegation were already mounted and ready to take a safe position outside the city.

"You knew," Gamaliel said bitterly. "She was still in the synagogue. You could have saved her."

"She is no longer my daughter," Hillel replied, tightening the strap on his sandal. "She made her choice. Now we make ours."

Gamaliel spat on the ground. "May God judge you for this, Father."

"As he will do you too, my son. I serve God. No one else," Hillel said, as mounted.

Behind them, fire was already rising over the rooftops.

Natronai found Isaac kneeling beside a wounded fighter, trying to stop the bleeding. Around them, bodies littered the square. The canopy lay in tatters. Flames licked at the colonnade.

"Where is she?" Natronai shouted. "|I thought you had her."

Isaac pointed to the alley that ran behind the amphitheater. "She's with one of our most trusted men. They took her into the cellar of the scroll house. Go! I'll hold the gate."

Natronai ran.

Dodging arrows, he dashed into the alley and barreled down the cellar steps. Inside the dim, dusty chamber, he found her.

Havilah was slumped against a barrel, her gown torn, her hands shaking.

"You're alive," she whispered.

He dropped beside her, pulling her close.

"I'm sorry," she wept. "I didn't know. I swear it."

"I know," he said. "It was never you. Isaac had warned me and I never listened."

They held each other as the sounds of slaughter rose outside. Their wedding had become a funeral. Their love, a symbol of betrayal.

Natronai wiped blood from her forehead. It wasn't hers. "You need to go. Now."

"I can't leave you," she said.

"You won't," he promised. "But if we die here, it's over. If we live, if even a remnant survives, then we rebuild."

A thundering crash above signaled the breach of the scroll house.

He rose and pulled her to her feet. "You have to go," he said, voice low and firm. "Now."

She shook her head, tears cutting paths down her soot-darkened cheeks. "No, I won't leave you!"

But Natronai was already signaling to two of his men, seasoned fighters from Sepphoris who had survived every ambush so far. "Take her," he ordered. "Get her to the ravine and then into the hills. Don't stop. Don't look back."

Havilah fought them, screamed his name, cursed them all. But the men obeyed, each grabbing an arm, half-lifting her from the ground. She struggled, kicked, pleaded, but they pressed on, weaving through burning doorways and shattered columns while behind them, Natronai turned to face the oncoming legionaries. His sword gleamed as he climbed the steps of the ruined scroll house, preparing to make a final stand, not for victory, but for defiance. As Havilah was dragged away, her last glimpse of him was not of a prophet or a groom, but of a warrior bathed in firelight, ready to meet death like a king.

The three of them vanished into the smoke that curled over Tiberias like the veil of a funeral shroud, dark plumes rising into the heavens from the heart of the once-prosperous city. The firestorm had begun as soon as the town was breached, stoked by Roman torches and vengeance. All the while, Havilah could not help but think about her father. He had disappeared well before the ambush began. The truth had come not with a whisper but with a scream: he had conspired, perhaps unwittingly or perhaps not, with the Romans. She remembered she had seen a letter in his study days before, bearing a Roman seal that had been broken open, but he quickly stuffed it away beneath his robe as soon as she entered the room. It was now obvious that her father, the one she had trusted above all, had played a role in orchestrating their doom.

Havilah could barely feel her feet. Her bloodied sandals slapped against the stone with each faltering step as she was dragged through a side alley by two men ordered to carrier her to safety. One was Eliezer, Isaac's body guard, nursing a mangled arm, and the other, Menash, one of Natronai's best scouts, whose leg now bled freely from a javelin graze. They had no time to feel the pain, no moment to rest. The full legion of Ursicinus had breached the city gates just after the wedding massacre. Now, Tiberias was burning, and the roads to the hills were closing like the jaws of a snare.

Behind them, the synagogue compound lay soaked in blood. Natronai had vanished into the smoke, sword drawn, yelling for the remnants of the wedding party to flee.

"This way," Eliezer hissed.

They ducked into a collapsed stable and crawled through a rear shaft leading out to a ravine that skirted the city's northeast walls. The escape plan had been Isaac's, drawn up in secret after long nights of poring over maps. He never did trust her father and just in case prepared for the worst. Patricius had resisted even taking a look at it, arrogant in his belief that Hillel was sincere in offering his daughter as a bride.

The survivors burst through the brush outside the city, the air thick with floating cinders and falling ash. Around them, others stumbled from the treelines: bakers, smiths, a few were the fleeing soldiers remaining from those that Isaac had stationed within the city. Children cried. Mothers held them silent. The hills would not offer safety for long.

A sharp horn pierced the wind.

"Romans," Eliezer said.

Cresting the western ridge was a cohort of cavalry, Ursinicus's scouts. Their armor gleamed like brass locusts in the rising sun.

"Run!"

The chase that followed was brutal. The Romans, mounted and tireless, picked off the stragglers one by one. Arrows blackened the sky. A child stumbled and was trampled. Menash was pulled under their hooves when his wound gave out. Eliezer and Havilah, mouths dry with dust and terror, dove down a steep escarpment and rolled into a narrow creek bed. They pressed their bodies to the wet stones as the horses snorted loudly above.

Nightfall came like a reprieve from a god who had turned his face. The Romans paused, perhaps regrouping, perhaps content to herd their prey toward their own encampment to feed the slave market. The pair crept northward in silence, following the route Isaac had laid out for retreat. A path that would take them supposedly safely back to Magdala.

By midday of the next day, they reached the outer edges of the hill camp where Isaac had hidden the five thousand. What they found was ruin. Corpses lay in tangled heaps, many still holding their weapons. The Roman legion had struck before dawn, using the element of surprise and overwhelming numbers. The Jews had never stood a chance. Isaac's foresight had placed them in the hills, but he had not counted on betrayal. Someone had leaked the fact that they were outside the city and Havilah did not need to guess who.

She walked the blood-soaked fields in a daze. Dogs fed on the dead. Fires still smoldered in the remnants of tents. Armor lay twisted like broken shells. The air reeked of death and urine and burned linen. Her father's name fell from the lips of survivors like a curse. They never even had a chance to charge towards the city to even attempt a rescue.

"Have you seen Isaac?" she whispered.

"Taken," someone muttered, a youth with a cracked helmet. "They paraded him through the ranks in chains before carting him south. Said he would be made an example in Caesarea."

"What about Natronai?"

No answer. Some that had also escaped from the city swore they saw him cut down by the Romans, others said he escaped surrounded by a band of zealots. Havilah clung to hope like a drowning woman clings to driftwood, but each passing minute made hope feel more like delusion.

The days blurred. She wandered the hills with the other survivors, hunted by the Romans, feeding on roots, finding shelter in caves. But the wrath of Ursicinus had not yet been sated. Word spread: Tiberias had been encircled and Sepphoris would be next.

Sepphoris, once a gem of Galilee, was to be made an example for letting itself become Natronai's base of operations. From a distant hill, Havilah watched with hollow eyes as the torches were set. Flames leapt from rooftop to rooftop. The wind carried the crackle of beams collapsing, the screams of those still trapped inside. Even the Roman soldiers watched in silence. It was not a battle. It was a grotesque purge.

Her father's legacy burned with it.

They say that Ursicinus declared it righteous vengeance, that the Jews had betrayed the Pax Romana and brought fire upon themselves. But to the few who watched from the crags and shadows, it was not justice. It was annihilation. It was genocide.

Three days later, Havilah found herself among a cluster of thirty survivors huddled near a spring on Mount Tabor. Of the five thousand man army Isaac had brought to Tiberias, only a few hundred still lived, scattered, leaderless, haunted. Some spoke of regrouping with the main body near Magdala. Others of fleeing east beyond the Jordan.

A council formed under the shade of a cedar grove. A rabbi from Sepphoris, a former sage turned fighter, a midwife, and Havilah herself.

"We must decide," the rabbi said. "Do we surrender? Do we scatter?"

"We wait," Havilah answered.

"For what?"

She looked southward, to the smoke rising still from the ruins of Sepphoris. "For Natronai," she said. "He will return."

"And if he does not?" the others questioned.

"Then we mourn," she answered, her eyes dry with no more tears to shed.

Eliezer placed a hand on her shoulder, feeling her loss and somehow knowing that Natronai would not return. He suggested they head towards Magdala with the hope that the main force under Ashurbanipol still was intact. They had no way of knowing but it was their only hope.

The night was still, unnaturally so, as if the earth itself had paused to mourn. The surviving few huddled beneath the canopy of Mount Tabor, but Havilah had wandered alone, beyond the dim circle of the firelight, until she reached a solitary cedar that stood like a sentinel overlooking the charred valley below. The smoke from Sepphoris still drifted faintly on the wind, a ghost clinging to the ruins of a world that had died. In her trembling hands, she held the blade Natronai had once given her the first night they stayed together, a small, curved knife engraved with the words al tikra'i bodedah; call her not forsaken.

With slow, deliberate strokes, she carved into the living wood. Two crossed spears. A six-pointed star between them. A new sigil for a cause now buried beneath the blood-soaked soil. Her fingers bled as she etched, her tears falling freely, mixing with sap and grief. She whispered prayers, ancient ones, half-forgotten ones, until the words lost meaning, becoming nothing more than breath and sobs. Her body ached from the days of running, from hunger, from sorrow too immense to name.

Then, standing before the mark she had made, Havilah felt the weight settle in her chest like stone. The hope that Natronai might have survived, the thing that had kept her moving, breathing, was gone. No one had seen him among the living. No sign, no word. Only the memory of him, alone and radiant in his final stand, consumed by flame and steel. She clutched the knife to her breast, knelt before the cedar, and pressed her forehead to the bark, whispering his name like a prayer. And then, with the last of her strength, she placed the blade where her heart beat fiercest, and ended her sorrow in silence, beneath the mark of a forgotten rebellion.

But the land would never be the same.

CHAPTER XXXV: REVENGE

In the ruins of Sepphoris, Roman patrols walked through embers, executing survivors, collecting valuables, and burning ancient records of Jewish civilization. Ursicinus stood near the blackened skeleton of what had been the synagogue where Natronai had given his first speech. His face bore no joy, only grim satisfaction of a war coming to an end.

"Let it be known," he told his aide, "that any city harboring rebellion shall face this fate. Write it into the proclamations. Carve it on stone if you must. No more talk of insurrection will be tolerated."

"What of the girl and their Messiah?"

Ursicinus turned toward the hills. "If they live, which I doubt, they will suffer. Their main camp has been dispersed and whatever remains of their army has fled across the hills to Arabia. I'm sure their Persian general is glad to be rid of this place. He had no reason to stay."

"Shall we pursue them?"

"I have no quarrel with the Persian. If he takes what remains with him back to Ctesiphon, I care little."

"But what if the girl and Natronai are with them," the aide was still concerned.

"It's impossible they made it that far." Ursicinus was certain. "We cut off every avenue. If they live then they will die a miserable fate in the wilderness. Let carrion strip their bones. Their story ends here. Now it is time to return to Caesarea and let Gallus deal with the matter," the general instructed. "But first we return to Tiberias and deal with a small matter there."

The year was early 353 and imperial retribution had turned decisive. Patricius, it was declared fell in battle, though no body was ever receovered and Sepphoris was turned into a pile of ash. Isaac managed to find his way to Sepphoris, only to be captured following the city's fall. He was sent to Caesarea in chains to stand before Gallus. The rebellion of Patricius had ended not with the clang of swords on shields, but with silence. Sepphoris, once proud and stubborn, stood no more. Its walls had been torn down stone by stone, its synagogues toppled, its markets turned into nothing but heaps of smoldering ash. Ursicinus, with the cold precision of a surgeon, had reduced it to an example, a warning to any city tempted to harbor insurgents. Sepphoris had been called the "ornament of Galilee," but now it was no more than rubble. The Roman legions had left their imprint not only in ruined streets but in the memory of every survivor, if such a word could still apply to those who staggered half-burnt and half-mad out of the wreckage.

Magdala had fared no better. If Sepphoris was dismantled, Magdala was erased. The flames had licked every corner of the fishing town, and where nets once dried along the shoreline, corpses now bobbed in the waves. Families had clutched one another as the soldiers set fire to the houses, and the shrieks of the dying echoed across the lake. The smoke drifted far over the Sea of Galilee, visible even from Tiberias, a black banner covering the sky, proclaiming Rome's vengeance.

Tens of thousands of Jews were dead. Some had fought with Patricius. Some had done no more than offer bread or water to the rebels. Others had simply been unlucky enough to live in the wrong place at the wrong time. Ursicinus's policy had been clear from the beginning: mercy was weakness, and weakness was rebellion's seed. He uprooted not only the rebels but the soil in which rebellion might grow. To him, no Jew was innocent, only complicit by blood or silence.

When the killing en masse finally ended, the army turned back toward Tiberias. It was there that everything had begun; Patricius's wedding, the spark that had lit the flames of revolt, the betrayal of alliances, the first declaration of defiance against Rome, following the spectacle in the arena. Ursicinus always intended to return there, not merely to claim victory but in particular to spit in the face of those who had thought themselves clever enough to bargain with an empire.

Rumor reached him before he even entered the city: Rabbi Hillel, the patriarch and Nasi of Israel, who had thought to broker safety through a false wedding and duplicity, it was now said muttered against the general. Hillel claimed Rome had broken its word, that Ursicinus had slaughtered the innocent and destroyed half the city of Tiberias itself in defiance of their agreement. He whispered of betrayal, of dishonor, of Roman treachery. Ursicinus smiled when he heard it. He welcomed such muttering. Let the rabbi speak, let him complain. He would silence him not with a sword but with the truth of power. And so, he ordered his retinue to prepare a meeting. The general would sit across from the rabbi, man to man, and peel from him the last shreds of dignity.

Hillel appeared to have aged a lifetime in weeks. His beard, once long and grey with solemn dignity, was now white and ragged, as if clumps of hair had been torn out by grief rather than years. His dead daughter was returned to him not as bride but as corpse. His city, Tiberias, had been battered by Ursicinus's soldiers, who treated it as a nest of rebels whether or not all its citizens had lifted a hand in defiance. His followers dwindled daily, those who had once called him wise now cursing him for their losses, whispering that his bargaining had saved no one.

Still, Hillel clung to the only thread he had: the supposed agreement he forged with the general. Had not Ursicinus promised him that if he delivered the leaders of the rebellion, Rome would spare the city? Had he not maneuvered to arrange the wedding, to lure Natronai and Isaac into a place where they could be taken? Was this not the very essence of his compromise?

But the Patricius was dead, or so the Romans said, though no body had been produced. Natronai had vanished like smoke, perhaps there was no body because some of his followers buried it before the Romans could find it and desecrate it. The wedding had ended in blood. Hillel's daughter had been crushed in the chaos. And half of Tiberias had burned. Collateral damage as far as the Roman general was concerned.

The rabbi muttered in the halls of his house, pacing as though the floor might collapse beneath him. He told his disciples that Rome had betrayed him, that Ursicinus had shown himself to be faithless. He still believed, somehow, that his words might carry weight, that he could demand an explanation, even compensation. But the disciples only exchanged nervous glances. They knew what Hillel failed to realize himself: a man who thinks he can negotiate with the devil will always be sold a one-sided bargain.

The arrival of Ursicinus was like a storm rolling into the city. His soldiers marched in disciplined ranks, the iron of their armor glinting under the sun, their banners fluttering with the imperial eagle. Behind them came the wagons of spoils, the chained prisoners dragged from Sepphoris and Magdala, their faces hollow with hunger and fear.

The people of Tiberias watched in silence. Some spat, some wept, some fell to their knees in desperate prayers. The city had already been bruised by Roman wrath, and none wished to provoke it further.

At the head rode Ursicinus himself. He sat tall in the saddle, his features hard, his eyes like carved stone. He was a man accustomed to command, accustomed to watching cities burn and not blinking. If he noticed the glares of the townsfolk, he gave no sign. To him they were not men and women but potential enemies, and therefore sheep to be culled at will.

When word came that Ursicinus would meet him, Hillel prepared himself. He rehearsed his arguments, his laments. He told himself he would speak with strength, that he would show the general that Rome could not easily crush a man of God as it crushed cities.

The general dismounted only when he reached the patriarch's house, where Hillel had been waiting impatiently. The rabbi was sitting in the audience chamber, trembling but trying to mask it with dignity. His hands clutched the staff that had once symbolized authority but now seemed more like a crutch for his faltering body.

The doors opened, and Ursicinus strode in. He removed his gauntlets slowly, deliberately, as though each movement was a statement. He let them fall onto the table with a metallic thud before he sat, uninvited, across from the rabbi.

He did not bow, did not greet, did not provide any honor or respect. He sat himself comfortably in the chair, wiping his boots into the tightly wound woolen rug as if the house were his own.

For a long moment he said nothing. His gaze pinned Hillel as a hawk pins a rabbit. Then, at last, he spoke.

"So. You wished to see me, Rabbi. You felt that you might have something to say. You have complaints?"

Hillel swallowed, summoning what remained of his last vestige of courage. He then straightened his back, willing his voice not to tremble.

"You have wronged me," he began. "You did not keep your word," he said. "We had a bargain. The city of Tiberias was to be spared. Yet half of it lies in ruins. My daughter is dead, though I gave her hand in marriage as you demanded. Thousands of innocents have perished. This was not the agreement. Men and women who never raised a sword now feed your slave markets."

Ursicinus leaned back in his chair and laughed, a harsh sound that filled the chamber. His lips curled. "Wronged you? I demanded? Do you imagine I give thought to you at all, Rabbi? Speak, then. Tell me all that is on your mind. Entertain me."

Hillel struck the floor with his staff. "We had an agreement. The city was to be spared. Yet half of Tiberias burns. My daughter lies in her grave. The people cry out in anguish. Was this Rome's oath?"

The general's laughter continued like iron scraping stone. "The agreement?" he questioned. "Do you truly believe there was an agreement? Let me remind you, old man: the bargain was that both leaders of the rebellion would be delivered to me at the wedding. Both. Where are they? The Patricius is still unaccounted for, his body has never been found. And as for Isaac, my men had to chase after him across the province to Sepphoris before they were able to subdue him and bring him in chains to me.

Tell me, did you hand them over? No. You failed. And you dare to speak of bargains. You gave me nothing. And you dare complain that I did not spare your walls?"

"I gave you my child," Hillel cried. His voice cracked. "I gave her as bride, as bait, as you demanded. She died in the chaos you unleashed. Do you mock a father's grief?"

"Mock?" Ursicinus leaned forward, eyes hard as flint. "No, I dismiss it. How can I demand that which was never mine. Your daughter was nothing to me. You were the one that gave her hand, you were the one to offer her as bait, because she was not mine to take. She died because you failed, not because I demanded anything of her. Do not insult me with your feigned father's grief when it is obvious that you cared nothing for your daughter. Do not blame Rome for the price of your own schemes that go awry."

Hillel's face flushed with anger. "Natronai is dead! The people say so. The fighting in the city proved it. Yes, Natronai vanished in the chaos, but I did all I could to bring him forth. Would you punish the whole people for what was beyond my control? You killed thousands who never lifted a sword. Women, children, the sick, the old. How could you dare to call them rebels?"

"Beyond your control," Ursicinus repeated with a sneer. "At last, you speak truth. It was always beyond your control. Did you think Rome needed your help to crush rebels? Did you think you were the master of events, when you were nothing but a pawn? Your daughter's marriage was no more to me than a stone cast into a river. She lived, she died, it mattered nothing. The city burned because you failed. That is the only truth."

The rabbi gripped the staff so tightly his knuckles turned white. "You still continue to mock me," he said, voice trembling. "But you cannot deny that you slaughtered thousands who took no part in the rebellion. Old men, women, and children. Tell me, what crime had they committed?" The rabbi slammed his fist on the table. "Justice? It is butchery! You will answer before the God of Israel."

Ursicinus leaned forward, his eyes glittering with cold amusement. "In war, there are no innocents. Every man is a fighter in waiting, every woman a mother of rebels, every child a seed of defiance. You want to know their crime; they were Jews, just as you are. To leave them alive is to sow the field with weeds. I reap, Rabbi, and I leave no weeds. You should be grateful I let you live at all."

Hillel's composure broke. He struck the floor with his staff, his voice rising. "Grateful? You have destroyed my family, my city, my people, and you tell me to be grateful? You promised me safety, and you gave me ashes!"

Ursicinus's laughter returned, louder this time, echoing off the stone walls. "Safety? You are a fool, Hillel. You betrayed your own kin, your own people, thinking you could save yourself. You imagined you had power to bargain with Rome. But what are you? A feeble old man clinging to titles. You betrayed your Patricius, this Natronai. You betrayed your daughter. And still you believed you could negotiate. You betrayed everyone, Rabbi, even yourself."

The words struck like blows. Hillel staggered, his shoulders sagging, his mouth opening and closing with no sound.

Ursicinus rose, towering over him. "You are alive because I allow it. Not because of any bargain, not because of any promise, but because your death would mean nothing. You are already dead in the eyes of your people. They see you for what you are: weak, pathetic, a tool discarded once it has served its purpose. Remember that, if you dare speak of bargains again. Your God is silent, Rabbi. He did not shield Sepphoris. He did not save Magdala. He did not protect your daughter. Where was He when my soldiers marched? Where was He when your people screamed? He was absent, or he was powerless. Either way, he was not there and even now he is silent."

Hillel's face went pale. He stammered words of scripture, half-remembered psalms. But Ursicinus cut him off.

Hillel sagged back into his chair, the fight draining from him. He whispered, "You leave me nothing."

Ursicinus's grinned wickedly. "Nothing is all you deserve. You live only because your death as I have said would mean nothing. I have broken you. Your people despise you. You are a ghost that still breathes. Be grateful, Rabbi, that I let you crawl in your shame." Having said that, he turned and strode from the chamber. The brazier's flame flickered in his wake, and then snuffed itself out, leaving Hillel in darkness.

Outside, the people of Tiberias whispered. Some cursed the rabbi openly, saying he had brought ruin on them by dealing with Rome. Others pitied him, seeing in his hollow eyes a man broken beyond repair. But one thing was absolute, none respected him.

Ursicinus, meanwhile, rode through the streets like a conqueror. He had not only destroyed cities but broken spirits. He had shown that Rome could not be bargained with, only obeyed. And as he departed Tiberias, leaving garrisons to keep order, he thought of Natronai's missing body. Somewhere, perhaps, the rebel still lived. That thought displeased him. For if Natronai yet breathed, then hope would linger in the land. A hope that would let them defy Rome's wrath, even if Natronai was nothing more than a survivor hunted without end.

Hillel finally stood and walked through the courtyards of his house, each step echoing. Servants no longer bowed deeply when he passed. Disciples no longer looked at him with reverence. Their eyes, once trusting, were now full of accusations. His disciples whispered among themselves. Some sneered openly.

"He sold us for ashes," one said.

"He killed his own daughter," another spat.

"He is no leader, only a coward who thought himself a prince."

Hillel heard every word. He said nothing. His lips moved silently, repeating prayers, but no one listened.

"You said Rome would spare us," one cried. "You told us there was a covenant between them and us. Where is your covenant now, Rabbi? Where is the Roman mercy you promised?"

Hillel tried to speak of circumstances beyond control, of chaos, of Natronai's disappearance. But his words fell like dust.

Another disciple spat at his feet. "You bargained with wolves," he said. "And you fed them your own daughter."

The rabbi staggered, clutching his chest as if struck. He wanted to defend himself, to claim wisdom, to remind them of his lineage, of his scholarship, of his piety. But the truth pressed against him like a weight: he had failed.

Still, he clung to the thought that the bargain had been real, that he had been wronged. If Ursicinus would have only admitted it, if Rome would only acknowledge it, perhaps he could salvage something, if not his reputation, then at least the dignity of vindication.

By the next Sabbath, the main synagogue of Tiberias was nearly empty when he entered. Men avoided his gaze. Women pulled their children close. The rabbi who once carried authority now carried only shame.

He tried to speak of mourning, of God's hidden purposes. His voice cracked. Few listened. Most walked out.

Hillel realized, with a bitterness sharper than death, that Ursicinus had been right. He was alive, but he was already dead.

CHAPTER XXXVI: AFTERMATH

In the villages of Judaea, in the markets of Galilee, in the whispers of the synagogues, the memory lived. Mothers told their children of Sepphoris's fall. Refugees spoke of the day Rome turned its face of iron against them. And always, beneath the whispers, was the question: was Natronai really dead or did he yet live, waiting, plotting, a flame hidden under ashes about to burst forth again?

A widow of Sepphoris wandered the wreckage of her home, clutching the charred remains of a child's sandal. She had buried her husband with her own hands, scraping soil over his blackened corpse with the broken fragment of a clay pot. The Romans had marched on, leaving the survivors to rot amidst the ashes. She muttered prayers with cracked lips, though she no longer knew if she prayed to God for deliverance or vengeance.

By the lakeshore of Magdala, a fisherman sat on the rocks, staring at the water where his boat once floated. The Romans had burned it, and with it, his livelihood. His sons had been dragged away in chains. He no longer had words; his eyes were empty, his back bent. When he saw the sails of Roman galleys gliding across the water, he spat into the lake, though the gesture brought him no satisfaction.

In Tiberias itself, the streets were filled with refugees. Children begged for bread; women huddled with infants against the walls of half-burnt houses. The air carried not only the stench of smoke but the bitterness of betrayal. Some cursed Patricius for leading them into rebellion. Others cursed Hillel for thinking he could buy peace with a daughter's hand and half-kept promises. The name of Ursicinus was spoken only with fear and dread.

The gates of Caesarea groaned open as Ursicinus led the victory procession. Citizens poured into the streets, eager to witness Rome's triumph over Galilee. Trumpets blared, standards fluttered, and at the center of the grim spectacle marched the prisoners, fifty of the rebel officers in chains, barefoot, their faces gaunt but unbowed.

At their head walked Isaac. His wrists were shackled, iron biting into raw flesh, yet he held himself with a strange dignity. He looked neither left nor right, though the crowds jeered, spat, and hurled stones. The Romans displayed him not as a man but as a trophy, proof that the rebellion had been crushed. But to those who watched closely, Isaac did not walk as a conquered man. He walked as one who carried a nation's grief and defiance on his shoulders.

Behind him shuffled the other rebels. Some of them were men barely old enough to grow their beards. They had been dragged from caves, from burning homes, from the smoking ruins of Sepphoris and Magdala. Yet they marched with their heads high, their eyes burning with the same fire. Rome could chain their limbs, but not their spirit.

The procession wound through the streets of Caesarea, past the amphitheater, past the marble statues of emperors, until it came at last to the governor's palace, where Constantius Gallus awaited, having traveled from Antioch for this very special occasion.

The great hall of Caesarea was stifling with heat and tension. Torches guttered in their sconces, casting long shadows on the marble walls. At the far end of the chamber, raised high upon a dais, sat Caesar Constantius Gallus, stern-faced and heavily guarded. Beside him stood scribes, notaries, and the imperial lictors bearing their fasces. Draped in imperial robes, crowned with the diadem, he radiated authority. His face was pale, his eyes sharp and cold. He was not a man given to mercy; he was a man who all had come to realize ruled through fear.

Dragged in chains, Isaac entered with fifty other rebels, their clothes torn from weeks of imprisonment, their bodies battered by whips and irons. Yet their eyes burned with something no prison could extinguish, defiance. They had been paraded through the streets of Caesarea earlier that morning, mocked by the crowd, their humiliation meant to break them before ever stepping into the presence of Caesar. But as they stood in the hall, backs straight despite their chains, it was clear they had not been broken.

Ursicinus stood at Gallus's side, armor polished until it no longer showed any stains of the war, his expression hard with satisfaction. The prisoners were forced to kneel before the dais. Chains clattered, but Isaac alone refused to bow. Soldiers shoved him down, but he struggled back to his feet.

Gallus's voice was sharp, carrying across the chamber. "You are their ringleader?" he demanded to know.

Isaac met his gaze without flinching.

"I am a son of Israel. No more, no less."

Gallus's lips curled. "Isaac ben Eleazar, called the right hand of the Patricius. You stand accused of sedition against Rome, of inciting rebellion, of desecrating the peace of this province, and of the slaughter of loyal subjects of the empire. What say you?"

"Given the opportunity, I would do it again," he said defiantly.

Gallus continued. "You have led your people into ruin. You have defied Rome. Do you know the cost of such folly?"

Isaac raised his head. His beard was matted with dust, his wrists raw from iron shackles, his voice rang clear and strong, echoing off the marble walls. "I say that the charges are all true. I rebelled against Rome. And I would do so again, and again, and again, until the last breath leaves my body and Rome is nothing more than a lost memory to history. For no man born of woman has the right to enslave my people in our own land. The cost of freedom is always high. But it is never too high. You call it folly; I call it faith. You think you have crushed us, but the spirit of my people cannot be chained and it cannot be crushed. We have endured Babylon, Persia, Greece, and now Rome. We will endure when your empire is nothing more than dust. We will endure against whatever the future holds. That is our legacy and there is nothing you can do to stop it."

Murmurs rippled through the chamber. Ursicinus's eyes narrowed, but Gallus gestured for silence. One of the scribes glanced nervously at Gallus, but the Caesar's expression remained unreadable, his blue-green eyes fixed upon the prisoner. " You confess openly then? You admit to treason?"

"I admit," Isaac said, his gaze unwavering, "to fighting for freedom. Call it treason if you will. Rome has ever called freedom by that name when it is not her own."

Ursicinus gave a sharp bark of laughter. "Arrogant even at the end."

Gallus raised a hand, silencing him. His eyes moved to the other prisoners.

"And you, the rest of you, do you too share this madness? Was it not for Patricius that you took up arms, for his blasphemous claim to kingship?"

Before anyone could stop them, one of the younger rebels cried out, his voice raw but proud:

"We fight for no man! We fight for the God of Israel and the freedom He promised His people!"

Another joined him: "Natronai was but one among us. He is not the cause, he is the brother who walked beside us."

"You speak as though your rebellion were noble," Caesar said. "But you led men to their deaths. You brought ruin upon your cities. Was it worth it?"

Isaac lifted his chin.

"Better ruin with honor than peace in chains. Better ashes with dignity than life as slaves. You ask if it was worth it, yes, it was worth everything. And if it takes another two hundred years, or two thousand, we will rise again. We will not be broken. We will not forget. This is our land, our covenant, our God. Rome is but a dark shadow passing across it."

A hush fell. Even some Roman officers shifted uneasily at the boldness of the words.

Gallus leaned forward. "And what about your leader, the one they call Patricius, or Natronai? Where is he? Does he live, did he abandon you, or is he dead?"

The chamber bristled with tension. Ursicinus's gaze swept the prisoners, demanding an answer.

Then, before Isaac could speak, one of the rebels shouted, "I am Natronai!"

Another joined: "I am Natronai!"

Then another. And another.

Within moments, the hall thundered with voices, all fifty prisoners crying out as one:

"I am Natronai! I am Natronai! I am Natronai!"

The sound shook the marble walls of the hall, a roar of defiance that refused to be silenced. Guards struck the prisoners with staves, but they shouted louder, their chains rattling like drums of war.

Gallus's face hardened, but even he seemed momentarily shaken. For here was no single rebel to crush, no single leader to execute. Gallus raised his hand again, commanding silence. The echoes of the declaration still rang from the marble as he spoke slowly, coldly.

"You all claim the mantle of the Patricius? You dare to equate yourselves with a pretender who eluded even death?"

The rebellion had no head to sever; it lived in every man, in every voice, in every Jew who longed for freedom.

Isaac raised his voice above them all.

"You do not understand, Caesar. Natronai is not a man but instead is another name for freedom. You cannot kill him, more than you can kill a dream, Caesar! For he is all of us. He is the fire that burns in every heart of Israel. Strike us down, and a thousand more will rise. Crucify us, and our blood will cry from the stones. Drive us into the sea, and our children will crawl back onto the shore, still crying out for liberty. We will never bow! We are Natronai. Every Jew who yearns for freedom is Natronai. And you cannot kill us all."

The chamber erupted, soldiers struggling to contain the chaos. But the cry had already been heard.

Gallus's jaw tightened. For a long moment, he said nothing. Then he gestured to the guards.

"Silence them."

A soldier struck Isaac across the mouth with the shaft of his spear. Blood trickled from his lip, but Isaac only spat it onto the marble floor. "Even now," he snarled, "you fear words more than swords."

Another prisoner cried out from the back:

"Rome fears truth because it cannot kill it!"

Others followed, their voices rising like a wave that battered against the imperial authority in the hall.

"You can crucify us, but we will not bow!"

"Our children will remember! Israel will live!"

The hall dissolved into chaos. Guards rushed forward, beating the prisoners with staves, but even under the blows the rebels shouted, their voices echoing like the roar of the sea. Gallus's face had gone pale with fury, but still he remained seated, gripping the arm of his throne until his knuckles whitened.

When silence was finally beaten back into the room, Constantius Gallus rose, his voice cold and unyielding.

"Enough of this foolishness. You would spit upon the majesty of Rome in the very face of the Caesar? You would turn this trial into mockery? These men are guilty of rebellion, guilty of defiance against Rome. There can be no mercy. By my decree, all shall be crucified. Let their deaths stand as warning to all who would rise against the empire."

The rebels lifted their voices in a final cheer, shouting 'Am Israel Chai', even as the guards dragged them away. Chains rattled, but their taunts carried through the halls.

Ursicinus stepped forward, bowing.

"It will be done, Caesar, but I thought you said there were to be no crucifixions."

"That was before I realized how impertinent these Jews could be. It is the only fitting punishment to teach these people a lesson once and for all."

The general smiled. "And most fittingly, I will carry it out outside the gates of Tiberias. Let that city, faithless and cowardly, see the cost of betrayal. Let them watch their leaders die."

Gallus gave a single nod and the prisoners were dragged away.

The march back to Tiberias was long and brutal. The prisoners staggered under the weight of their crosses, beaten and bloodied by soldiers. Yet they sang psalms as they walked, voices rising over the sound of marching feet.

The people of Tiberias lined the roads, silent, ashamed. Some wept. Some turned away. By mid-morning, the place was already thick with crowds, Romans, Greeks, Samaritans, and Jews alike, drawn as if by morbid gravity to witness the punishment. Soldiers barked orders, clearing a path. Lictors swung their rods at anyone who pressed too close. Some whispered prayers. But none dared intervene.

At the head walked Isaac, bearing his cross with steady steps. His body was broken, but his eyes still blazed with fire. The people watched in silence as he passed, some weeping, some trembling, some daring to look on with pride.

A woman cried out from the crowd, "Isaac! Forgive us!" and a centurion struck her with the flat of his blade. Isaac turned his head just enough to meet her eyes, his voice hoarse but steady:

"There is nothing to forgive. Stand tall. Do not bow."

Outside the gates of Tiberias, fifty crosses were raised. Soldiers hammered nails into wrists and feet, each blow ringing like a curse across the valley. The rebels were nailed to the wood, their cries of pain mingling with their cries of defiance. Blood soaked the earth. The sky darkened with vultures circling overhead.

When Isaac's turn came, he was thrown backward onto the wood. The nails were driven into his flesh, and though his body shook, he did not scream. Instead, with each hammer blow he forced words out between clenched teeth: "Shema Yisrael, Adonai Eloheinu, Adonai Echad. Hear, O Israel, the Lord is our God, the Lord is One."

The crowd shuddered. Many fell to their knees, repeating the words through their tears. More nails and Isaac continued to raise his voice his voice. His words rang out across the crowd, over the soldiers, over the city walls: "We will rise again! We will be free! Israel shall never die!"

The other rebels took up the cry, their voices ragged but fierce. Fragments of psalms were shouted, prayers echoed across the hillside. It sounded like a broken liturgy, jagged and raw, but it carried the cadence of worship.

"Out of the depths I cry to you, O Lord!" one man shouted.

"Though I walk through the valley of the shadow of death," cried another.

"I fear no evil, for You are with me!"

The soldiers cursed and struck them, but the voices would not stop. The people of Tiberias wept openly now, their shame turned to mourning, their mourning to resolve.

When the crosses were raised upright, the prisoners hung like fruit on a tree of sorrow. Blood streaked down their arms, sweat glistened on their faces, but still their eyes were not broken. Isaac, suspended between heaven and earth, raised his head and spoke, not to God, but to the people gathered below.

"You see us nailed here as criminals," he cried, his voice cracked but unshaken. "But we are not conquered. No iron can bind the soul. No empire can chain the will of a people to be free."

The soldiers jeered, some throwing stones at his body, but Isaac only lifted his head higher, his voice carrying like the wind.

"You think you will kill the spirit of Natronai by killing us, but Natronai is every one of us! He lives in you, in your sons, in your daughters. He lives in the unborn children yet to walk this land. Rome crucifies fifty men, but Rome cannot crucify the nation of Israel!"

A murmur ran through the crowd. Even those who had come in fear, or to mock, felt something shift inside them. The other prisoners, though writhing in agony, continued to chant together. Weak voices joined into one, ragged but undeniable:

"The Lord is my light and my salvation, whom shall I fear?"

The words carried like a hymn, floating across the waters of the Galilee.

Ursicinus watched, arms crossed, unmoved. To him, it was justice. To the people, it was a revelation. He approached the crucifix where Isaac hung. "Do you have any last request," he asked. "Though we are enemies, I can admire courage and I will grant you one last boon."

His voice hoarse and cracking, Isaac made his last request. "Bring the patriarch here so I can look upon him. That is my only request."

Ursicinus immediately gave the order to one of his tribunes to go to the house of Hillel and bring him before Isaac."

It took time to retrieve the Nasi of Tiberias. More time than Isaac could afford to lose. Finally, Hillel was dragged from the crowd and held beneath Isaac's weakening frame.

"Look at me, Rabbi!" Isaac commanded but Hillel refused.

"Make him look," Ursicinus ordered and two of his soldiers forced Hillel's head to look upward.

Isaac, near the end, gathered his remaining strength. His chest heaved as he forced the blood and phlegm into his throat and spat it directly into Hillel's face."

It was the first time any in the crowd cheered that day. So many wishing they could have done the same. Ursicinus roared with laughter.

Isaac shouted one final time, his voice breaking but still defiant, "Do not weep for us! We are the seed! From this hill, from this blood, Israel will rise again. We will rise again. We will be free!"

This time a roar broke from the crowd, some in grief, some in anger, some in hope. Soldiers rushed into the crowd to silence them, striking down men and women alike, but the cry could not be smothered, it could not be extinguished.

And so, they hung, fifty men, battered by the wind whipping at their bodies, their voices echoing until the last fell silent. Yet in the silence that followed, the people whispered among themselves, repeating Isaac's words like scripture. *'We will rise again. We will be free.'*

The crosses stood for days, a forest of defiance outside the city. Every passerby was forced to look upon them, to see the price of rebellion. But for the Jews of Galilee, they became something else, not symbols of defeat, but of promise. A reminder that even broken, even crucified, their spirit was Invictus. And long after the bodies had been taken down, the memory remained.

EPILOGUE

Emperor Constantius summoned Gallus and Constantina to Mediolanum. Constantina left first, in order to gain some of her brother's trust, but suddenly died from a fever at Caeni Gallicani in Bithynia. Gallus, whose bonds to Constantius had now been severely weakened, remained in Antioch, afraid to answer the summons.

Seeing his cousin's refusal to meet, Constantius tried to lure Gallus, sending the tribunus scutariorum, Scudilo, to tell Gallus that the Emperor wanted to raise him to the level of Augustus. Letting pride march before wisdom, Gallus took Constantius's bait and left Antioch to meet him. Believing the honor to be true, Gallus had the audacity to stage a chariot race in Constantinople's Hippodrome and crowned the victor, an honor that was only reserved for an Augustus. This insolence enraged Constantius. In an attempt to further isolate Gallus from any form of military protection, Constantius had the garrisons removed from all of the towns in Gallus's path as he headed to Mediolanum

When Gallus arrived at Poetovio in Noricum, Barbatio, one of the officers who had been supporting Gallus's dismissal within Constantius' court, surrounded the palace of the Caesar and arrested him, stripping Gallus of the imperial robes, but assuring him that no harm would come to him. It was a lie designed to render Gallus complacent and it worked. Gallus was led to Pola, Istria where he was interrogated by some of the highest officials of Constantius' court, including the eunuch praepositus sacri cubiculi, Eusebius, and the agens notarius rebus, Apodemius. During the questioning, Gallus tried to put the blame for all of his actions on Constantina, saying that she advised that her brother's expectations would be the harsh manner in which he dealt with the Judea problem. All of his responses were sent to the Emperor, who still waited in Mediolanum.

Constantius II sat rigidly on the gilded throne in Mediolanum, reading the report from the two inquisitors, his face an impassive mask carved from years of rule and suspicion, but his clenched jaw betrayed the fury boiling beneath. The scroll he held trembled slightly in his hand. The chronicling of the debacle that transpired under the command of his cousin, Gaius Vettius Aquilinus Gallus, Caesar of the East was more than he could tolerate. As far as je was concerned, Gallus had proven himself, yet again, to be a disgrace to the imperial purple, having the inability to distinguish between ruling as a diplomat and that of a tyrant.

The Jewish revolt, which Gallus had promised to contain, had spiraled into a full-blown regional catastrophe. Instead of swift suppression, Gallus allowed the situation to fester, misjudging the zeal of the rebels and the cunning of their leaders. It had required Ursicinus, the empire's most brutal general, to crush the uprising. But

Ursicinus, though loyal, had acted with excessive brutality. Three towns, Magdala, Sepphoris, and Bethar had been reduced to smoldering ruin, their populations either slain or scattered. Tiberias had been reduced to half of its former self. Entire villages were emptied. Temples pillaged. And with their destruction came the most devastating consequence as far as Constantius was concerned, the tax registers had vanished, the collectors slain, and the imperial coffers had been bled dry.

Constantius was livid not only because the treasury's expected revenue from Palestina and parts of Syria had plummeted, but because Gallus had allowed his name, the name of the House of Constantine, to be dragged through the ashes and rivers of blood. The Senate whispered of the Emperor's incompetence for appointing his cousin to the position in the first place. Now, as a consequence, the governors in Asia Minor delayed shipments and grain levies, uncertain of which town might next fall to chaos. Worst of all, in the middle of the report was the explanation that Gallus, amid the unrest, had staged a chariot race in the Hippodrome of Constantinople, crowning the victor as if he were Augustus himself.

Constantius's fingers tore the parchment. He turned to his chamberlain, eyes blazing. "Gallus has not merely failed me, he has humiliated me," he spat. "Losses in Armenia, sedition in Judaea, and now the ruin of three cities under Roman protection? Tell me, Gallineus, how do I maintain divine favor when the East is scorched by fools and pretenders?"

Gallineus bowed his bald head. "Sire, his removal is all but assured. The people murmur. The army is unsure. And the provinces, well without the benefit of their taxes, they will turn away. And now there is word that the Samaritan chieftain Baba Rabbah is taking up where this Natronai has left off. Gallus has plunged a knife into the heart of the Empire."

Constantius rose from his throne like a thundercloud incarnate. "Then what do you suggest I do next, Gallineus?"

"The answer to that, Excellency is easy. Let Eusebius know that Gallus no longer has your favor or protection," he said coldly. "Eusebius will know what to do. Your cousin will learn what becomes of those who mistake your silence for forgiveness. It will be the last mistake he makes."

As far as the emperor was concerned, what Gallus had done was not just reckless, it was an affront to the majesty of the Empire. There could only be one punishment to remedy the insult to Rome and Constantius agreed that it would be the last mistake his cousin ever made.

Back in the provinces of Judaea and Galilee, Hillel ben Judah, lived long enough to see the ruin of everything he had gambled his reputation upon. To his contemporaries in Tiberias he was not a hero, nor even a wise leader, but a man who bargained with Rome, betrayed his own, and thought himself a master of politics when he was little more than a pawn in the games of Emperors.

His defenders in later centuries tried to veil the truth with pious legend. They claimed it was Hillel who established the fixed calendar of the Jews, sparing the exiles from uncertainty as they wandered far from the Land. But history itself betrays the tale. The calculations of the Hebrew calendar in the form it eventually took was not finalized in his day. At most, Hillel may have given his assent to the beginnings of a mathematical system already in circulation, but he was no architect of time, no Moses of the moons. The honor he coveted, the credit of giving structure to eternity, was never his.

Instead, Hillel II lived in shadows, waiting for vindication from emperors. When Julian ascended the throne in 361 CE, turning his back on Christianity and promising to restore the ancestral faiths, the Jews of the empire whispered of a miracle. Julian, styled "the Apostate," granted them permission to rebuild the Temple. Hillel, old and desperate, clung to the hope that at last he would be proven right, that his compromises with Rome had purchased the people their survival until this very hour. He boasted that the nation would rise again, that Jerusalem would be theirs once more, and he quietly told his followers that it was all due to his patience and diplomacy when dealing with the Romans.

But fate mocked him. as Julian's reign lasted scarcely two years. Struck down in Persia, the dream of rebuilding Jerusalem vanished with him. The Temple remained a heap of stones. The hopes Hillel had staked his legacy upon turned to dust. Hillel lived to see the faith of his people suppressed further under the Christian emperors that came afterwards. Sequentially, each was harsher than the one before, and Hillel's name became a bitter reminder of promises unfulfilled.

The final humiliation came under Theodosius, when as Emperor, he eliminated the judicial role of the Sanhedrin, reducing it to nothing more than an old boys club. What was once the heart of Jewish life and law was now stripped of any and all authority. Past decrees were declared void. The family authority and heritage that Hillel had sacrificed his own daughter to preserve was dissolved by imperial edict. He had thought to keep power by appeasement, only to live long enough to see it extinguished forever.

Thus ended the career of Hillel II: not in vindication, not in triumph, but in silence and disgrace. A man who imagined himself a savior of his people, only to leave ruins in his wake. The very bargains he struck for survival turned to shackles; the empire he flattered crushed the Sanhedrin he sought to protect and stripped him of the patriarchy he hoped to preserve. His name would linger, attached to legends of the calendar, but the truth was harsher.

What he reaped was what he had sown: betrayal answered by betrayal, compromise ending in destruction, ambition swallowed in humiliation. In the end, the fate of Hillel was not unlike the fate of Israel in those dark centuries, surviving, yes, but broken, scattered, and waiting for redemption in another time and by another hand. Yet fate does have sense of karma, even for one such as Hillel II. One hundred and thirty years later, the last of the Nasi line, Gamaliel VII was struck down by an exiled

Byzantine general named Patricius, who served a descendant of Natronai's family, the Exilarch Zutra II. It would appear that Natronai finally had his revenge.

AM YISRAEL CHAI

www.ingramcontent.com/pod-product-compliance
Lightning Source LLC
LaVergne TN
LVHW041612070426
835507LV00008B/199